Saving LIVES
& Saving MONEY

Also by Newt Gingrich

Gettysburg Co-authored by William Forstchen

Lessons Learned the Hard Way: A Personal Report

Renewing American Civilization

1945 Co-authored by William Forstchen

To Renew America

Contract with America: The Bold Plan to Change the Nation

Window of Opportunity: A Blueprint for the Future

Saving Lives & Saving Money

TRANSFORMING HEALTH AND HEALTHCARE

Newt Gingrich

with Dana Pavey and Anne Woodbury

The Alexis de Tocqueville Institution   Washington, DC

The Alexis de Tocqueville Institution, Washington, DC 20003

Copyright 2003 by Gingrich Communications, Inc.

Trademark 2003 Saving Lives & Saving Money by Gingrich Communications, Inc.

All rights reserved

PRINTED IN CANADA

ISBN : 0-970-54854-0

We Dedicate This Book

Newt Gingrich

To my mother, Kit Gingrich, and my in-laws, Alphonse and Bernita Bisek.

Dana Pavey

To my family and friends, thank you each for teaching me how to obtain my own wholeness. You continue to show me that I cannot control the ocean, but you also continue to teach me how to surf.

Anne Woodbury

To my family—who is the passion behind this book, and Martha Beighey—my rosy example of active, healthy aging!

Vince Haley

To my father, Dr. Richard L. Haley, and my stepmother, Betty Ruth Haley.

Sarah Murphy

To my parents, Margaret Anne Hufnagel and Fred A. Hufnagel Jr., and their teams of doctors at the University of Virginia Hospital.

Bill Sanders

To my brother, Jeff Sanders—for having a few more visits to the doctor than me—but he's always been a little bit taller and a whole lot stronger.

Mike Shields

To my son, Aidan David Shields-Eads, who would not be here without Newt and Anne.

And to all the friends and family who supported us in this effort, and to all the people who want and deserve longer lives with better health.

Charts and Graphs

Contents

Newt's mother, Kit Gingrich; standing (L to R) Mrs. Callista Gingrich;
Callista's parents, Bernita and Alphonse Bisek.
Newt's motivation for *Saving Lives & Saving Money*. 2002

Newt listening to and taking notes from Dr. W. Edwards Deming,
the guru of quality. July 21, 1991

Pictured (L to R) Newt, Secretary of Defense Dick Cheney,
and Republican Minority Leader Bob Michel. July 20, 1989

Kathy G. Lubbers and her husband, Paul A. Lubbers, PhD. 2003

Newt with President George Bush in the White House Oval Office. June 30, 1992
Courtesy of the George Bush Presidential Library

Newt with Secretary of Health and Human Services Lou Sullivan
in Washington, DC. July 22, 1991

Secretary of Health and Human Services Tommy Thompson and Newt. 2003
Courtesy of House Photographer

Speaker of the House Dennis Hastert with Callista and Newt Gingrich.
Hastert chaired the House Republican Task Force on Health from 1991–1998. 2003
Courtesy of Steve Rusnak, Office of Photography, U.S. House of Representatives

Pictured (L to R) Cyril Brickfield, AARP Executive Director; Newt;
John Denning, AARP President; and Kermit Phelps, AARP Chairman of the Board of Directors
at the AARP Congressional Reception. January 28, 1987
Courtesy of AARP

Newt with Secretary of Defense Dick Cheney in Washington, DC. June 1992

Secretary Thompson, Newt Gingrich, Dana Pavey, and their associates had a lunch meeting
to discuss the opportunities and future of healthcare. 2003
Courtesy of House Photographer

FOREWORD

Writing about health and healthcare is a big job. Writing about transforming the entire American healthcare system is even more daunting. In *Saving Lives & Saving Money*, Newt Gingrich has done an admirable job of both. He has clearly and comprehensively described the problems with our current healthcare system, explained why it cannot continue to stagger along and, most importantly, offered his own ideas about how to transform our current mess into a 21st century system that saves lives and saves money.

Gingrich believes that our healthcare system is beyond reform—that it needs to be transformed into something totally different than it is today. "'Reforming,'" Gingrich says, "is the process of trying to make the current pattern work. 'Transforming' is about developing new and very different patterns."

Volumes have been written about the problems with our healthcare system, and hundreds (if not thousands) of conferences are held every year with experts discussing how addressing a specific piece of the problem will improve the system. Yet with all the talking and tinkering, costs continue to rise while quality care continues to decrease.

Newt Gingrich has never been one to tinker. He is a big-idea person and, moreover, he has the ability to link big ideas into something even larger still. He believes it is time to focus the healthcare debate where it truly belongs—on people's health. That is what Gingrich does in *Saving Lives & Saving Money*. The gap between the health and healthcare we should have and what we actually have is appallingly huge and will only get larger if we don't transform the system. And in the process of improving our health, the nation can also save billions of dollars if we make substantial changes in the way we practice health and healthcare.

Gingrich is proposing nothing less than dramatically changing one of the largest segments of our economy. His ideas for transforming the system are not academic theories. They are based on real-life examples of entre-preneurial changes people are making across the healthcare system throughout the country, and he offers specific examples to back up his claims and allow people to find out more.

Transformation of America's healthcare system is one of the biggest chal-lenges facing our nation. In 2011 the first members of the 76 million baby-boomer generation will begin turning 65. This will have a dramatic and lasting impact on our healthcare system simply because older people tend to use healthcare more. Transformation does not happen overnight. As Gingrich points out, it took us twenty years to transform our welfare sys-tem. We don't have twenty years to get our healthcare system in order. We have to start work on it now.

Gingrich's ideas are influencing how we at AARP are thinking about our national role in health promotion and disease prevention and in our advo-cating for system change. He writes: "The healthcare debate is not about Democrats and Republicans. It's not about liberals and conservatives. The health debate is about your life and the lives of your family. The healthcare debate is about your money and your family's money." I would only add, it's also about your future—and America's.

Whatever your views and your state of health, you will find *Saving Lives & Saving Money* bold, enlightening, and provocative. While you may not agree with all of Gingrich's ideas, this book will engage you in thinking about—and probably acting on—health and healthcare. That's important because, as he observes, transforming our nation's healthcare system will take all of us to make it happen. And indeed, it must happen. Our health, our families, and our futures depend on it.

> *William D. Novelli*
> *AARP Executive Director and CEO*

INTRODUCTION

It's Your Life and Your Money:
What Is at Stake in the Health Debate?

Saving Lives & Saving Money is a new approach to the challenge of creating a better system of health and healthcare for the 21st century, a system that saves lives and saves money. Our goal was to establish principles of transformation and present stories of actual companies, organizations, and projects that are successfully trailblazing this process. Their achievements not only offer conceptual proof that those principles work but they also provide us with the opportunity to use or copy the ideas that are already saving lives and saving money.

There is an enormous gap between the health and healthcare you and your family should have and the health and healthcare you most likely will have if we do not transform the current system.

We wrote this book to let you know that you can make a difference over the next few years by insisting the debate be focused on your health. The difference you make will be reflected in how long you and your loved ones might live, the quality of life you have, and the amount of money and time you will need to spend on healthcare.

We hope to create a movement of innovation and improvement in which thousands of people and institutions are working to develop a better health future by producing better outcomes at lower costs. We have developed a series of recommendations that we believe policymakers—both public and private—can use to develop better systems of health and healthcare. However, change must come from the American people. So we have also outlined ideas, resources, and tools that you can use in your daily life to spur and support this process of transformation.

We know there will be many false steps, missteps, and failures between here and the life- and money-saving system of 2010 or 2015. And while we believe that our vision outlines the right principles to guide the transformation of American healthcare, we do not believe we have all the answers for dramatically improving the largest sector of the economy and the most complex area of American life.

It is a simple, stark fact that we could have a dramatically better system and that such a system would save hundreds of thousands of lives and billions of dollars every year. It is also a fact that mechanisms to achieve this system are already saving lives and saving money.

For example:

- Today, if you were to be admitted to an intensive care unit, you could be supervised by an intensive-care doctor and nurse 24 hours a day, 7 days a week. You would be saved from avoidable mistakes, treated for problems at their earliest symptoms, and know that if a crisis were to occur at two o'clock in the morning, a fully awake, intensive-care team is prepared to respond. As a result, you would leave the intensive care unit sooner and save money. This currently exists and you can find out more at www.visicu.com.

- Today, you could assess your own symptoms and evaluate possible diagnoses. Your doctor could be accessing expert systems that help make decisions based on the most recent breakthroughs and studies of the best outcomes. Your doctor would have more knowledge with less wasted time because you could prepare the information before even visiting the office. You could also keep a record of that information for future reference should you have other problems. This technology is already available, and you can learn more about the services at www.pkc.com and www.worlddoc.com.

- Today, you could be visiting a clinic with electronic medical records, electronic lab reports, and electronic drug prescriptions. The entirely electronic clinic saves money and lives because it is far more accurate. This system exists at the Mayo Clinic in Jacksonville, Florida.

- Today, you could visit a hospital that has dramatically fewer medication errors. These institutions insist their doctors use computerized physician order entry with an expert electronic system that checks for inappropriate prescriptions and ensures the pharmacist receives the correct information in a readable form. You and your family would experience fewer medication errors and unnecessary hospital-induced illnesses, saving you pain, time, and money. Electronic physician order entry is being used at Vanderbilt University Medical Center in Tennessee, Danville Regional Medical Center in Virginia, Latter Day Saints Hospital in Utah, and virtually the entire Veterans Health Administration. Find out more at www.va.gov/vista_monograph.

- Today, if you or a family member has diabetes, asthma, or cardiovascular disease, you could participate in a health-management program that is keeping people healthy without hospital stays or emergency-room visits.

You can see programs like these in Florida where Pfizer is helping Medicaid patients manage their health, at www.pfizer-healthsolutions.com/healthystateframe.htm, and in five Georgia hospitals where Currahee Health Benefits Solutions is helping hospital employees with their health management at www.currahee.net.

- Today, if you have an elderly relative who is ill and in a long-term-care facility, they could have a personalized, highly individualized program that would probably be able to substantially reduce their daily medications. They would be cared for by people who know their medical condition. As a result, your relative would have fewer hospitalizations, less illness, and a happier, longer life. You can see this model in action at nursing homes that offer the Evercare program at www.evercare-online.com.

The debate in Washington continually centers on marginal changes that offer little improvement to the individual. Most states have also failed to meet the challenge of planning a better health future, and in state after state, the failure to transform Medicaid is now leading to tax increases. Often Medicaid is the monster that eats the state budget. It is crowding out education, highways, public safety, and other traditional services as health-care costs continue to rise.

In the private sector, corporate leadership narrowly focuses on containing costs. Twenty years ago executives agreed to pay managed-care companies to control their healthcare costs. In order to control the costs, the managed-care companies imposed increasingly restrictive external controls on healthcare providers. Frustrated by their resulting inability to provide the necessary care, doctors promptly told patients that they were receiving less care and their lives were being threatened to save the insurance companies money. Although the insurance companies were angering the only people who directly interact with patients, they really did not care as long as the corporate executives were happy and kept renewing the contracts.

Neither the corporate executives nor the insurance companies properly recognized that patients are voters, and these voters were not happy about their healthcare arrangements. Backed with the moral authority of their doctors who define quality in healthcare, the voters complained en masse to their elective representatives in Congress. This team would become an overwhelmingly powerful political force that wanted change. The result has been a decade-long fight over patients' rights.

Between fear of lawsuits and fear of governmental control, the managed-care process collapsed, which is just as well because it never really managed care anyway. Managing care requires gathering and analyzing data about care. Insurance companies were not interested in this data; their focus was exclusively on cost. (They would have been better described as managed-cost companies.) Systems that actually focus on managing care (like the Mayo Clinics and Kaiser Permanente) have entirely different and better relationships with patients, because people trust their providers' focus is on health, not money.

With managed care collapsing and health costs rising, some corporations are now shifting toward a new cost-control system. They are trying to dump an increasingly larger share of the costs and risks onto their employees. When this is done in a too aggressive manner, it leads immediately to labor problems. The Hershey and General Electric strikes are early symptoms of how people react to employers forcing them to take on additional risks and costs.

In the midst of uninspired political debate, corporate maneuvering, and health budget cuts, predatory trial lawyers file more lawsuits, blackmail more doctors, and drive information about quality underground. We cannot build a quality program in health because no rational person will voluntarily tell the truth about errors if that simply makes them a larger target for ruinously expensive lawsuits.

Faced with the growing burden of regulation and red tape, the spiraling costs of liability insurance, and the growing risk of being sued by hungry trial lawyers, doctors and nurses are leaving the profession in alarming numbers. The result is that many cities are experiencing a dire shortage of nurses willing to work as nurses (although there are thousands in the community doing other jobs) and a crisis in finding doctors for some specialties. In some cities there are no obstetricians taking on new patients, and in other cities fewer and fewer doctors will perform surgery.

Unfortunately these symptoms lead to nothing more than arguments that merely shift the deck chairs on the Titanic. Politicians and lobbyists have learned their lines over the last twenty years. They do little more than posture and repeat their fruitless positions. And the media does little more than echo them.

The danger for you and your family is that our current public health policies, reinforced by our healthcare policies, are making it more likely that you will get sick and more likely that you will receive inadequate care. Subsequently, the cost of your sickness will become a larger and larger portion of your family budget either directly (you pay) or indirectly as an employee (your employer takes more and more out of your total compensation to pay for health costs) or indirectly as a taxpayer (the cost of Medicare, Medicaid, and other services).

The bottom line is that you and your family are both physically and financially at risk in the current system of health and healthcare.

There have been some glimmerings of hope in the last two years. Four public officials in Washington have begun to talk about the need for profound change in our system of health and healthcare.

President George W. Bush, Secretary of Health and Human Services Tommy Thompson, former Secretary of the Treasury Paul O'Neill, and Senate Majority Leader Bill Frist, a heart and lung transplant surgeon whose knowledge of health and healthcare is unparalleled among elected officials, are all ready to roll up their sleeves and get to work on the issue.

The president has been calling for a profound rethinking in our system of medical justice, new approaches to quality, and a shift to a market-oriented system of choices controlled by the individual. He is calling for new efforts to insure every American and for access to drugs for senior citizens through a modernized and improved Medicare system that will be able to absorb the baby boomers when they retire.

Secretary Thompson has become a champion of preventive care and an intense advocate of better personal health. His public and personal focus on obesity and exercise has changed his own life as he has lost weight, and it has made him an example of the changes we need. He is committed to using information technology to improve the quality of healthcare and lower costs while preparing the nation for the threat of a biological attack. He is dedicated to creating a high-quality, citizen-oriented Center for Medicare and Medicaid Services to replace the centralized control and petty red tape of the stodgy healthcare-financing system.

As the chief executive officer of Alcoa, former Secretary O'Neill improved the quality of care for his employees by introducing the Toyota Production System into his company. He learned that focusing on quality and improving value and outcomes leads to dramatic increases in productivity and declines in cost in both the manufacturing arena and in worker safety.

As a civic leader, Paul O'Neill brought that commitment to quality and value into the Pittsburgh health system by helping to create the Pittsburgh Regional Healthcare Initiative (PRHI), www.prhi.org. Like Alcoa, PRHI is based on the philosophy that healthcare outcomes will improve if the focus is placed on the quality of care delivered and that will lead to better health and a less expensive healthcare system.

When he became Secretary of the Treasury, Paul O'Neill brought that same passion for quality and transformation in health to Washington. He used every opportunity to educate Washington leaders about the great opportunities for getting better outcomes at lower costs even though it wasn't in his direct job description.

In a very important step toward increasing an individual's control over his or her own life, the Treasury under then Secretary O'Neill ruled that flexible spending accounts could carry over from year to year, a critical move that increased personal control of health spending. Americans with flexible spending accounts are no longer forced to choose between spending wastefully at year's end and losing their account balance every December.

As a surgeon, Senator Frist understands that the health and healthcare system is the largest challenge in American public life. While his new job as Senate majority leader will force him to focus on many issues beyond the healthcare system, Senator Frist will undoubtedly remain committed to transforming the system to save lives and save money.

However, these four can no more transform the health system by themselves than First Lady Hillary Clinton could in 1993. Ultimately the healthcare system cannot be solved inside the Washington political structure. Most political leaders will not organize a parade, but they will gladly jump in front to lead one. It is the American people who must engage in saving their own lives and saving their own money. Only then, with the backing of the country, will political leaders in Washington put their weight behind the campaign. The tragedy is that the current government/corporation /interest-group-dominated system of healthcare is resistant to innovation and new approaches. Without citizen participation, lobbyists and powerful special interests will continue to block any real improvements to protect their sacred cows and feed their special interests with our money and at the expense of our health.

We wrote *Saving Lives & Saving Money* to encourage you to become involved in helping think through the health system as it affects you and your family. With your voice and your effort, you can become a force for change. To bring about the level of transformation necessary will not be easy. But it is important to understand that it is not impossible. I am familiar with the process and strategy required to bring about large-scale change. I led the 1994 effort that resulted in the Republican Party becoming a majority in Congress for the first time in 40 years. As a result, Congress passed welfare reform, increased defense spending, balanced the budget, and cut taxes for the first time in sixteen years.

Saving Lives & Saving Money is the first step; it is a scouting report on the opportunities and technologies that are saving American lives and money now in the real world. It is not based on theory but on four years of research and on programs that are already working today. There are hundreds of entrepreneurs developing better ways of saving lives, caring for people, handling health information, and accounting for health expenses. Many of these entrepreneurs are medical doctors and nurses who decided there had to be a healthier, smarter way to get the job done. Others are technical experts who have seen the power of computers, information systems, and quality programs in other parts of our economy and who have believed they could dramatically improve the health-delivery system. Finally, some are public health experts who know that a better system of activity and nutrition, combined with a sense of personal responsibility for our own health, will save millions of lives and billions of dollars in the next generation. Throughout the book we will refer to the achievements of many of these people. Whenever possible, we include Web sites so that you can go directly to the source and see these breakthroughs for yourself.

We believe there will be a large, loosely knit movement of people working toward better outcomes at lower costs. We believe we will ultimately save lives and save money by focusing on the breakthroughs that work, the principles that sustain them, and the policies that encourage them. We also believe that saving millions of American lives and billions of dollars in the next generation is a job that will require many people and will transcend the efforts of any one person or group.

If you find the core principles in this book make sense and you would like to participate in creating better outcomes at lower cost and advancing a 21st Century System of Health and Healthcare, we encourage you to join the Center for Health Transformation at www.healthtransformation.net. This center was created by individuals, organizations, policymakers, and corporations who wanted to unite their efforts to pursue and advocate the transformed system of health and healthcare outlined in this book. If you are interested in membership in the center, have comments or suggestions about this book, or would like to tell us about a hospital, doctor, pharmacy, or other health professional, company, or individual who is developing a new approach that saves lives and saves money, we would like to hear from you. We are constantly looking for breakthroughs.

In addition, we invite private-sector companies and organizations, trade and professional associations, and state and local government leaders seeking individualized consulting assistance in applying these principles or creating a transformational plan to visit the Gingrich Group at www.gingrichgroup.com.

If you would like to receive book reviews, general ideas, and concepts beyond the field of health and healthcare, you can visit my site www.newt.org.

We believe that with your help—in your own life as a patient, as a purchaser of healthcare, as a voice in your community, as a voter—you can help shift America to a better system of health and healthcare and realize the promise of a healthier future for you and your family.

Remember, we need your help because this is too big a change for Washington to accomplish without you. Only when citizens are involved will we get the breakthroughs we need. Only when citizens are involved will we save lives and save money. In a free society, your involvement is exactly what should be necessary to transform a big issue like health and healthcare.

Transforming health and healthcare is a big canoe. We need all the paddlers we can get. We hope you will decide to become one.

CHAPTER ONE

Why the Best of the Past
Is Not Good Enough for the Future

The proposal to transform the 20th century American pattern of health and healthcare into a 21st century system should not be interpreted as an attack on the achievements of the past or a sign of disrespect for the hard work and great medical accomplishments of the last century. Nor should it be seen as an attack on, or disregard for, the hard work and dedication of thousands of doctors and nurses who save lives every day.

The 20th century was a time of enormous progress in human health. Infectious diseases like yellow fever, smallpox, and cholera were brought under control while basic research extended the range of knowledge about human biology. Two generations of hard work on cancer treatment may have advanced us within sight of actually eliminating cancer as a major threat. Research on the role of nutrition, activity, and attitude has dramatically expanded our understanding of how humans remain healthy and minimize disease.

We are the first generation in history to have significant numbers of people living into their eighties, nineties, and beyond the century mark. This achievement is largely a tribute to dramatic progress in public health, nutrition, and medical services.

No one who compared the health of Americans in 1903 and 2003 could have anything but admiration and respect for the extraordinary accomplishments of scientists, doctors, and public officials in creating a better world. The last century has clearly been one of remarkable achievement.

Yet the question we must ask is not how good was our past, but rather can our future be better. We must have the same courage in meeting the challenges, solving the problems, and seizing the opportunities of our generation that the doctors, scientists, and public leaders of 1903 had for their generation.

Faced with the opportunity of a far better future, defensive assertions that American doctors are the best trained medical staff in the world do not excuse the industry for neglecting to utilize the available technology to advance care delivery. The massive explosions in knowledge about biology, pharmacology, and best outcomes may render the current system of memorization and individually focused training in medical schools obsolete in the 21st century. Indeed, given the nature of modern informatics and the growth of team medical practice involving many people beyond the individual doctor, would it not be better to rethink medical learning from the ground up? Medical education should include a significant amount of public health, teamwork (maybe nurses and doctors should work together from day one in medical school), considerable education into medical informatics, less memorization, and greater usage of sophisticated, modern information systems and expert problem solving built into computerized databases.

Doctors' resistance to adopting information-based systems with greater transparency must be abrogated in light of the series of reports revealing the prevalence of medication errors, hospital-care-induced illnesses, and medical mistakes. How many deaths are necessary before medical arrogance is considered an inadequate defense for a system that clearly could be improved overnight if only the will were there to insist on the improvement? There is a growing gap between the achievements of the past and the needs of the future, a gap between the application of quality and information technology in other industries and our quality-ignoring, paper-dominated system of healthcare that is creating an environment in which major changes will become inevitable.

We call that environment "the perfect storm."

The Perfect Storm

The blockbuster 2000 hit movie, *The Perfect Storm,* was based on a book written about "the storm of the century" that hit off the coast of Gloucester, Massachusetts in October of 1991. The strongest storm in recorded history, this perfect storm was actually two separate storms and one hurricane that combined into a single fury of 100-foot, unnavigable seas. The movie surmises what the *Andrea Gail*, captained and skippered by skilled and experienced sailors, may have gone through as the crew fought the storm. No matter how skilful the crew and how well equipped the boat, their fate was sealed.

America's healthcare system is nearing the edge of its own perfect storm. The system is broken—qualitatively in the product it delivers and financially in the amount it costs. It cannot be repaired well enough to face the impending tempest. This is a tempest brought about by a huge increase in the number of older adults needing more healthcare as the baby boomers retire and a growing public health crisis of nutrition-activity-attitude manifesting itself in an alarming increase of teenage diabetes and general obesity. In addition, there is an explosion of new knowledge that is introducing new opportunities and, in some cases, new costs into the system. No single modification or even a series of modifications can save the current system. It is not about trying harder, tweaking the tax system, or increasing government regulation. Tinkering around the margins has brought us to where we are today. It is time to apply what we have learned to completely redesign and build a new ship of health and healthcare.

A National Academy of Science report released in November of 2002 by a panel of experts appointed by the Institute of Medicine stated, "The

American healthcare system is confronting a crisis. The healthcare delivery system is incapable of meeting the present, let alone the future, needs of the American public."[1]

To date, American institutions lead the world in medical research and specialty healthcare. However, the American health and healthcare system is at its breaking point. The balance of this chapter reports on the trends that have already impaired and will incapacitate the system's ability to meet the minimum standards for Americans if not transformed.

The combined forces of the perfect storm:

- An unsustainable trend of increasing costs for healthcare
- The unacceptable number of medical errors resulting in human pain and suffering, unnecessary death, and unnecessary cost
- A disregard for serious focus on quality and outcomes
- Absence of a true market system in healthcare
- Skyrocketing insurance premiums
- An increasing reliance on government to pay for healthcare and bureaucracy to manage it
- Costly administrative burdens and inefficiencies
- An enormous growth in our elderly population and the consequent increase in demand for healthcare
- Predatory trial lawyers driving up medical malpractice insurance
- A shortage of healthcare providers
- An egocentric medical culture making teamwork and new learning very difficult
- Millions of Americans who do not have health insurance

Skyrocketing Healthcare Costs with No End in Sight

Since 1965 the amount that Americans spend on healthcare as a share of the gross domestic product has doubled. We are paying a larger share of a much larger economy for healthcare than we did 40 years ago. This includes expenses that we pay out of our pockets and through our taxes to support government insurance programs like Medicare and Medicaid. In 1965 the per person expenditure in the United States for health and healthcare was $205. In 2000 this number was $4,637. In the year 1965, $205 had the same purchasing power as $1,119.78 in the year 2000. So even after inflation, the total per person expenditure on healthcare has gone up 300%.[2]

Research experts, the media, political leaders, and employers cite the metrics of rising healthcare spending, particularly on prescription drugs, as a key contributor to the perfect storm. However, the debate has the wrong focus. The fact that expenditures are rising, in and of itself, is not bad. For example, much of the growth in the last 35 years can be attributed to leaps in medical care that have provided us with the opportunity to spend money in order to live longer and healthier. As Americans, we place a high moral value on our health and the health of our community. It costs more money to treat a patient with cancer than it would to let the person die. Of course no one in America would argue that saving the life of a cancer patient by using breakthrough drugs, specialized care, and new devices is a bad idea. In reality it is impossible to place a value on how much of our GDP we should spend on health and healthcare services. The optimum dollar amount may be 6% or it may be 20%.

However, as long as the dollars are spent in a bureaucratic system without quality controls, we have no way of knowing what the right value should be. If the American people voluntarily decided that for *their* health, and *their* needs, out of *their* pockets, they wanted to spend *their* money, that number would be in *their* control.

Today citizens and employers continue to funnel more of their income into a health system they cannot control. Taxpayers purchase care for other Americans in a healthcare system that they do not control. Without quality-control requirements, the health system is charging, and will continue to charge, whatever it can. Therefore the steady increase of a larger share of a larger gross domestic product is an indicator of dysfunction in the current system. This is the heart of why the rising health expenditures are an issue—a bigger share of a bigger economy is paying for bureaucratic structures operating without standards of quality or controls. It is a healthcare system out of sync with the American people.

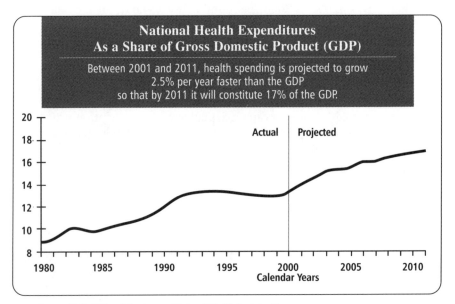

**National Health Expenditures
As a Share of Gross Domestic Product (GDP)**

Between 2001 and 2011, health spending is projected to grow 2.5% per year faster than the GDP so that by 2011 it will constitute 17% of the GDP.

*Source: CMS, Office of the Actuary, National Health Statistics Group
June 2002 Edition, Centers for Medicare & Medicaid Services, Section I. Page 24*

Employer Cost Shifts

As the economy slows, both government and employer resources are being diverted to health and healthcare from other parts of their budgets. In 2002 employer-sponsored, health-insurance payers experienced a 12.5% increase in their premiums on top of double digit premium increases in 2001. According to a survey of business leaders, over the next five years the cost of insurance premiums will rise 17% each year.[3] According to Harris Interactive, 59% of employers say healthcare costs are out of control, up from 21% in 1995.[4] In response, employers are shifting a portion of their healthcare costs to the employee by increasing co-payments and deductibles, having the employee pay a larger share of the insurance premiums, implementing strict drug formularies, and restricting coverage. Predictably, employees are unhappy about these cost-shifting tactics. The employees of Hershey Foods, and more recently General Electric, went on strike to protest the portion of the increased costs they must now pay.

The Silent Epidemic: The Moral Unacceptability of Medical Errors

According to the report, *To Err Is Human,* by the Institute of Medicine (IOM), between 44,000 and 98,000 people die needlessly every year due to medical error. To put this in perspective, 98,000 medical-error deaths is the

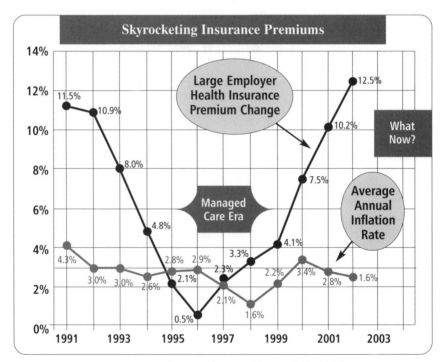

Source: Employer Premium Info: www.hschange.org/CONTENT/472/table1.shtml
Inflation Info: http://inflationdata.com/Inflation/Inflation_Rate/HistoricalInflation.aspx

equivalent of a jumbo jet full of passengers crashing every single day, killing more than 250 Americans. Even using the lower estimate, medical error deaths still rank as the eighth leading killer in America. Medical errors in hospitals alone kill more people in a given year than motor vehicle accidents (43,458), breast cancer (42,297), or AIDS (16,516), yet the study received surprisingly little media attention. Additionally, the IOM numbers do not include the deadly mistakes made in home care, ambulatory care, outpatient visits, or nursing homes. Most of the care providers we interviewed indicated that the total number of deaths by medical error is likely to be substantially higher than those contained in the IOM report.[5]

The estimates in the report have been vigorously challenged by many healthcare executives, care providers, and hospital administrators. One expert wishing to discredit the study declared that the real number of deaths caused by medical error was likely to be half that reported by the IOM. Even if that were true, and using the lower estimate, the results are still an appallingly unacceptable 22,000 needless deaths because of avoidable errors, the equivalent of a New York to Washington shuttle flight crashing every other day killing everyone on board.

According to the IOM report, the total cost of preventable medical errors from lost income, lost household production, disability, and the additional healthcare costs is between $17 billion and $29 billion annually. At least half of that estimate is the cost attributed to fixing or living with the mistake.

Consider this: Healthcare is the only industry in America that can give you a disease and then charge you to cure the disease it gave you. Clearly this is an outrageously wrong principle. In the airline industry, for example, we have correctly insisted that safety transcends not only profits but also management styles, corporate cultures, pilots' preferences, fears about privacy, or any other excuse.

Adding insult to injury are the errors that do not actually result in death. Out of every 100 hospital patients, 5 or 6 will be the victim of a preventable error. In addition, 5% to 10% of all hospital patients—2 million people per year—contract an infection while staying in the hospital. It is estimated that hospital-acquired infections, which are not considered medical errors, are responsible for over 88,000 deaths every year and cost over $4.5 billion.[6]

If the American media were to report the daily death toll from medical errors with the same intensity as the tragic, but far less significant, stories of the OJ Simpson trial or the disappearance of Shandra Levy, the country would be outraged, prompting political leaders to demand action. Yet there has been no response proportional to the crisis. As one point of comparison, 6,000 people die annually from workplace injuries. The Occupational Safety and Health Administration (OSHA) that employs over 5,200 workers with a 2003 budget request for $437 million dollars, was created in response to our concerns about workplace safety.[7]

> **Pittsburgh Regional Healthcare Initiative** is adapting the Toyota Production System (TPS) for the healthcare setting by creating problem-solving laboratories called Learning Lines in several hospital units across the community. Each TPS Learning Line focuses on the individual patient's needs. When a problem arises, those on the Learning Line intervene to solve it immediately.
>
> The TPS approach sets PRHI apart from many other healthcare reinvention efforts. With TPS, everyone in the care continuum works toward the ideal: delivering patient care on demand, defect free, one-by-one, immediately, without waste, in an environment that is physically, emotionally, and professionally safe.
>
> *Source: www.prhi.org*

Medication errors alone kill 7,000 people each year adding $2 billion to the overall cost of healthcare, a cost 4.5 times the size of the OSHA budget.[8] Yet there is no coordinated government response to lower the error rate and save lives and suffering.

The enormous number of needless deaths from medical errors (44,000), hospital-induced infections (88,000), and medication errors (7,000) is not only unacceptable, it is un-American.

A Disregard for Quality and Outcomes

Although every error is different, there is overwhelming agreement that the principle cause of error is not the individual care provider but a hopelessly flawed system. While most industries have benefited from systems overhauls, the healthcare industry has escaped comprehensive quality approaches, such as those from Edwards Deming, or the application of Total Quality Management, Six Sigma, or the Toyota Production System (TPS).

Former Secretary Paul O'Neill, while chairman and CEO of Alcoa, used a total systems approach to worker safety, which resulted in America's safest workplace. He applied the principles of the Toyota Production System to his manufacturing practices as well, reducing Alcoa's costs by $1.1 billion since 1998. However, as any Alcoa employee will tell you, the company is still not satisfied. Alcoa's mantra is Zero is possible. Alcoa's goal will be reached when no work-related injuries occur.

Although every quality program differs somewhat in approach, a key principle of each—which is not present in hospitals—is data transparency. If a hospital's goal is to decrease medication errors by 50%, it must have the baseline data on how many medication errors have been occurring in order to know when success is achieved. Most hospital administrators would tell you in confidence that they do not adequately collect the kind of comprehensive data that could provide a benchmark for future improvement.

One of our friends was recently in an intensive care unit for four days due to multiple blood clots in his legs, putting him at serious risk of a heart attack or a stroke if the clots were to travel to his heart or brain. To dissolve the clots, the hospital was giving him the blood thinner, Coumadin. The day he was released from the hospital, a nurse reviewing his discharge orders indicated to him that the circled medications needed to be taken that evening. Later that night, he reviewed his exit instructions that indicated he was to take the Coumadin that evening. He remembered that while in the hospital, he had been given 1 pill but his instructions specified that he was to take 2.5 pills. He called the hospital and spoke to a nurse who told him to follow the instructions and to take 2.5 pills. Two days later, a blood test revealed that his blood was dangerously thin. He told the doctor that he thought he might have been double dosed. The doctor responded that he had no way of knowing because the written medical records were at the hospital, so the doctor was unable to review them. At this point, the doctor was rightfully concerned about how to fix the blood level but shockingly unconcerned about why it had gotten so low. The doctor took him off the Coumadin for a couple of days and told him to have his blood rechecked. When he did, his blood was too thick, putting him again at risk of a heart attack or a stroke. Four days after he left the hospital, he and his care providers had no idea how much Coumadin he should take. Had there been a medication error? Clearly no action was taken to identify it as such, and there was definitely no "after action review" or "lessons learned" to prevent the same type of error from happening again.

His story is similar to dozens and dozens of other stories we heard and is typical of the state of our healthcare system. Particularly striking to us was that this friend is a very successful business executive. Having earned an industrial engineering degree, he had risen through the ranks and gained recognition from applying efficient systems improvements at a very large plastics company. He was so successful he eventually bought the company. If a mistake like this were to be brought to his attention in his own factory, he would have demanded that the root cause of the error be found and a systemic solution put in place to ensure it did not happen again. Yet he did not demand the same from the doctor even when his life was at risk. Are we willing to accept that the perfection of a plastic bucket is more important than a human life?

This type of data transparency is often lacking in hospitals for three principle reasons: the threat of trial lawyers abusing such knowledge to generate more lawsuits, a lack of market incentives encouraging quality reporting, and the failure of the federal government to value lives in hospitals as much as it values lives in airplanes. Without the collection of and access to good data, it is impossible to implement a quality systems approach. Our healthcare will continue to suffer until the industry implements an outcomes-driven, data-transparent system that focuses on quality by uncovering errors, determining root causation, and implementing a systemic solution to ensure the error is avoided in the future.

The Unempowered Consumer

Like education, healthcare is currently one of the few industries not properly influenced by market dynamics. The essence of the problem is that the consumers (the patients) are not the buyers. They do not possess the financial leverage, which consumers have in almost every other sector of our economy, because they do not directly pay the bills.

The associates in our company, the Gingrich Group, and our research director at the American Enterprise Institute attend a variety of healthcare conferences, seminars, and lectures. One of our associates, after attending a managed-care conference where there were numerous educational seminars, remarked on this simple fact: Insurance companies do not see patients as their customers, they see employers as their customers and, to a lesser extent, doctors and hospitals. This conference, like most others, did not have one seminar about the patient.

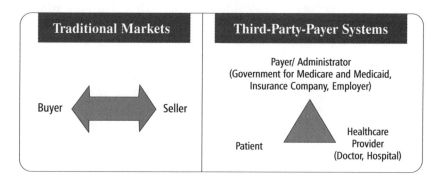

A healthcare system that has designed the patient out of the financial decision-making process is at the heart of the perfect storm. All the other elements we discuss in this chapter are large storms with high winds. The third-party-payer system is the hurricane.

The third-party-payer system stems from corporate and governmental attempts to centralize power and decision making into their bureaucracies. Feeling burdened, private sector employers have sought solutions through legislation at the state and federal levels, giving these governments enormous control over the healthcare system. But instead of relief, employers are confronted with a government that continues to compound the problems. Whereas employers are held accountable to the employees and shareholders, the government is more difficult to hold accountable. Examples like the now-defunct Soviet Union have confirmed that centralized government control employing coercion through regulation or edict is not a good solution. America is the best current example of a democracy in which people loan their power to the government but remain the ultimate decision makers.

This attempt at centralized governmental control has spawned many of the raging storms we have today—dissatisfied patients, restricted access, huge numbers of uninsured, unacceptable medical mistakes, a lack of information technology, and upwardly spiraling costs. These issues are exacerbated by our growing reliance on the government to pay for services.

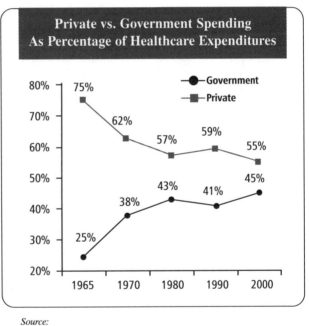

Source:
http://www.cms.gov/researchers/pubs/datacompendium/2002/C2pg14.pdf

Today government officials have ample reason to be even more concerned than employers. Medicaid, the health insurance program for low-income Americans, is the single largest expenditure for most state governments. In fact the amount states are paying for Medicaid has doubled in the last ten years.

On the federal level, the government pays for Medicare, which is the nation's largest health insurance program and covers nearly 40 million Americans. Medicare spending increased 11.6% in 2001 and 11.7% in 2002. Costs will continue to rise between 6% and 8% every year through 2011.[9] Even though the baby boomers will not become eligible for Medicare until 2011, the Department of Health and Human Services believes Medicare spending will grow by 73% under existing law even before the boomers qualify.[10]

Administrative Burdens

The U.S. healthcare system is drowning in bureaucracy and paperwork. Nowhere is this more true than in the doctor's office. A PricewaterhouseCoopers' study estimated that 1 hour of care requires 30 minutes of paperwork, and 1 hour of emergency room care requires a full hour of paperwork.[11] It is my understanding that in 2000 the Center for Medicare and Medicaid Services had 138,000 pages of regulations—more than IRS tax regulations. In addition, each insurance company imposes its own paperwork requirements on providers to settle claims, give permission for procedures, and evaluate whether doctors are providing too much care. Families and caregivers spend significant time and energy trying to determine what is and is not covered under their insurance policy. Some doctors' offices have to cope with over 30 different sets of rules and paperwork just to get payment for the services rendered.

The administrative burdens are magnified by the medical and insurance industries' reliance on paper. They are slow to adopt the efficiency advances made possible by computer software and Internet communication. An Efficient Healthcare Consumer Response (EHCR) assessment study recently concluded that implementing an electronic information system could eliminate approximately 50%, $11 billion of the total $23 billion, of processing costs in the healthcare supply chain.[12] However, the government budget analysis used today would not credit the investment in new technology as a savings. Therefore the capital needed to avoid future costs is not, and likely will not be, made available.

For two generations we have been shifting money away from the people who actually give care and toward those who administer the caregivers.

The results are declining incomes and plummeting satisfaction among providers, major components of the perfect storm.

Demographics

As the baby-boomer generation is getting older and people are living longer, America is aging.

In 2000, 34.7 million Americans, almost 13% of the population, were over 65 years of age. By the year 2030, 70 million Americans, 20% of our population, will be over 65. The fastest growing segment of the population is centenarians, individuals over 100 years of age, followed by the 85 to 100 year olds.

America's healthcare system is not prepared to meet the needs of our growing senior population. For example, it is expected that the number of people living in long-term care facilities will double or triple by 2030. The long-term-care profession does not have the workforce nor the institutions to meet this increasing demand.

Litigation Costs Are Hurting Patients

There is no legal protection for doctors and other care providers who report errors. Doctors who admit that an error has been made are exposing themselves and/or the hospital to a lawsuit. The possibility for data transparency is eliminated because the predatory behavior of trial lawyers has created a litigious culture in America that intimidates doctors and hospitals from reporting errors, which leave patients to die every day. The problem is only getting worse.

Because of an increase in the number of frivolous lawsuits in America, malpractice insurance premiums are skyrocketing. This trend is literally killing patients in two fundamental ways. Care providers and institutions are less motivated to uncover and investigate mistakes, and unaffordable malpractice premiums are causing a massive exodus of physicians from private practice. The premiums in some states such as Mississippi, West Virginia, Nevada, and Pennsylvania have reached such a critical level that

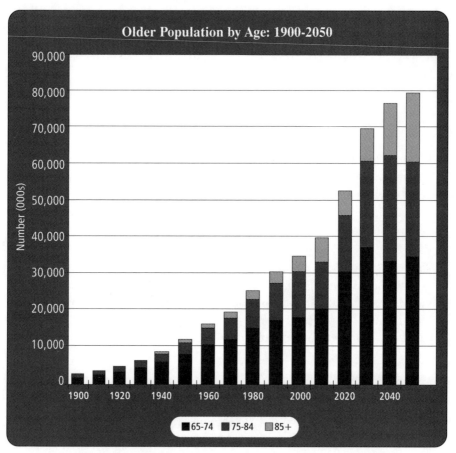

Chart developed by the U.S. Administration on Aging based on Census Bureau data.

whole communities have been left with a dangerous shortage of available physicians. This void especially impacts high-risk patients such as those who are pregnant.

A recent poll of West Virginia physicians conducted by Harris Interactive revealed that over 50% of physicians believe that their ability to treat their patients with high-quality care has decreased over the last five years, despite advances in technology and medical knowledge, because their funds have been diverted to malpractice insurance. Two out of three doctors have considered moving to another state to practice medicine.[13]

By 2005, 2.4% of the GDP will be spent on litigation costs. According to a study by the National Center for Policy Analysis, the money that we spend on litigation alone could pay for the healthcare needs of millions of people.

Shortage of Care Providers

Predatory trial-lawyer behavior is not the only dynamic causing a shortage of healthcare providers. Working conditions in the average doctor's office, hospital, and nursing home have been deteriorating. The increased demand for technologies and the aging baby-boomer population are squeezing government budgets. Because the government accounts for 45% of all healthcare spending, their tactics to control costs have hit the system like an atomic bomb. Decreased reimbursement rates from the govern-

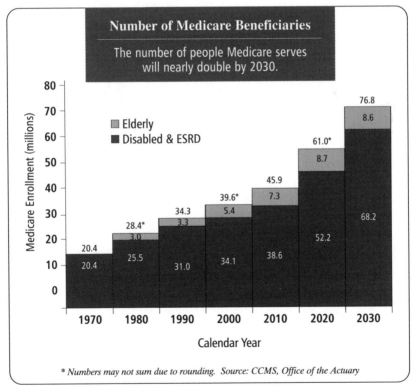

Source: Centers for Medicare & Medicaid Services, June 2002 Edition, Section III.B.1. Page 4

Key Findings of Report

Sicker and Poorer: The Consequences of Being Uninsured

- The uninsured receive less preventive care, are diagnosed at more advanced disease stages, and once diagnosed, tend to receive less therapeutic care (drugs and surgical interventions).

- The uninsured are 30% to 50% more likely to be hospitalized for an avoidable condition. The average cost of an avoidable hospital stay in 2002 was estimated to be about $3,300.

- Having health insurance would reduce mortality rates for the uninsured by 10% to 15%.

- Better health improves annual earnings by 10% to 30% (depending on measures and specific health condition) and increases educational attainment.

- Children in poor health miss more school days and have lower cognitive development.

- Lower educational attainment due to poor childhood health contributes to lower wages and lower labor force participation, which increase the likelihood of not being insured as an adult and the odds of continued poor health.

*The Kaiser Family Foundation Report
can be found at
http://www.kff.org/content/2002/20020510/.*

ment are hurting the bottom line. Doctors and other care providers are forced to see more patients for less time in order to maintain their standard of living. Some doctors are now even charging a "membership fee" of $1,500 to reduce the number of patients they treat.

By far the healthcare-provider profession facing the biggest shortage is nursing. In 2001 there were more than 126,000 registered nurse (RN) vacancies. By 2020 the shortage is expected to rise to 400,000 unless we can find ways to reverse this trend.

Shortages are already affecting patient care. Ninety percent of long-term care facilities admit that their ability to provide even basic care for their patients is being jeopardized because of the nurse shortage. As the 76 million baby boomers begin requiring even more from our healthcare system, this number will skyrocket. Given the current trends, the RN shortage will exceed 1 million by the year 2011.

Just as healthcare providers are retiring in increasing numbers, young people are choosing more lucrative, less stressful, and more stable professions. Medical school applications have fallen for the fifth year in a row.

Many of these same dynamics are also contributing to a shortage of physicians. Dr. Richard "Buz" Cooper of the Institute for Health Policy at the Medical College of Wisconsin led a team of researchers in a comprehensive study of the future population of physicians. The study, published in early 2002, revealed a 200,000-physician deficit by 2020.[14]

The specialty area that will be the most in demand is geriatric care. The Alliance for Aging Research has documented a need for 20,000 geriatric-trained physicians to adequately care for the 35 million older people in America. However, of the 650,000 licensed physicians in this country, fewer than 9,000 are qualified in gerontology. By 2004, due to physicians retiring and Medicare's trend of cutbacks, that number is estimated to drop to as few as 6,100. In 2030, America will need 36,000 gerontologists, but with the current trends, we may fall short by 25,000! That means two out of three seniors who need a gerontologist will not be able to find one.

The increase in drug utilization has resulted in a booming job market for pharmacists. In mid-October, however, there were less than two active pharmacists for each dispensing pharmacy. The National Association of Chain Drug Stores conducts an annual survey of pharmacy job vacancies. The vacancy rate in 2002 was 7% for retail pharmacists and 9% for hospitals and health systems nationwide. Despite the attractive job market, young people are less drawn to pharmacy as a line of medicine since income and advancement potential are more limited and red tape, frustration, and litigation seem to be increasing.

Other health professions are also experiencing shortages. An increase in availability and usage of new lifesaving technologies has resulted in a demand for trained technicians, yet the pressures of the perfect storm have caused a shortage again. The American Hospital Association found vacancy rates of 18% for radiological technologists and a 12% shortage of lab technicians.

The Culture of Medicine

The current culture of medicine is the fuel that feeds the perfect storm. According to the IOM, it takes seventeen years for an innovation to be thoroughly disseminated throughout the medical system.

Doctors are notorious for resisting any change that does not have a clear financial or personal benefit to them. Despite what many argue, they are not technology resistant. Doctors were some of the earliest adopters of pagers, for example, because they allowed the doctor more personal freedom out of the office. However, their zealous adoption has not carried over to more recent innovations or to those that provide a less personal benefit.

The e-Health Initiative released a survey showing that only one in four hospitals have a computerized physician order entry system, a system that can drastically reduce medication errors. And in those hospitals, only 15% of the physicians use the system. Eighty-five percent of doctors, nearly six out of seven, refuse to use the new system even when they know it saves lives, avoids unnecessary illnesses, and saves money. There is no other place in American life where personal prejudice is allowed to risk the loss of life or the imposition of unnecessary illness.

There are clearly destructive cultural dynamics present in healthcare that are not present in other industries. Imagine, for example, a manufacturing company in 1925 rejecting the truck in favor of the horse-drawn carriage because switching to the automobile would require a huge capital investment and retraining of their workforce. The company would soon be out of business. The market would demand it.

Healthcare, by contrast, lacks true market dynamics. This means that, as the consumer of the service, you do not have the financial power to force change in the system. Nor does the current system have the flexibility to incentivize physicians to change their behavior. Therefore there is little or no market incentive to decrease human suffering, save lives, or realize cost savings. Patients are primarily at the whim of doctors' personal preferences and knowledge levels when it comes to advances in the practice and administration of medicine.

Physicians are trained to be a "one man band." They spend a lot of money to cram as much knowledge and gain as much experience as possible in school and residency so they can treat any condition a patient might present. Doctors are trained to be confident, directive, unswerving, and to question all assertions. They are at the top of the medical "food chain." Patients, in general, perpetuate that culture by passively relying on doctors to manage their health. Until the popularization of the Internet, doctors and other trained care providers had a virtual monopoly on health information. Today medical information is readily available to anyone who seeks it.

Uninsured

American civilization is generally compassionate and generous; we do not like to see people in need. As in the movie, *John Q*, it is un-American for a child to die because his father does not have insurance, cannot afford to pay the hospital, and does not qualify for Medicaid. Audiences are so outraged that they cheer when an armed father holds caregivers and patients hostage to get his son the necessary medical care. The value we place on human life is so strong that we justify this behavior.

The number of uninsured in America is a threat to our civilization. Although we have seen a decrease in the number of children without health insurance coverage, Census Bureau numbers indicate the number of uninsured in America rose to 41.2 million in 2001. In a country that embraces access to affordable, quality medical care as a cultural value, it is unacceptable to have so many uninsured. It is the prospect of 100% coverage for all Americans that is the attraction of a single-payer system like those in Canada and England. The plight of the uninsured is consistently ranked at the top of our agenda in public-opinion polls.

The Kaiser Family Foundation commissioned a study to review all the major research of the last 25 years in order to define the value of insurance. What difference does insurance really make? What is its true value? It concluded that insurance is better for the patient, better for the wallet, and better for society. Insurance dramatically decreases both financial costs and human suffering.

Consumer Dissatisfaction

The "consumer revolution" has contributed to our discontentment with an industry that fails to utilize modern information technology systems that have added more control and convenience to almost every other sector of our lives. We have 24/7 access to cash through ATMs, instant access to a wealth of product and service comparison information through the Internet, automatic deposit of our paychecks and automatic withdrawal for monthly bills, on-line restaurant and tee-time scheduling, and overnight delivery from almost anywhere in the world. Even the bureaucratic poster child, the IRS, allows us to file our taxes on-line.

Yet these conveniences have not rooted themselves in mainstream medical offices. Most doctors do not use e-mail, and few offices will allow you to leave a non-urgent message on voice mail during non-business hours or lunchtime. Few individuals have access to their personal medical record on-line. Even scheduling a medical visit can be a laborious process; it may be weeks or months before an appointment is available. Most patients still receive written prescriptions that they have to drop off at a pharmacy and then wait 30 to 60 minutes for it to be filled.

Convenience aside, the chief concerns for most Americans are access, quality, and affordability of healthcare. Recent studies indicate that concern is growing. For example, a survey sponsored by the Consumer Health Education Council found the following results.

- When asked what the most important issue facing America is today, healthcare received 19% of the votes. Terrorism and national security was the only category that ranked higher.

- Over half of consumers, 55%, were confident they will get

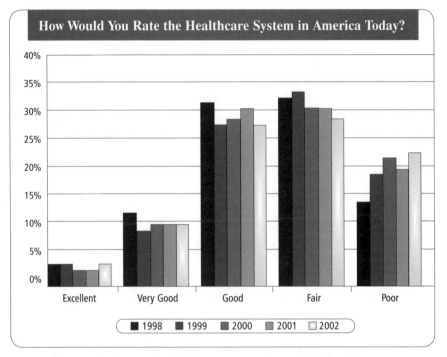

How Would You Rate the Healthcare System in America Today?

Source: Employee Benefit Research Institute, Consumer Health Education Council, and Mathew Greenwald & Associates, Inc., 1998-2002 Health Confidence Surveys. www.ebri.org/hcs/2002/hcs-conf.pdf

the healthcare treatment they need. When asked how confident they are that they will get needed treatment ten years from now, that number drops to 34%.

- Fifty-five percent do not believe they have enough choice about who provides their medical care, and 70% believe they will not have enough choice ten years from now.

- When asked to rate the healthcare system in America, 54% gave it a ranking of fair or poor, a 5% increase from 1998.

Americans are increasingly dissatisfied with the healthcare system and the ability of the system to meet future challenges.

Biological Warfare Threat

The current healthcare system is not nearly prepared to meet the challenge of a biological, chemical, or nuclear attack. The events surrounding September 11 comparatively understressed the system. The anthrax incident involved five tragic deaths and nineteen infections but was far smaller than a possible biological event that could infect millions of people. Nor did the terror of September 11 stress our national health system. Because of the high percentage of deaths among the casualties at the World Trade Center, a relatively limited number of individuals actually needed serious medical care.

The threat of a biological weapon is a grave concern. Secretary of Defense Donald Rumsfeld warned Americans in a speech at the Reserve Officer's Association in January of 2003.

> *It should be noted that biological weapons, which Iraq and North Korea both possess, can be as deadly and arguably a more immediate danger because they are simpler and cheaper to develop and deliver, and are even more readily transferred to terrorist networks than would be nuclear weapons.*
>
> *His [Saddam Hussein's] regime has large unaccounted for stockpiles of chemical and biological weapons including VX, sarin, mustard gas, anthrax, botulism, and possibly smallpox.*
>
> *The recent Dark Winter exercise, conducted at Johns Hopkins University, simulated a biological attack in which terrorists released smallpox in three separate locations in the United States. Within two months, the worst case estimate indicated that up to 1 million people could be dead and another 2 million affected. Biological weapons must be of major concern, let there be no doubt.* [15]

A biological weapon used against the United States would paralyze our healthcare system. People would panic and civil order would be threatened with collapse. The cost of not developing the information technology and surge capability in our medical system could result in thousands, if not hundreds of thousands, of people dying. There could be a crisis as early as tomorrow morning and we are unprepared to deal with it effectively.

Conclusion

The macro-level picture we have painted in this chapter leads to one conclusion—the current health and healthcare system is politically and financially impossible to defend and is the wrong model to achieve or maintain good health. The current model lacks effective systems, information technology, financing mechanisms and incentives, and costs far more than it should. While failing to emphasize quality, it distributes power to everyone but the individual patient.

Health and healthcare is the largest problem in American domestic policy today. As we try to achieve quality healthcare at reasonable costs, we are trapped by a focus on tactical or, at best, operational changes within the existing vision and strategies of healthcare. We are trying to invent marginal improvements instead of transforming the system. Why create a better iron lung when we can eliminate the threat of polio with the Salk vaccine? We need a transformation because the current system is unnecessarily costing both lives and money.

[1] Robert Pear, "U.S. Urged to Test Solutions to a 'Crisis' in Health Care," *New York Times,* (Washington: 20 November 2002): 19.
[2] As reported on <www.cms.gov/researchers/pubs/datacompendium/2002/02pg14.pdf> as of 24 April 2003.
[3] *Managed Care Weekly Digest*, "Businesses anticipate increases in healthcare insurance costs," (7 April 2003): 6.
[4] As reported on <www.harrisinteractive.com/news/newsletters_healthcare.asp> as of 24 April 2003.
[5] Linda T. Kohn, Janet M. Corrigan, and Molla S. Donaldson, ed., "To Err Is Human," (Washington DC: Institute of Medicine, 2000).
[6] As reported on <www.cdc.gov/ncidod/eid/vol4no3/weinstein.htm> as of 24 April 2003.
[7] As reported on <www.osha.gov/as/opa/oshafacts.html> as of 24 April 2003.
[8] See note 5; D.W. Bates, et al., "The cost of adverse drug events in hospitalized patients," *JAMA* 277, vol. 4 (1997): 307-311.
[9] As reported on <www.nasbo.org/Publications/PDFs/medicaid2003.pdf> as of 24 April 2003.
[10] As reported on <www.hhs.gov/news/press/1996pres/960425.html> as of 24 April 2003.
[11] As reported on <www.ihaonline.org/frimailing/2001/Email%20fm05-04-01.pdf> as of 24 April 2003.
[12] As reported on <www.csc.com/newsandevents/news/1227.shtml> as found on 23 April 2003; Efficient Healthcare Consumer Response initiative study, EHCR Assessment study is available to HIDA Members and Educational Foundation Associates for only $25. Call the HIDA office at 1-703-549-4432.
[13] Harris Interactive report: "The Increasing Impact of eHealth on Physician Behavior," (20 November 2001).
[14] *Health Affairs*, Jan/Feb 2002
[15] As reported on <www.defense.gov/speeches/2003/s20030120-secdef.html> as of 24 April 2003.

CHAPTER TWO

Why Reforming Healthcare Is Doomed to Fail and Only a Process of Transforming Health and Healthcare Can Succeed

We have an opportunity to save millions of lives and billions of dollars over the next generation. This concept is not merely an interesting or idealistic slogan. It is literally possible to properly design a system of health and healthcare that will save millions of Americans from getting sick, enable even more to manage their own health, and lead to a revolution in the quality of healthcare that will save countless lives and billions of dollars.

This is not a question of cheaper care being worse and more expensive care being better. This is a question of transforming current patterns of medicine, health, and healthcare into a system that will empower individuals with the knowledge to take control of their health and, when necessary, their own healthcare. The result will be healthier Americans and a less expensive health system.

Accomplishing these changes is possible and necessary. Unfortunately it cannot be achieved by merely "reforming" the current system. Any health "reform" within the current model is doomed to fail since it can only lead to a more complicated, more expensive, more bureaucratic system of ever greater mediocrity.

On the other hand, it is possible to develop new patterns and incentives that will transform the current system into one that is more desirable, affordable, and significantly more successful.

Reforming is a process of trying to make the current pattern work. Transforming is developing a new and very different pattern. Making a better horse and buggy was reforming. Inventing the internal combustion engine for cars, trucks, and airplanes was transforming. Developing longer hours for bank tellers was reforming. Inventing the automatic teller machine so people could get cash 24/7 almost anywhere in the world was transforming.

Politics is almost always about reforming and almost never about transforming because interest groups make transformation too complicated and too hard to understand. The old interest groups and the old arguments dominate politicians, their staffs, and the news media. The future has no interest groups. There are no paid lobbyists for the future. There are no editors with an intellectual investment in covering the future. There are no political reporters or columnists whose careers have come from describing the future.

Reforms are easy to cover. Minimum wage fights, taxing the rich, more money for this group or for that, these are the kinds of fights politicians know how to describe in speeches and that reporters know how to cover.

Obscure entrepreneurs, who are even now inventing the future as well as delivering better care at lower cost, are a difficult story to get the media to cover. Start-up Web sites that bring 21st century medical knowledge directly to individuals and families do not fit into the present editorial definition of news. Most start-ups have neither the time nor the money to hire a lobbyist. They are literally not in the room when the bigwigs gather at political action committee fundraisers in the major hotels of Washington or in the state capitols.

The currently powerful interest groups are based on the guilds and structures of the past. Invariably they absorb all the available money from government, leaving the future once again starved of resources.

Bureaucracies simply compound the bias toward the past. Bureaucrats know the past. That is what they regulate, study, and discuss. Bureaucrats do not know the future nor do they contemplate it. It might be dangerous. It certainly is not something for which they want to make exceptions. Start-ups might fail. Entrepreneurs might deliver on only half of their promises. After all, career bureaucrats are not visionaries. They do their jobs, protect their turf, and diligently adhere to the status quo. The thought of answering to a congressional hearing or to the news media understandably keeps them very risk adverse.

Americans know instinctively that too much power in centralized bureaucracies and too much money in government is inherently dangerous because it leads to corrupt, slow, ponderous, red-tape-ridden systems that deny the future by propping up the past.

Throughout the Soviet era, American leaders said repeatedly that centralized command and control bureaucracies would not work. We argued that a dynamic, entrepreneurial, customer-oriented free market would always develop more and better products and services than a centralized bureaucracy. We argued that markets led to better decisions than red tape. We said that the customer and not the bureaucrat should be the arbiter of what is purchased and, therefore, what kind of production is needed.

That we were right in the 1980s about the Soviet Union was proved when the Soviet empire collapsed and disappeared in 1991. We lecture the same principles to other nations today. Yet we fail to adhere to our own recommendations when we come to the politics of healthcare.

The current model has moved government control and purchase of healthcare from 25% of the total in 1965 to 45% today.[1] Even after the Clintons' big government health plan was rejected in 1994, America has continued to move toward government and bureaucratic control of the health process. If you add insurance company bureaucrats in large private plans to the equation, public and private bureaucracies shape two-thirds or more of all health decisions in America today.

Trying to reform this bureaucratically dominated collection of special interest groups is, as I have seen over the last 29 years, a hopeless cause.

Instead, we have to accept that this model has failed and turn our attention to transforming it into a very different system of health and healthcare.

My belief that we have to replace the current healthcare pattern with a 21st century pattern is based on years of involvement and study of healthcare by myself and many others.

When I first ran for Congress in 1974, doctors, hospitals, and patients were already complaining about the bureaucracy, red tape, and costs of healthcare. Doctors were in distress over the threat of litigation, blackmail by trial lawyers, and fears that a trial lawyer could ruin their lives. Small-business owners lamented the high cost of health insurance and doctors complained about all the paperwork and how long it took the insurance companies to pay. Even worse than private insurance, doctors said, was Medicaid, which had more paperwork, more regulations, and lower payments.

When I finally won election to Congress in 1978, President Jimmy Carter was trying to pass a cost-control bill aimed at hospitals. The hospitals and their allies rallied grassroots support and defeated the Carter proposal. Year after year since then, some 29 years since that first campaign, I have studied the health issue and listened to people complain with increasing intensity.

In 1991 I worked with Republican Minority Leader Bob Michel to create the House Republican Task Force on Health. A then-unknown Illinois Congressman named Denny Hastert chaired that Task Force. He is now, of course, Speaker of the House. We worked to develop a positive, market-oriented solution to the rising cost of healthcare. Unfortunately we failed to carry it in the House.

Then in 1993, former First Lady and now Senator, Hillary Clinton led a determined effort to overhaul the entire health system. At first the Clinton proposal for radical health reform seemed to gain ground. However, as people realized how complicated it was and how much it extended government into their personal healthcare, support for the plan quickly eroded.

Finally in 1994, it collapsed from its own weight as Democratic leaders in the House and Senate refused to even bring it to a vote.

We are once again faced with dramatically rising health costs. There are strikes in the private sector as employers try to shift some of the costs onto their employees. Doctors are leaving their practices in protest against the rising cost of malpractice insurance due to unrestrained litigation. The red tape is worsening, the quality of service is declining, the states are facing budget crises in Medicaid, and a growing number of reports indicate that the quality of care provided is so poor that for some it is life-threatening. According to one study, there are an estimated 2,000,000 hospital- and 1,500,000 nursing-home-induced illnesses annually.[2] A previously cited report indicated between 44,000 and 98,000 deaths occur in hospitals each year from medical errors. And another found it can take up to seventeen years for a new, improved medical procedure to reach every doctor. In effect, for seventeen years, your care provider could be giving you less than the best care.

When I stepped down as Speaker of the House in January 1999, I resolved to focus a great deal on rethinking the healthcare system. At more than 13% of the total GDP and growing rapidly, it is the largest single sector of our economy. One projection is that healthcare spending could be one out of every four dollars of GDP by the time the baby boomers have all retired.

Not only are the economics of health immense but they are also literally a matter of life and death. As more Americans grow older, the question of health and healthcare will only become even more important.

As a senior fellow at the American Enterprise Institute, I have been examining the healthcare system for the last four years. With strong support from Anne Woodbury, vice president for health at my consulting firm, the Gingrich Group; our associate Sarah Murphy; and Dana Pavey, our director of research at the American Enterprise Institute, we have been interviewing experts, analyzing data, visiting medical entrepreneurs, and examining success stories.

Two things have become very clear to us.

First, there are thousands of dedicated, inventive, persistent, and creative people who are discovering better solutions for American health and healthcare. Every day these pioneers save lives and save money by doing things smarter and better.

Second, there are enormous, deep, entrenched barriers to change. In fact, the current system is badly designed and dominated by the self-interested forces of the past.

After four years of work, we concluded that it was impossible to reform the current system. At its core, the design itself is hopelessly flawed because it is based on the wrong principles. Every effort at reform simply makes the current system more complicated and leads the entrenched forces of the past to modify their behavior just enough to protect their pocketbooks, their status, and their self-interests regardless of what the new rules require.

The current system cannot be reformed because

1. The very principle of a third-party-payer system is profoundly wrong. Trouble always arises when you have a triangular-payment model where one person pays, a second person provides a service or product, and a third person receives the service or product.

The consumer pays less than the cost of the service or product or, indeed, nothing at all. Yet he feels entitled to expect only the best. Under this model, the sky is the limit. The consumer has no sense of gratitude because he assumes it is the provider's duty to give him whatever he wants. The payer has no commitment to the highest quality service and convenience because he is not receiving it. The payer is focused on a system that will minimize his expenditure of money, and he resents every penny the provider charges and every demand the receiver makes. The payer sees himself as caught between the greedy and the demanding. And the service provider is confused and frustrated because he can never please either the payer or the consumer.

In a third-party-payer system, unhappiness is maximized and conflict is virtually guaranteed. This problem would occur in any third-party transactional model where it is applied.

The first step toward a sound, responsible system of health and healthcare is to find a positive, incentive-led method of returning to the binary buyer-seller system in which the individual has an economic interest in his or her own health and is the primary guardian of how his or her own money is spent.

2. The current system is profoundly misfocused in defining the doctor as the center of the system and acute care as its primary interest. Both assumptions are wrong and are mutually reinforcing. We should optimize health by creating systems that enable people to sustain their own health instead of attending to an individual's health only retroactively when they are in need of acute care.

The greatest opportunities in healthcare occur before someone needs acute care. To save lives and save money it is paramount to focus on keeping people healthy, diagnosing their health challenges early, and teaching them to manage their own health before they develop chronic conditions. This is more than patient-centered care. This is individual-centered health and healthcare, because our first goal is for the individual to embrace his or her own nutrition-activity-attitude pattern to avoid becoming a patient in the first place.

If you already have a chronic condition, the healthcare system should educate and empower you to manage your health with minimum engagement of the acute-care system. Managing your own health with a chronic condition like diabetes, asthma, arthritis, or cardiovascular disease has to be undertaken by the individual with coaching by a doctor or nurse. It is impossible for the doctor or nurse to manage an individual's chronic disease. Unfortunately, because the doctor is regarded as the center of the current system, medical culture trains patients to rely on doctors to maintain their health, absolving them of personal responsibility. Individual self-awareness and self-management is the biggest need in healthcare today.

However, as long as people lack the power and responsibility to choose, it will be extraordinarily difficult to get people to take primary responsibility for their own health. In order to reinforce the shift toward personal responsibility, we must reengage the individual financially through individual purchase of healthcare.

We all understand the phenomenon of personal interest being tied to financial interest in other parts of the economy. No one washes a rental car. If you own it, you take care of it. If you rent it, you expect the owner to take care of it.

When people feel ownership, they learn to maintain and repair their car; refill the gas tank rather than run out; change the oil instead of having the engine seize; and wash the exterior to minimize rust. Similarly, homeowners learn how to hire painters, electricians, plumbers, roofers, and in some cases, to do all of those things themselves.

When we reconnect individuals' economic interest in their own health with systems of information that enable them to understand and manage their health (with doctors and nurses as partners, but with the individual clearly and ultimately responsible for his or her health), then we will be on the verge of truly saving lives and saving money on an enormous scale.

Virtually every expert agrees that better public health policies—emphasizing nutrition, exercise, attitude, and early diagnosis—are key to saving lives and saving money. They agree that an individual-centered program of health management is critical. And they agree that the current doctor-centered, acute-care-focused system encourages the wrong attitude and behaviors.

Providing both the financial control and the information for individuals to regain control of their health and their family's health will be very controversial. It will be especially resisted by those who gain the most money and status by claiming that health is a mystery beyond the understanding of patients. However, patient education, knowledge, and financial control are essential for achieving a healthy system.

3. One reason healthcare reform fails is because the activities of healthcare are simply too complex to be reformed by a political process. What we now have is a massive, almost incomprehensible jumble of activities that we label healthcare. This system is at least 30 times more complex than the

Defense Department. Reform efforts are compounded by the enormous political leverage the power centers in healthcare wield to simply block changes they think will hurt them.

The result is that leaders are constantly caught in the dilemma of too much or too little change. If you try too much change as the Clintons did in 1993, every interest group will attack you and the effort will collapse. If you try small incremental changes, the affected interest groups will fight ferociously to protect their turf. The fight for even small changes is exhausting. Even if you win a small change, the system simply reorganizes itself around the reform and continues with business as usual. Cut the amount paid per visit, and suddenly doctors will discover that people need significantly more visits. Squeeze hospitals, and the home-health business will suddenly blossom. Shift spending toward generic drugs, and the price of generic drugs will start rising. Focus on the rising cost of prescription drugs (the 2002 problem), and suddenly consolidated hospitals with strong market dominance in cities start raising their rates faster (the 2003 problem).

Thus the current collection of interest groups and activities we lump together as healthcare is virtually unreformable in any meaningful way. Transformation is the only successful and logistically possible option.

4. The rejection of new ideas and new technologies is inherent in the current system. For 30 years healthcare providers have spurned an electronic information system. Start-up entrepreneurs with new ideas are simply repudiated. Serving patients better, saving money, and even saving lives simply fail to penetrate as reasons to use new technologies. Without them we continue to needlessly lose lives. Our authorities shrug and say there is nothing they can do about it.

They are wrong.

When people are being killed by arrogance and obstinacy, something can be done. When people are being given additional illnesses and health problems through willful refusal to learn habits that work, something can be done. When money is being wasted extravagantly because a few people hide behind their guild and refuse to be held accountable for basic modernization, something can and must be done.

Transforming: The Creation of Large-Scale Change

We are proposing very bold ideas. In that sense, transformation is like crossing a mountain range. It is a major systems change and not just marginal improvements on one part of the system or another. Once you get the majority of people over the intellectual mountain range to a better health future, they will never want to go back to the old system. In essence, each mountaintop represents a concept that, once accepted, affords climbers a glorious view of the benefits as they travel to the valley below, where they are confronted with another mountain until they have crossed the range. That process is transformation, one conceptual challenge at a time. But once across the range, it is intellectually impossible to go back.

The rise of the automobile is a good example of a major and successful systems change. The first transformation was from the horse and buggy to the automobile. The next great breakthrough came when Henry Ford designed interchangeable parts, which led Ford to his second breakthrough, the assembly line. The result was an explosion in productivity and lowering of costs. However, Ford's market was still riding horses or walking. He wanted to have the longest feasible production run in order to drop the cost of cars as dramatically as possible. So he offered his customers the one-size-fits-all Model T. It came in any color—as long as it was black. But people were happy because they most valued an affordable car in this phase of the automobile revolution. The Model A was merely a reform. It was larger, more comfortable, and more powerful, but every car was still exactly the same and available only in black.

It was about that time that General Motors hired Alfred Pritchard Sloan. Sloan's response to the Henry Ford model transformed the automobile industry. He did not start by thinking about how to produce cars; he started by thinking about America. In 1921 Sloan believed that Americans would get richer and would want to demonstrate their success. Expecting that people would want to project their new economic status, Sloan pioneered the concept of the annual model change.

He pursued neither a manufacturing strategy nor a narrowly drawn business strategy but instead a social strategy that had economic and manufacturing components. Traveling to a different region for one week every quarter, Sloan personally sold cars to better understand his customers. By answering their questions, he got the earliest indicators of how people's tastes were changing.

Where Ford had pioneered the lowest-cost production run, Sloan pioneered the customer-defined manufacturing process. Each was a great breakthrough for its era.

The history of the automobile is an example of truly large-scale transformation. It took many different changes to arrive at today's modern mass-production, consumer-oriented, multi-model system of automobiles. Nevertheless, a requisite entrepreneurial attitude produced the large-scale changes required. Sloan successfully integrated those changes into the world in which he was living. His design in the 1920s would have been wrong in 1905. Ford's design in 1905 was right, but he failed to adapt to the new model when the old model had fulfilled its mission and people were ready for social status as well as transportation.

By the 1960s the quality ideas developed by Dr. W. Edwards Deming and Joseph M. Juran spurred another transformation with the even more productive and lower cost Toyota Production System.

Because I wanted to understand the quality concept as he did, I took a 60-hour tutorial with Deming when he was 90-years old. He had taken the Western Electric production model, which we used brilliantly in the Second World War, and extracted the fundamental principles that made it work. After WWII we were indisputably the most productive country in the world. Deming went to Japan in 1951 and presented a three-day seminar to the leaders of 75% of the industrial capital of Japan. Having paid close attention to Deming, Toyota simply created a better production system. Today the Japanese award for the best company each year is named after Deming.

We can apply a similar concept of large-scale transformation to healthcare. Think about a world where 23 seconds is too long to wait for an ATM machine to dispense money; self-service gasoline can be paid for electronically and so accurately that many customers no longer keep the receipt;

and travelers can go on-line to choose their flights, purchase their tickets, and pick their own seats. That is the world we live in today. In that context of sophisticated, but increasingly inexpensive, information systems, we can certainly create a healthcare system designed around the health of the healthcare consumer.

Applying the Concept of Transformation to Health and Healthcare

The balance of *Saving Lives & Saving Money* outlines how we can apply this concept of transformation to create an entirely new approach to a 21st Century System of Health and Healthcare. We outline new opportunities that exist and the real success stories on which public policies can be built to save lives and save money. We describe the kind of ongoing transforming process that could be launched at the federal level, in every state capital, and by health payers in the private sector. We also emphasize Internet-based opportunities for you to learn more, connect with others, and participate in creating this new system.

Transforming healthcare is a massive task. It took from 1970 until 1996 for welfare to be transformed. Nevertheless, Americans were convinced that requiring people to work or attend school was better than having them stay at home waiting on the next check from the welfare office. We were told for years that welfare could never be reformed and, in fact, that was true—it had to be completely transformed. We were told to be realistic and settle for small changes in an inherently bad system. However, the American people insisted that we transform the system from dependency to opportunity, from waiting passively to learning and working.

By 1996, after 26 years of effort, the American people had spoken decisively. Congress passed welfare reform three times. The first two times President Clinton vetoed it. Then a widely circulated Public Agenda Foundation study called *The Values We Live By* reported that 92% of the American people favored changing the system, including 88% of the people on welfare.[3] The third time Congress passed it, President Clinton signed the bill.

The results have been spectacular. Welfare officials evolved from advocates of dependency to counselors of opportunity and self-reliance. The welfare rolls shrank by approximately 60%. Child abuse declined, spousal abuse declined, marriage increased, and income went up for those who left welfare for school and work.

Transforming healthcare will happen much faster than transforming welfare did. Everyone has a stake in their own health and in the health of the ones they love. As the American people come to realize that a transformed system will save hundreds of thousands of lives, improve the quality of life for millions of others, and save billions of dollars, there will be a rapidly growing demand for real change.

What follows are real examples of the specific steps that need to be taken today to save lives and save money.

[1] As reported on <www.geomedics.com/ebook/healthysystem/index.htm> as of 23 April 2003: 39
[2] The costs of adverse drug events in hospitalized patients as cited in: Adverse Drug Events Prevention Study Group. *JAMA* 277, vol. 4 (1997): 307-311.
[3] Public Agenda, *The Values We Live By: What Americans Want From Welfare Reform,* (New York: 1996): 18-19, 24-25; and *Closing Gateway,* p.20.

CHAPTER THREE

The Principles of a 21st Century
System of Health and Healthcare

It will be impossible to transform the current system with incremental reforms. Each of the changes and policy initiatives will be successful only if they occur in a broader context driven by an overarching vision. Former British Prime Minister Margaret Thatcher, one of the great change agents in British history, had a firm principle, First you win the argument, then you win the vote. Putting ideas and proposals in the context of the big picture is vital to achieving success. People have to learn where you intend to go, think through the argument about your vision, compare it to the other options, and then conclude you are right before they commit themselves to a major change.

One of the key principles I have learned from spending more than two decades working with military leaders is to plan back from victory. It is imperative to first define success so you know when you have reached it. In fact, without a clear vision and an understanding of the principles underlying that vision, it is impossible to know whether you are working toward success or merely staying busy. Without an idea of where you are going, all of your efforts are just meaningless activity. What we need is progress. And progress is defined by a clearly stated goal or vision.

20th Century Current System	21st Century Transformed System
Provider Centered	Individual Centered
Price Driven	Values Driven
Knowledge Disconnected	Knowledge Intense
Slow Diffusion of Innovation	Rapid Innovation and Speed of Diffusion
Care Is Reactive, Episodic, and Disjointed	Use Genetic, Outcomes-Based Knowledge to Create a Preventive, Self-Managed, and Health-Oriented System of Continuous Involvement Using the Nutrition-Activity-Attitude Model
Paper Based	Electronic, Information Based
Triangular Third-Party-Controlled Market	Binary, Market Mediated
Adversarial Government Manages by Process	Collaborative Government Manages by Outcomes
Limited Choice	Increased Choice
Outcomes Undermeasured and Ignored	Outcomes Measured and Improved
Expensive, Predatory Trial Lawyer-Enriching System of Dispute Resolution	Fair, Affordable System of Health Justice That Protects Individuals and Encourages Access to Quality Care
Overall Cost Increase	Overall Cost Decrease

Four years ago, when our group started this project to rethink our system of health and healthcare, we were struck by how little work had been done to define success for a health and healthcare system of the 21st century. What would the optimal system of health and healthcare in America look like?

We talked with thousands of people, met with hundreds of companies and associations, and reviewed mountains of research. We tried to capture good ideas and working models (many of them are listed in Transforming Examples, Appendix A of this book) and determine what made them successful. We synthesized all this information in a list of "Principles of a 21st Century System." We drafted, sought advice, redrafted, sought advice, and redrafted again. The chart on the previous page summarizes what we believe are the principals of the current system and those of the 21st century system. The balance of this chapter describes them in more detail.

The 21st Century System Is Individual Centered
As Opposed to the Current Provider/Payer-Centered System

Our healthcare system—doctors, nurses, hospitals, insurance, prescription drugs, medical devices, medical schools, and other elements too numerous to mention—exists because of us, the individuals. Any system that does not put the interests of the individual first, such as the current one, must be transformed.

We purposely use "individual centered" as opposed to "patient/customer/consumer centered" because the goal of the 21st Century System of Health and Healthcare is to keep the individual healthy so he or she does not have to become a patient.

The 20th century system of healthcare does not allow you to own your own medical records or control your healthcare dollars, and it limits your access to expert providers. In the 21st Century System of Health and Healthcare, you will own your medical record, control your healthcare dollars, and be able to make informed choices about healthcare providers. In the 20th century system of healthcare, you are not expected to be knowledgeable about your own health. In the 21st Century System of Health and

Healthcare, you are expected to bear the primary responsibility for managing your own health in consultation with your doctor.

The 21st Century System Is Values Driven
As Opposed to the Current Price-Driven System

The system of the 21st century focuses on measuring and delivering quality healthcare based on the premise that focusing on quality will inherently decrease costs. Former Treasury Secretary Paul O'Neill, when he was CEO of Alcoa and co-chairman of the Pittsburgh Regional Healthcare Initiative, and Don Berwick, president of the Institute for Healthcare Improvement, have pioneered the translation of the teachings of popular industry quality experts such as Edwards Deming and Joseph Juran to the healthcare profession. They passionately believe that a quality-focused system results in better overall outcomes at lower overall costs and that the principles of quality, which have revolutionized almost every other industry, can have a dramatic effect on the healthcare industry as well.

Students of Deming and Juran know that statistical information and systems analysis are vital to the development of quality. They also know that the revolution in manufacturing productivity over the last 50 years has largely been brought about by innovative thinking.

That same revolution in outcomes can be achieved in health and healthcare if we have the courage to insist on applying sound principles to systems that historically have rejected sharing knowledge and have refused to be systematically self-critical.

This is not an idle proposition. Thousands of lives and billions of dollars a year are at stake in the quality revolution. We must have the firmness those lives deserve because they can be saved. We should have the determination those dollars deserve because they can be put to better use. The time for the quality revolution is now, and it should occur in every sector of health and healthcare in America.

The current focus on lowering and managing the cost of healthcare ignores the impact of the quality of care being received. Excuses for managed-care companies to neglect preventive care, such as the individual will not be in the system long enough for preventive care to pay off, merely reveal the immoral anti-humanism of such healthcare providers. In the airline industry, we insist on safety first and profits second. In providing care we should insist on value for the patient before the provider or insurer can try to make a profit. Any other focus risks lives and is inherently immoral.

A values-driven system will balance the cost with the overall benefit. It asks, "What is best for the long-term needs of the individual?" as opposed to "What is best for the short-term needs of the quarterly report?" The frenzy of cost-cutting and cost-shifting tactics used by healthcare payers (employers, insurance companies, and the government), such as stricter prescription-drug formularies, eliminated metal-health benefits, higher deductibles, and the like, may relieve some short-term financial strain, but the longer-term implications will reveal that those decisions were not based on a true value assessment of what was best for the patient. Healthcare administrators have an obligation to measure the benefits they manage, such as absence of illness, quality of life, or productivity, on a long-term horizon.

The 21st Century System Is Knowledge Intensive
As Opposed to the Current Knowledge-Disconnected System

Receiving the best healthcare hinges on the availability of correct information. It is imperative that the trained professionals paid to help you stay healthy or become healthy have the most up-to-date information to provide the most efficient and comprehensive care possible.

This includes a baseline of vital information about you as the patient. It will likely consist of a complete medical and family history including the list of prescription drugs, over-the-counter medications, any herbal treatments or supplements you may be taking, and results from tests administered at the request of other care providers. Most of us have experienced the frustration of being asked to fill out a patient history report for ourselves or a loved one at the inception of an emergency room visit. It is truly unacceptable to be asked to remember every detail of our past medical care during what is often a stressful—but critical—emergency visit.

Intuitively we know that, if Amazon.com can track every purchase we have made with them, electronically synthesize that information, and recommend other books we may enjoy, a hospital can surely keep track of vital health information for emergencies.

The job of the provider is to match your personal information against up-to-the-minute breakthroughs in science and medicine that may influence your diagnosis, treatment, and potentially save your life. The 21st Century System of Health and Healthcare empowers patients, doctors, nurses, and other care providers with the tools they need to access the knowledge they need, the moment they need it.

MEDLINE is a very comprehensive source of life science and biomedical bibliographic information. Compiled by the National Library of Medicine, it contains nearly eleven million articles from 4,300 different publications. Thankfully, the amount of scientific evidence to guide medical care is voluminous, and it is growing exponentially. However, no matter how well-intentioned and intelligent the care provider may be, it is impossible for any one person to synthesize all the available information and consider all of the permutations of the interactions and potential treatments, even if the information is readily available.

The creation of sophisticated information technology systems in the last five years has leapfrogged the ability of providers to have information and decision-support tools to help synthesize the massive amount of information necessary to make good health decisions. Technology tools created by companies such as SKOLAR and PKC Corporation (see Transforming Examples, Appendix A) are increasing effectiveness of care providers and resulting in dramatic increases in the quality of care patients receive.

It is difficult to overstate how big a change in medical school, in licensing tests, and in daily practice this principle will require. We are proposing the move from a memorized, comfortable, customary practice of past knowledge to a system in which the doctor and nurse are embedded in an electronic web of constantly changing information so that both the patient information and the best practices information are available at the moment the doctor or nurse needs it. This will be a vastly more powerful and more efficient system, but it is a shift comparable to that from a local newspaper to Newscorp's worldwide media reach. This change is central to our future, but its complexities should not be underestimated.

The 21st Century System Rapidly Diffuses Innovation

> *"Knowing is not enough; we must apply. Willing is not enough; we must do."*
> - Johann Wolfgang von Goethe

No matter how useful an innovation, it is purposeless unless used. We expect our healthcare providers to have all the latest information about medical breakthroughs in order to provide us with the highest quality care. Yet in *Crossing the Quality Chasm,* the Institute of Medicine made the following statement:

> *The lag between the discovery of more efficacious forms of treatment and their incorporation into routine patient care is unnecessarily long, in the range of about 15 to 20 years (Balas and Boren, 2000). Even then, adherence of clinical practice to the evidence is highly uneven.*[1]

A 21st Century System of Health and Healthcare would not only invest in new innovations and discoveries, but also build a system that rapidly diffuses new innovations and discoveries to the people that can use them. The pace of change in modern society is so rapid, especially in biological knowledge, that it is impossible to expect any one person to know about every new discovery even in their specialty.

We must design the system to be easier for you and your doctor to access new discoveries and innovations about your particular illness or set of symptoms. We must expect the government to use their regulatory authority effectively and efficiently to allow innovations to rapidly permeate the system.

Evercare, a comprehensive health management approach for Medicare's frail elderly, is delivering dramatic increases in quality care for patients at a dramatic decrease in cost to the government (see Transforming

Examples, Appendix A). When I learned about their outcomes two years ago, I was surprised to find they were operating in only 60 counties. In order for Evercare to be considered a payable service by Medicare nationally, the company would have had to apply in every one of the 3,000 counties in the United States separately. When Tom Scully, chief federal administrator of the Medicare and Medicaid Services programs, learned about this, he issued a block waiver so Evercare could bypass the process of petitioning each county. He is now exploring the possibility of creating a review board to issue these block waivers to technologies and innovations proven to increase quality and decrease costs. This bold and systemic change to accelerate the adoption of a proven, innovative program is government at its best. And it is what we should expect.

The 21st Century Is Health Oriented As Opposed to Sickness Oriented

Most of us have heard the old cliché, An ounce of prevention is worth a pound of cure. Your medical system obviously has not, as evidenced by its focus on reactive acute care after you become sick instead of working to keep you healthy.

In the 20th century system, patients do not figure into the model until they are already ill. At that point care is administered (much more than would likely have been necessary if preventive care had been utilized) episodically and disjointedly because an acute-care-focused system can't really keep up with the emergency needs of the population.

The 21st Century System of Health and Healthcare will partner with you first to prevent illness and then to care for you as a patient if you become ill. It will put greater emphasis on the interaction between nutrition, activity, and attitude in preventing disease. It will emphasize and incentivize you to be self-aware and provide you with the tools to self-manage any chronic disease you may have. While this does not eliminate the need for health professionals, it returns control of your health back to you.

Unfortunately the current medical system is neither financially incentivized nor intellectually prepared for a shift to this health-oriented, wellness model of disease avoidance and care minimization. The starting point should be optimizing health and creating systems that allow people to sustain their own health. In order to receive the highest quality healthcare, cut medical costs, and decrease pain, we must broaden the health policy dialogue to include health, wellness, prevention, and preemption.

The 21st Century System Is Electronically Based
As Opposed to Paper Based

The objective fact that paper and the telephone remain the primary means of information flow in our medical system is evidence enough that our current system is both inadequate and dysfunctional. A system in which saving money, saving lives, and producing a better outcome are not reason enough to use new technologies is inconsistent with the American spirit and need not be accepted.

A transformed 21st Century System of Health and Healthcare would have its foundation in secure electronic information sharing that maintains an individual's right to privacy. Paper-based records and handwritten prescriptions would be as obsolete in the new 21st century system as leeches are in the current system. Every hospital, long-term care facility, and doctor's office would be required to use an electronic system to order prescription drugs. Medical schools would include electronic software and Internet-based systems in their curriculum when they train students to use diagnostic tools such as the stethoscope and thermometer. A specialist in London would be able to review your complete electronic medical record, including x-rays and lab results, within seconds of your decision to seek his or her help while on a vacation or business trip.

The current system's reliance on paper is costing lives, increasing needless suffering, and unnecessarily inflating costs. It is impossible to argue against an electronic system of information. Even as a free-market conservative who believes in minimal government involvement, I would argue that it is justified to mandate the use of electronic systems to drag the medical system into the 21st century and save lives and save money.

*The 21st Century System Is a Buyer/Seller-Mediated Market
As Opposed to a Third-Party, Bureaucratically Controlled Market*

The first step toward a 21st Century System of Health and Healthcare is to return to the classic, binary system in which the individual has an economic interest in his or her own health and is the primary guardian of how his or her money is spent.

Returning financial power to the individual is the only way to grow a system of health and healthcare congruent with the culture of America and the opportunities of the 21st century. In every other sector of the American economy, with the unfortunate exception of education, we trust individuals to make their own decisions. We do not need a third party to tell us how and where we can spend our money when we are purchasing a home, buying a car, or contracting with an Internet service provider. Yet with our most important decisions—decisions about our health—we are subject to third-party involvement and approval. No wonder we are dissatisfied with the current system. It is also not surprising that doctors and other care providers are also dissatisfied. Their ability to help you make the best decision for your particular situation is thwarted by a third party who lacks their knowledge and training but is restricting their options.

A 21st Century System of Health and Healthcare will give you control of the care you receive by enabling you to purchase your own care.

*The 21st Century System Practices Collaborative Governance
As Opposed to Adversarial Government*

There will always be a role for government in ensuring the safety of the 21st Century System of Health and Healthcare. Every time I eat a hamburger, I am confident that what I am eating is in fact hamburger because of the USDA requirements and regulations. I like that. What would be absurd is if the USDA required that every hamburger be a certain diameter with a certain circumference and that a form be filed on each one produced. That is one differentiation between a collaborative and an adversarial government.

The healthcare industry is largely affected by the government in its role as a regulator and as the largest single payer for healthcare services. The traditional, 20th century role of government in healthcare is adversarial because it manages by process instead of outcomes, guaranteeing a lack of information and engendering hostility.

There is presently zero incentive to collaborate with the government. I recently learned that when one of the healthcare professional organizations partnered with the government to accomplish a specific goal, the result was a decrease in reimbursement rate for the healthcare profession. The organization worked with the government to solve a problem, and when the problem was solved, the overall cost decreased. In response, the government cut their reimbursement. Improving the system to save money ended up costing them money. With these realities, it is no surprise that the private sector is so reluctant to work with government.

In a 21st Century System of Health and Healthcare, collaborative government would partner with private industry to identify ways to improve outcomes of care in an industry setting. I firmly believe that the government should insist on those outcomes and not be mired in process management.

The 21st Century System Increases Choice As Opposed to Limiting Choice

The 20th century system, particularly in managed care, was characterized by limiting our choices and freedoms. Many of us are bound by the limitations of insurance-company formularies and preferred-provider networks. We are limited by what kind of insurance we are provided through our employer or through the government. Patients are limited by the doctor's knowledge or bias because it is the doctor who filters the information on treatment and drug options.

A 21st Century System of Health and Healthcare will increase the power and freedom of the individual to choose and provide the necessary information for good choices. It will not handcuff you to a specific insurance plan because that happens to be the only one offered by your employer.

Although some would argue that we are welcome to purchase our own insurance on the free market now, I disagree. The current system and our current tax laws are so biased in favor of larger purchasers that we really do not have any practical choices.

Under the current system, it would take a major effort to find out what drugs, both brand and generic, are available for a certain diagnosis, which ones are on your insurance's formulary, and the total price, not just your co-pay, of the drug at the different pharmacies in your area. We cannot have free-market choices without usable information sources to filter our options. The 21st century system will increase choice by allowing you to access information at one comprehensive portal on the Internet.

The 21st Century System Measures and Improves Outcomes

In our current system, it is impossible to obtain any data related to outcomes from a provider or an institution. It would be challenging to call any local hospital and find out how many heart surgeries they completed in the last year. More importantly, they would not be able to tell you what the current health is of the patients on whom they operated. How many days did the average patient remain in the hospital, and how did it compare with the national average? How many patients acquired a hospital-induced illness? What percentage of the patients were hospitalized again within six months?

The current reimbursement method and the threat of predatory trial lawyers are the two principle reasons that outcomes are not measured or are ignored in our current system. Reimbursement is the amount of money an insurance company or the government, in the case of Medicare or Medicaid, pays a doctor, hospital, or long-term care facility to provide a particular service or procedure. Because the government is the largest health insurer in America, its decisions on reimbursement lead all the others. In our current system, a check is written to the doctor for a procedure but there is no measure of whether that money benefited the patient, whether it produced a valuable outcome. Equally troubling is the opinion among healthcare providers that honesty about problems or quality indicators would simply draw the attention of trial lawyers. As you can imagine, this is a strong deterrent for healthcare professionals to measure outcomes. The right to sue is overwhelming the right to get the best quality care.

Outcomes measurement is a foundational principle of the 21st century system. With electronic medical records and claims systems, it would be possible to aggregate information from a particular doctor or hospital annually and report out certain risk-adjusted metrics.

We should incentivize providers to achieve certain outcomes. For example, the national rate for hospital-induced illnesses is about 4%. If Medicare had an incentive program in which hospitals reporting an error rate under 1% received a substantial bonus (say one-half the amount they saved Medicare by creating fewer hospital-induced illnesses), we would begin to see dramatic decreases in hospital-induced illness. In order to institute incentive programs, however, the system would need to more aggressively rely on electronic information sources and the participants would need protection from predatory lawsuits.

The 21st Century System Has a Health Justice System That Protects Individuals and Encourages Quality

The current system of health and healthcare permits trial lawyers and frivolous lawsuits to manipulate the system at enormous cost to society. Because of high premiums and a predatory trial-lawyer environment, patients' access to healthcare is being thwarted. Doctors are closing their practices or eliminating certain lines of service because of the fear of being sued, especially if they are in a high-risk specialty like obstetrics. The American College of Obstetrics and Gynecology has issued a red alert in nine states and placed four more on the watch list.[2] The medical litigation system is jeopardizing women and their unborn babies by inducing the flight of physicians willing to deliver babies. Consider some recent incidents where the litigation crisis has sacrificed care.

- In Pennsylvania, after 150 years of providing obstetrical care, Mercy Hospital closed its maternity ward—the only one in South Philadelphia—because insurance premiums for its group of four hospitals swelled to $22 million from $7 million in 2000.[3]

- In Arizona a woman had to give birth by the side of the road before she could reach the only remaining maternity ward in a 6,000 square mile area.

- In West Virginia and northern Mississippi there are no neurosurgeons because of out-of-control liability costs.

- In Washington state, clinics serving a collective total of 60,000 patients were forced to close because of the insurance burden. Almost immediately the ER at the nearest hospital developed a five-hour wait.

A 21st century system of health justice would fairly and justly compensate individuals who have been victims of egregious errors and bad medicine while preserving the access to quality care for the collective body of patients. Medical malpractice insurance would be available in every state for a reasonable fee. The system will have information transparency because reporting mistakes will no longer equate to professional suicide. Mistakes will be analyzed until the root cause is found so future mistakes are avoided and quality controls can be implemented.

The 21st Century System Will See an Overall Cost Decrease As Opposed to an Overall Cost Increase

It is impossible to have a 21st century system with the principles listed here and not see an overall decrease in the cost of healthcare. Today the cost of our system is spinning out of control. It is only projected to get worse. For example, if Congress adds a prescription drug benefit to Medicare that is similar to the House bill passed in 2002, the cost of the drug benefit over 75 years will equal the current national debt. To pay for those kinds of programs we must transform the system. Implementing a 21st century health system will save billions of dollars and countless lives.

Here is one notable example of how a quality-focused system would decrease healthcare spending. Approximately 20% of Americans account for over 80% of healthcare spending.[4] The large portion of this small concentration of individuals has two conditions, heart disease and/or diabetes. Together, heart disease and diabetes account for $300 billion in direct healthcare costs—over 23% of the total healthcare spending in the United States. Any quality improvement effort in the area of diabetes and heart disease will result in significant cost savings. Yet the widely accepted protocols of blood-sugar testing, retinal eye exams, aspirin use, and beta-blocker use are only followed 18% to 40% of the time.[5] This low level of compliance with national guidelines results in avoidable patient suffering and an increase in high-cost, acute medical care.[6]

We can afford a Medicare drug benefit, and we can afford to sustain the baby boomers when they retire, if we have a quality-focused system that is lowering overall costs through better health and better practices. However, if we fail to shift to a values-oriented, health-focused system, we will either be crushed by tax increases or watch Medicare go bankrupt as the baby boomers retire.

Quality or bankruptcy may literally be the choice we face.

[1] Institute of Medicine, *Crossing the Quality Chasm,* (National Academy Press, 2001): 145. Taken from a study done by E. Andrew Balas and Suzanne A. Boren. "Managing Clinical Knowledge for Healthcare Improvement," *Yearbook of Medical Informatics*. (Bethesda: National Library of Medicine, 2000): 65-70.

[2] As reported on <www.acog.org> as of 24 April 2003; staff communication with Kathy Lubbers 24 April 2003.

[3] Laura Bradford, "Out of Medicine; As premiums soar for malpractive, doctors get harder to find," *Time Magazine,* (16 September 2002).

[4] As reported on < www. nbch.org/documents/outmgmtexecsum1.pdf> as of 24 April 2003.

[5] As reported on < www. nbch.org/documents/outmgmtexecsum1.pdf> as of 24 April 2003.

[6] As reported on <http://www.nbch.org/documents/outmgmtexecsum1.pdf> as of 24 April 2003.

CHAPTER FOUR

Health First,
Healthcare Second

The healthcare system is laboring under the misconception that its primary goal is to reactively respond to acute-care needs. This dangerous premise fails to recognize that proactively keeping people healthy with preventive care can do more to improve and prolong the quality of life at a lower cost than reactive acute care will ever be able to do. The purpose of this chapter is to show how each of us, by taking personal responsibility for our health first and relying on the healthcare system second, can save our own lives and our own money.

Nutrition - Activity - Attitude

Although your genetic predisposition plays a large role in your health, evidence shows that a formula balancing nutrition, activity, and attitude defines an individual's path to the best possible health.

A tremendous amount of research is now underway to explore the nutrition-activity-attitude process by which people optimize their health. This process affects all of us as individuals long before we become patients. You have experienced these three factors working together. When you eat the right food, engage in healthy activity (a broader word than exercise), and maintain a positive state of mind, you are likely to feel significantly better than when you eat the wrong food, do nothing, and have a bad attitude.

However, this process is about more than giving you a day-to-day edge; it is about maximizing your quality of life. Think of this: Physical inactivity and failing to eat the right things are responsible for more than 300,000 preventable deaths each year.[1]

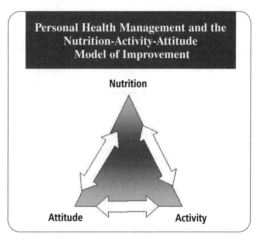

By utilizing this model, you can go a long way to preventing the onset of many debilitating diseases. With the right food, the right activity, the right attitude, and access to the right information, we can be dramatically healthier than with the wrong ones. You may have been dealt a certain genetic deck of cards, but how you live out those cards can make a remarkable difference in your life, in some cases decades of good health and independence.

For example, nutrition-activity-attitude can reduce cardiovascular disease. Clinical studies conducted by Dr. Dean Ornish, founder and president of the Preventive Medicine Research Institute and a clinical professor of medicine at the University of California, San Francisco, have demonstrated that lifestyle changes may begin to reverse even severe coronary heart disease without drugs or surgery. According to Dr. Ornish, his studies "have proven that [a] very low-fat, whole foods, plant-based diet can reverse the progression of even severe heart disease in most people. In addition, the studies also indicate that this diet may stop or reverse the progression of early prostate cancer as well."[2] His work uses sophisticated, high-tech, state-of-the-art measures to prove the power of low-cost, low-tech interventions.

Last November Dr. Ornish reported in the *American Journal of Cardiology* the results of a five-year Multicenter Lifestyle Demonstration Project. It concluded that 77% of people who were eligible for bypass surgery or angioplasty were able to avoid it by making comprehensive lifestyle changes instead.[3]

Furthermore, a system based on the nutrition-activity-attitude model of treating diseases would dramatically reduce or eliminate the problems associated with type 2 diabetes and the impact of arthritis.[4]

Unfortunately the model of nutrition-activity-attitude has been undervalued by the medical profession and underemphasized in American culture. We may intuitively know its importance, but the reality is that we often fail to heed the message.

Nutrition

According to the Centers for Disease Control and Prevention (CDC), more than 60% of all U.S. adults are overweight and one-fifth of Americans are considered obese, up from 12% in 1991. Obesity among children is also growing and the CDC has labeled the phenomenon an "epidemic." Because obesity contributes to the development of many other diseases, such as heart failure and diabetes, it has to be considered a major health threat. Despite this, it is combative with a nutrition-activity-attitude approach.[5]

Today over 42 million Americans suffer from arthritis.[6] Sadly, virtually none of those 42 million patients are being educated by their doctor, or by society, on how a nutrition-activity-attitude model can help them achieve better health and reduce pain. In fact, many of the most useful products are very inexpensive and can be found at the grocery store rather than the drugstore. But doctors are prescribing only heavily promoted and expensive branded drugs, and excluding other worthwhile diets, products, and activities.

Activity

Physical activity is another key indicator of your ability to live longer, healthier, and happier. Activity can include regular exercise, but routine daily activities can make a big difference as well. Take the stairs instead of the elevator or escalator. Instead of parking next to the door, find a spot that allows you to walk across the lot. Walk around your neighborhood for half an hour in the evening. Developing habits as simple as these is a major step toward better health.

The benefits of regular exercise should not be underestimated. It reduces your risk of dying from coronary heart disease and of developing high blood pressure, colon cancer, and diabetes. It helps maintain healthy bones, muscles, and joints. According to the Centers for Disease Control and Prevention, exercise classes and home-based exercise can reduce the risk of hip fractures 40% to 60%.[7]

SilverSneakers is a company that has used exercise and social activity, combining better activity with better attitude, to dramatically improve the health and quality of life for seniors (see Transforming Examples, Appendix A). The SilverSneakers fitness program was developed by Mary Swanson in Tempe, Arizona. Having worked in healthcare and managed care, Mary was frustrated by the reactive nature of most insurance companies. She believed the evidence that exercise and social interaction could dramatically improve health and dramatically decrease overall medical costs, especially for those over 65. Mary decided to open her own business, Healthcare Dimensions, and launch a senior-friendly program. She partnered with local community health centers and workout facilities to design exercise classes and activities specifically for seniors. These centers have special senior aerobics classes, cycling classes, and they even have their own T-shirts. Insurance companies pay a nominal fee per month to make the SilverSneaker's Fitness Program available to their members that are 65 and older. For those who participate in the SilverSneaker's Fitness Program, high-risk sedentary behavior is reduced by 70%, and 44% of enrollees report increasing their frequency of physical activity by an average of two days per week. The latest internal statistic shows that the SilverSneaker program reduces medical claims costs between 5% and 8%, demonstrating that it not only enhances the health of the participants but also improves the health of the company's bottom line. This program has been so successful that it is now active in eleven states.[8]

Attitude

Studies have shown that your mental outlook on life and your sense of connection to others have dramatic implications for your health. For example, men who have high hostility levels are more likely to have a heart attack. In fact the only measurement that predicted heart-disease risk more accurately than hostility was HDL "good" cholesterol levels.[9] Hostility levels may be a better predictor of heart disease than traditional factors such as high cholesterol levels, high blood pressure, and being overweight.

Yet our current medical system finds it very hard to suggest to patients that they need to work on their hostility quotient to avoid a heart attack. We can prescribe a tranquilizer, but we can't prescribe a hobby or an attitude change. Over time it is clear that the attitude change may make the prescription unnecessary.

Programs like SilverSneakers positively affect both mental and physical fitness. Getting together with other people on a regular basis seems to dramatically reduce depression. This is especially important among older women who are more isolated and more likely to experience depression than men. Notice the difference in cost and outcome between prescribing an expensive anti-depressant drug and simply helping people get together a couple of times a week. The outcome is clear.

Group support, positive attitude, and faith can also have a significant impact on your overall health outcome. The University of Texas asked a group of people two questions before they had open-heart surgery, "Are you a member of a group of people that get together on a regular basis like a civic group?" and "Do you draw strength from your religious faith?" They followed up on the patients six months after surgery and found a sevenfold difference in mortality. Of those individuals who answered "No" to both questions, 21% were dead. Of those who answered "Yes" to both questions, only 3% were dead. Of the people that answered "Yes" to one of the questions and "No" to the other set of questions, less than 5% were dead.

David Spiegel at Stanford found similar results. He studied two groups of women with metatastic breast cancer. Half of the women were in a support group that met once a week for a year. The other half were not in a support group. After five years, he found that women who were part of a support group lived on average 36.6 months compared with 18.9 months for the women without a support group, a significant difference.[10]

In 1998 I had the pleasure of hearing Dr. Thomas T. Perls, co-author of *Living to 100*, speak. Perls and his colleague, Margery Hutter Silver, studied over 100 North Americans who lived to be centenarians. Although his findings placed a very high value on genetic predisposition, they also emphasized the nutrition-activity-attitude model. For example, their evidence suggests that your brain cells can be renewed and extended if you continue to learn new skills and keep your mind sharp. Key factors of longevity include controlling your blood sugar, consciously resisting stress, and having a positive outlook on life.

Start with the Children

The education system should provide the skills American children will need for a lifetime. It is our goal that they learn how to read, write, and do arithmetic. But we are not teaching them to be healthy, productive citizens of society. Today's children are not learning that their health depends upon what they eat and how much they exercise. Nor do they understand the overall approach to wellness. We educate them on the consequences of drinking alcohol and driving and the potential consequences of unprotected sex. But that is not enough. We need to teach them the concept of wellness first, how to be an informed consumer of healthcare, and what the consequences are if they fail to take charge of their lives. Health educators and school nurses are utilized now as medical drug dispensers rather than interactive resources for wellness education. We need to reengage the population by teaching and practicing health education.

Today's educational system has slowly drifted to the point of being counterproductive to health and wellness. Physical education (PE) is declining. Only a quarter of high school students participate in daily PE, down from 42% in 1991. In fact half of high school students are not enrolled in PE at all.[11]

"It makes great common sense to physical educators that active, physically fit children will perform better academically," said NASPE Executive Director Judith C. Young, Ph.D. "Now the California Department of Education has provided specific evidence. NASPE urges further research to examine relationships between physical activity and academic perform-ance. In addition, information is needed which compares the students' physical education programs to their various levels of fitness."[12]

"In the study, reading and mathematics scores were matched with fitness scores of 353,000 fifth graders, 322,000 seventh graders, and 279,000 ninth graders. Key findings of the study included the following.

- Higher achievement was associated with higher levels of fit-ness at each of the three grade levels measured.
- The relationship between academic achievement and fitness was greater in mathematics than in reading, particularly at higher fitness levels.
- Students who met minimum fitness levels in three or more physical fitness areas showed the greatest gains in academic achievement at all three grade levels.
- Females demonstrated higher achievement than males, partic-ularly at higher fitness levels."[13]

School lunches also contribute to instilling unhealthy eating habits in chil-dren. Most lunches are high in carbohydrates and fail to offer a variety of healthy alternatives such as soymilk. Foods containing soy protein are effective in reducing cholesterol, treating kidney disease, and may cause calcium to be better utilized, helping to ward off osteoporosis. This is a case where the politics of the dairy industry have overwhelmed the nutri-tional needs of children.

We should also be evaluating soft drink consumption. One school district in California, the Los Angeles Unified School District, recently banned the sale of soda on the district's 677 middle and high school campuses.[14] The school district serves 748,000 students. Milk, beverages with at least 50% fruit juice, and sports drinks with less than 42 grams of sugar per 20-ounce serving will now be available. Health advocates say this measure is designed to discourage growing teens from packing on pounds at a time when childhood obesity has become a growing problem.

The soft drink industry took issue with the sentiment that soda was some-thing for teenagers to avoid and contended that other factors contributed to the obesity problem. While the industry is clearly defending its turf, it offered more evidence of a growing problem. The industry group cited a lack of physical exercise as the greatest culprit and noted that school dis-tricts across the United States are ignoring recommendations from the sur-geon general that students should get an hour of physical activity every day to stay in shape.

I am not arguing for banning soft drinks or whole milk. I am arguing that balance is important and that offering healthy alternatives is also impor-tant. People, including children, should know that indulgence in sugar-based drinks and foods is fine as an occasional behavior but not as a stan-dard consumption. The soft drink companies should be challenged to pro-duce healthy alternatives or to expect to have reduced access to young peo-ple as a market. The earlier you learn good habits, the healthier you will be. That is why healthy parenting is an important part of each child's upbringing. Similarly, having healthy diets and healthy physical-education programs in school is a vital part of our public health strategy. And devel-oping healthy habits and monitoring your health as an adult can make a very big difference in the quality of life you experience.

It's Never Too Late to Start

For those people who are living with a chronic disease such as cancer, dia-betes, heart disease, or arthritis, it may seem that you have missed your opportunity to live healthier, happier, and longer. You may think your only option is to visit the doctor and maintain your medicine regime. Although these two factors are vital to fight your disease, applying the nutrition-activity-attitude model can make a substantial difference even now.

Your Life, Your Health

Many years ago someone warned me that I could spend a certain amount of time exercising or I could plan on spending the same amount of time in the hospital. They asserted that I had no choice about spending time on my health, but I did have a choice about how to spend that time.

Whether the question is exercising (or activity) on a regular basis, watching what you eat for cholesterol and weight purposes, being careful about drinking and driving, or a host of other common sense, but often ignored, health indicators, the fact is that maintaining your health and optimizing the quality of your life is a one-day-at-a-time process.

It is your health, and you have the opportunity to maintain independence by managing it intelligently. It is up to you.

[1] As reported on <www.wire.ap.org/APpackages/obesity_flash/> as of 23 April 2003.
[2] D. Ornish, et al., "Intensive lifestyle changes for reversal of coronary heart disease. Five-year follow-up of the Lifestyle Heart Trial," *JAMA* 280 (1998): 2001-2007.
[3] D. Ornish, "Avoiding Revascularization with Lifestyle Changes: The Multicenter Lifestyle Demonstration Project," *American Journal of Cardiology*, 82 (1998): 72T-76T.
[4] As reported on <www.silversneakers.com/news_item.php?id=11> as of 23 April 2003; Neal Barnard, MD, *Foods That Fight Pain* (New York: Harmony Books, 1998).
[5] As reported on <www.wire.ap.org/APpackages/obesity_flash> as of 23 April 2003; As reported on <www.cdc.gov/nccdphp/dnpa/obesity/trend/prey_char.htm> as of 23 April 2003.
[6] As reported on <www.cdc.gov/nccdphp/arthritis/index.htm> as of 23 April 2003.
[7] As reported on <www.cdc.gov/.mmwr//preview/mmwrhtml/rr4902a2.htm> as of 23 April 2003.
[8] Mary Ferron, correspondence with author (April 2003).
[9] D. Ornish, "Avoiding Revascularization with Lifestyle Changes: The Multicenter Lifestyle Demonstration Project," *The American Journal of Cardiology* 82 (1998), 72T-76T; D. Ornish, communication with Kathy Lubbers 24 April 2003; Sid Kirchheimer, "Hostility Predicts Heart Disease," *WebMD Medical News* (18 November 2002); Raymond Niaura, et al., "Hostility, the Metabolic Syndrome, and Incident Coronary Heart Disease," *Health Psychology*, (November 2002); As reported on <http://my.webmd.com/printing/article/1675.65822> as of 23 April 2003.
[10] As reported on <www.med.stanford.edu/school/Psychiatry/PSTreatLab/abstracts.html#metastatic> as of 23 April 2003.
[11] Centers for Disease Control and Prevention, "National Youth Risk Behaviour Survey." <http://www.wvdhhr.org/bph/oehp/hp/card/phyeddef.htm>
[12] Judith Young, communication with Jackie Cushman, 24 April 2003.
[13] California Department of Education, news release " State Study Proves Physically Fit Kids Perform Better Academically," 10 December 2002); As reported on <www.cooperinst.org/ftgmain.asp> as of 23 April 2003; The newly completed research study individually matched scores from the spring 2001 administration of the Stanford Achievement Test, Ninth Edition (SAT-9), given as part of California's Standardized Testing and Reporting Program, with results of the state-mandated physical fitness test, known as the Fitnessgram, given in 2001 to students in grades five, seven, and nine. The Fitnessgram, developed by the Cooper Institute for Aerobics Research, assesses six major health-related areas of physical fitness including aerobic capacity (cardiovascular endurance), body composition (percentage of body fat), abdominal strength and endurance, trunk strength and flexibility, upper body strength and endurance, and overall flexibility. A score of 6 indicates that a student is in the healthy fitness zone in all six performance areas, and meets standards to be considered physically fit.
[14] Hil Anderson, "Soft drinks expelled from L.A. Schools," *LA Times*, (27 August 2002).

Personal Control of Healthcare Dollars

Better Health at a Lower Cost

It is financially imperative that we transform the business of health and healthcare in America. Healthcare encompasses more than 13% of our economy's gross domestic product (GDP). By comparison, the defense expenditure is slightly more than 3%. Although there is not an ideal percentage for health's share of the GDP, considering the enormous amount that is currently spent on healthcare as a nation, we should have the greatest access, highest quality, and best outcomes—but it should also be at the most reasonable cost.

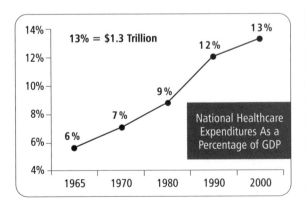

National Healthcare Expenditures As a Percentage of GDP

Third-Party-Payer System Doesn't Work

The current third-party-payer system is producing neither positive health outcomes nor acceptable financial outcomes. Most privately insured Americans are insured through their employer or the employer of their spouse. However, before 1942, the few people who bought health insurance did so in the individual market. It was only after the government implemented wage and price controls to control inflation during World War II that companies began offering to pay health insurance for their employees as a way to attract the best talent from a slim pool of workers. This benefit was also excluded from the employee's taxable income. Thus by a quirk of wartime, anti-inflation policy, the United States moved away from individuals insuring themselves to a world in which virtually all private insurance is employer based and bought on a third-party basis. This special tax treatment of health insurance is a major reason health insurance is primarily offered through the place of work while other forms of insurance (auto, housing) remain in the individual market. Over 55 years later, the employer-based system is still the model for most private health insurance in the United States.

The bureaucratic control of healthcare was based on the theory that bureaucratic rules and regulations would lead to wiser choices and would save money. Taking power away from both patient and provider was an enlightened step in an earlier era convinced that professional administrators knew more than either the individual, on whose behalf they were making a decision, or the doctor, who they were second-guessing. Bureaucratic "gatekeepers" were the order of the day for both private companies and governments.

Ironically the result of this 60-year evolution in taking power away from both patient and provider has been to shift money toward red tape, increase the cost of time and administration, and increase patient and provider dissatisfaction while failing to keep costs under control.

When we first began this project, we wanted to meet with those in the private sector who had the most to gain financially by increasing the quality and decreasing the cost of healthcare—employers. After speaking with numerous CEOs and CFOs, we learned that the average company's management leaders did not see the trends and debates in healthcare as vitally important or urgent to their bottom line. Although there were clear exceptions, such as Paul O'Neill at Alcoa, the general impression we received was "The VP of human resources is doing a good job if he or she keeps the issue away from my desk so I can focus on making money and running the company. Besides, paying attention to trends in health is what we are paying the insurance companies to do." Although innovative and entrepreneurial company leadership is dedicated to "driving the cost out" of the manufacturing side through quality programs such as Six Sigma or Total Quality Management, health benefits became the forgotten cost center when it came to applying quality principles to managing cost, profitability, and benefits effectiveness.

When we first visited the directors of health-benefits departments at otherwise sophisticated, large companies, we learned that most saw little hope for real change in the health system. Some were frustrated that their entrepreneurial ideas never seemed to make it onto their boss' list of priorities. Some had grown a large system of bureaucrats defending the status quo. Others saw themselves as victims of an out-of-control system who were helpless to elicit change. Probably the most troubling attitude was, "we pay an HMO or a third-party administrator to manage our health benefits." Again, there are clear exceptions, some of whom we will highlight later in this chapter. However, the void of systematic entrepreneurship, quality expertise in healthcare, and practical healthcare experience was the rule not the exception. The resulting short-sighted, cost-cutting, and cost-shifting tactics used by benefits designers are causing volatile relationships with employees, lowering company productivity, and will in the long term inevitably cost much more money and many more lives than a quality-focused approach.

With double-digit insurance premium increases, and no end in sight, corporations are now scrambling to identify areas of immediate relief in healthcare costs that will not jeopardize employee satisfaction and productivity. Senior executives have been faced with a financial crisis and, as they look more closely at the rising costs of healthcare for their company, they are now discovering that the visibility and accountability they expect in every other area of their companies is rare in healthcare.

The financial burden represented by skyrocketing premiums is only the tip of the healthcare challenge. Beyond the clear financial costs, there is a human price paid by the employees and their families as they get less adequate care. There is a labor-management price to be paid as employers shift more of the risk and the financial burden on employees. And there is a reduced-productivity price from a healthcare system doing little to prevent ill-health.

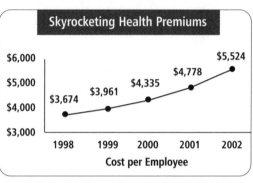

Source: The Houston Chronicle, April 24, 2002

Today many employers are using the same tactics with their employees that managed care used on their clients in the mid- and late-1990s including blanket reductions in benefits with increasing premiums and co-pays and the implementation of multi-tiered drug formularies. We have seen where those tactics lead us, yet we patronize the same frustrating patterns. A successful change in the trajectory of healthcare is going to require innovation, leadership, creativity, risk taking, and bucking the norm. It is going to require truly entrepreneurial health purchasing and a binary (buyer-seller) system that returns purchasing power to the individual.

Until recently, insurance companies could get by with sharing minimal amounts of information. Companies paid them a lump sum of money to manage their employees' needs and, as we saw earlier, companies were not particularly interested in accountability or information transparency—this was the essence of managed care. However managed care turned out to be managed costs. This worked for the short term. But cutting health benefits and creating barriers to care has taken a toll. As long as premiums were not painful, the companies could ignore where the money was actually being spent. Health expenses were seen as a sunken cost and simply endured. Now those costs are rising dramatically once again. The painful lesson is that letting insurance companies manage the health of employees and health expenditures is a road to higher costs and less employee satisfaction.

Despite all of the money spent on healthcare, Americans are increasingly dissatisfied with their system of healthcare and the providers of healthcare are increasingly dissatisfied with their careers. We have managed to create a steadily more expensive system that satisfies none of its participants. It is as though we bought a Ferrari that could only go 40 miles an hour or a diamond that did not sparkle. There is a disjunction between money spent and satisfaction achieved. While the rest of our world is modernizing in the information age, healthcare continues to be costly, ineffective, and outdated.

According to the 2002 Economic Report of the President to the Congress, "In most market settings, consumers' purchase decisions are based on good information on the value of the products they buy. But in healthcare the lack of good information on the success of different treatments—in terms of the best outcomes per dollar—means that individuals and families have difficulty making informed decisions, and insurance companies are not rewarded for altering their coverage to encourage high-value care. Effective competition to help all Americans get the care that best meets their needs requires innovative, market-oriented healthcare policies."[1]

Tragically the current system of third-party payment, third-party paperwork, and third-party oversight psychologically conditions us to minimize our own sense of self-reliance, maximize our willingness to let others worry about our health, and place the burden on others for "fixing" us when something goes wrong. This is a cultural and psychological formula for bad health and high costs.

The Transformational Binary Market-Oriented System

To design an affordable 21st Century System of Health and Healthcare, we have to reverse the financial incentives and encourage people to take charge of their own health and healthcare. The system would center on the individual who could direct the system by emphasizing personal choice. That would make our healthcare industry dramatically more responsive to the market, encouraging it to become more competitive, flexible, and innovative. In every other market sector, that process of individual choice has meant higher quality, greater efficiency, and lower costs. Lower costs could help more people afford healthcare and health insurance, enabling us to get closer to full coverage for every American.

The optimal 21st Century System of Health and Healthcare is built around you, the individual. It is not built around the physician's schedule or the hospital's billing system or an insurance company's formulary or bottom line. Only a patient-centered, binary model of healthcare will maximize the opportunities for better health at lower cost and incentivize all parties to work toward that goal. However, as the entire system of healthcare is transformed, roles will change. You will become the primary guardian of how money is spent on your healthcare. No longer beholden to insurance companies' regulations, doctors will be driven by market forces to provide better care at lower cost. And the insurance companies will no longer be financing the care of people incentivized to abuse their bodies. The system will empower patients to take control of their lives and their health, doctors to practice the best medicine possible, and insurance companies to create plans according to market forces thereby returning personal responsibility to each individual.

Expanding Coverage Through Market-Based Changes

There are three steps that should be taken to lower the cost of health insurance for small businesses, individual purchasers, and the working poor. First, every individual should receive the same tax treatment for buying insurance. Second, while people should be able to purchase insurance individually, they should also be able to buy that insurance as part of a pool or association. Third, individuals and small business should be able to buy insurance under the same rules as big businesses. Each step will lower the cost of insuring everyone, and each is worth a brief explanation.

First, it makes no sense to give big companies and well-paid executives a tax benefit for buying health insurance but then deny that benefit to the self-employed, workers in (typically small) firms who do not offer health insurance, and individuals who are unemployed. The current system favors large and successful corporations at the expense of individuals and small businesses. The answer is to simply allow the same tax deductibility for individual purchasers. That would be a first step toward making health insurance available for every American.

Second, while we favor individual purchasing of insurance (just as individuals purchase cars, houses, clothing, vacations, and almost everything else they need) in order to give individuals more market leverage and keep costs down, people should have the option to buy into a very wide range of groups and associations, including allowing existing insurance companies to offer association plans. Health insurance is designed so that individual insurance is the most expensive way to buy it. This is true for two reasons. The cost of selling to one person is much more expensive than the cost of selling to many people, so the individual purchaser is paying a very high cost for the sales organization and the administrative overhead. Furthermore, health insurance profitability can be dramatically enhanced if the company can measure your health status and either charge you an extra premium for any risk you have or simply avoid insuring you if they think you might be unhealthy. The result is a risk-based transaction cost that makes individual insurance consistently much higher than group insurance.

The answer is to allow every American to buy into group risk pools. Whether the association is based on professional identity (a Farm Bureau Insurance risk pool, a National Federation of Independent Businesses risk pool, a Chamber of Commerce risk pool), or on common interests (a Wildlife Federation risk pool, a National Rifle Association risk pool, your local church, synagogue, or mosque, etc.) the goal is to find inexpensive groupings which create large enough risk pools that the cost of the transaction drops toward that achieved by large companies. If most of the purchasing were done on the Internet, the transaction cost of the sales force and the company bureaucracy would be further reduced and insurance would be made even more widely accessible.

In addition, creating a national reinsurance pool that would eliminate the extraordinarily high-cost outliers could lower the cost of insurance even further. A national reinsurance risk pool would cover those cases where insurance premiums today increase dramatically in pools that have individuals with an expensive disease. These cases actually ruin small risk pools and create very big incentives for insurance companies to "cherry pick." Instead, a universal risk pool, where private-sector specialty firms could compete for these cases based on outcome and cost, would cover these very expensive situations. If the cost of this reinsurance system were spread across all insured Americans, it would enable our society to offer the best care to even the rarest and most difficult cases without having small risk pools see their insurance costs skyrocket if the pool contains one or more of these very expensive cases.

Third, small businesses and individuals should have the same nationwide health insurance purchasing protection that big businesses have. Under the federal Employee Retirement Income Security Act (ERISA), large corporations are able to insure themselves and are exempt from state mandates for all kinds of coverage. The result is that big companies can insure their employees and families for less than small businesses. Thus the small business, which has the hardest time affording insurance, has to pay a higher price because of various state mandates while the big corporation, which can most easily afford the insurance, is protected by the federal government and pays less per employee than its small neighbor. This is clearly wrong and should be changed. Allowing individuals and small businesses to purchase insurance through associational risk pools covered by ERISA would significantly lower the cost of insurance.

These three steps would make health insurance more affordable for the working poor, individuals, and small businesses, and that would make America a healthier country.

The Power of Personal Responsibility

The nature of insurance and market dynamics dictates that there will always be a role for large aggregators of lives whether that is employers or group associations. However, the cornerstone of change is to return as much market power as possible back to individuals. The trade-off for informed patient choice is an increase in personal responsibility and accountability.

In order to achieve a binary system that both empowers and incentivizes the individual to take responsibility for his or her health and returns market dynamics to the system, each of us should have the option to own a personal health account. This account, similar to a flexible spending account, will allow you to choose how your money is spent without limitations imposed by an insurance company; give you the ability to shop around for the best price and best service for your medications, your hospital procedures, and even your physicians; bring market forces into play so you are paying actual costs for the goods and services you use; save lives; and save money.

The Bush Administration took a very important step toward creating personal health accounts when the IRS changed its regulations in June of 2002 to allow the balance on a health reimbursement arrangement (HRA) to be carried over year-to-year. "Today the Treasury Department and the Internal Revenue Service issued guidance that clarifies the tax treatment of health reimbursement arrangements (HRAs) in which the employee's health benefit arrangement provides for employee-controlled reimbursement of medical costs. With this new guidance, we clear the way for employers to adopt health plans with patient-directed features so that employees have more choice and greater control over their healthcare coverage," stated Treasury Secretary Paul O'Neill.[2] This was a significant step in the right direction. But we need more steps. We need the law changed so we have the tax incentives for companies to create personal health accounts. The effects of competition and personal choice are key to building a healthier America and a healthier American system of health and healthcare.

Employers already contribute a certain amount of money to the healthcare expenses of each of their employees. Under a 21st century system, employers would contribute money for each employee's healthcare expenses directly into his or her personal health account. Each employee is personally responsible for spending in this account according to his or her individual health needs. Let's suppose, for instance, your employer put money into your personal health spending account each year and provided insurance coverage beyond that amount. We will use $1,500 for this example. With the first $1,500 in your control, you would pay your health expenses.

This would substantially lower the cost of the insurance your employer is buying for three reasons. First, the risk for the first $1,500 in expenses would no longer be covered by the insurance company. Second, the many small bills that come from doctor and dentist visits, filling prescriptions, and other small purchases would no longer be reviewed and processed by the insurance company. Third, because you would be empowered and incentivized to be responsible for your own healthcare dollars, you would learn more about your own health needs and how to manage them. This would lead to healthier lives and significantly lower lifetime costs.

Personal health spending accounts would be personal, portable, and tax free. This means that if you did not spend the entire $1,500, at the end of the year it would carry over tax free and earn interest, growing like an IRA or a 401K. Because most younger workers do not use healthcare services nearly as often as they will when they are older, their money could potentially build dramatically over their first twenty or thirty years of employment. Therefore, an employee who buys their own insurance policy could raise the deductible yearly to match the amount saved in their interest-earning health account so the cost for insurance would continue to decline while the size of the account continues to rise.

The personal health account shifts the incentives and the psychology toward a healthier system of self-learning, self-monitoring, and self-accountability. Since it is your money, you have a real say in your health choices. Since you have a real say—and there are real financial consequences from making good and bad decisions—you will spend more of your time learning, thinking through, and managing your own health. Personal health accounts would dramatically simplify the process of paying for healthcare and would take a lot of the bureaucratic cost out of the system. You would have a health debit card drawing on your personal health account for all certified health purchases like the doctor's office, drugstore, etc. You would then be your own gatekeeper in spending your money on health and healthcare.

Your interest in your own personal health account would continue to grow because there would be an amount at which you could withdraw some of the money as taxable income, which you could then spend as you wished. Alternatively, you could keep your money in the account and continue the tax-free buildup of savings. Thus your personal interest in being healthy would be tied to a financial interest in staying healthy, and you would have real resources to manage your interest in your own health intelligently.

You should be empowered to access information about best treatments, medications, and providers. Having access to knowledge and spending accordingly will force the healthcare industry to improve because competition drives quality. Doctors will have to tell you up front what they are charging for an office visit. With this information consumers can compare costs—which they will want to do because they are paying the bill. Bringing market forces to play in the healthcare industry will push costs down as informed consumers choose the goods and services that will provide the best health at the lowest cost.

You will pay your doctor on the spot with your health account debit card when service is rendered. Doctors will no longer have to keep clerical people to fill in all the forms, determine your insurance provider, compute your co-pay, or endure the time value of money while waiting to be paid by an insurance company deliberately stretching out the payments so it can profit from the interest generated from funds it is not paying.

Since the personal health account is your money, you can purchase services that traditional healthcare insurance may not cover. For example, you would be able to pay for preventive care, health management, alternative medicine, non-prescription drugs, mental health services, or even a health club membership if they are part of a wellness program. Since it is money that you have earned, you are the gatekeeper of what you think would most keep you healthy. The focus will shift from maneuvering through the paperwork and regulatory process designed for the benefit of others to considering the choices that you believe will lead to better outcomes for yourself.

Since consumers will pay the doctor and hospital directly, and insurance will apply only after you have spent your personal health account, doctors and hospitals will rapidly learn to pay more attention to their patients. Moreover, they will need to provide the best healthcare for the least expense in order to retain business. The consumer's power to choose introduces competition and market forces into the healthcare industry.

The market will require a transparency of information from healthcare providers in order for consumers to be appropriately informed of the cost of goods and services they are purchasing. This transparency will have a ripple effect on the industry, causing a complete shift in the medical culture. Costs will go down, lives will be saved, and people will experience a higher quality of living.

A Personal Story

Personal health accounts will return responsibility to the individual; they will incentivize individuals to managing their own health. However, even without these accounts, there are already examples of people taking charge of their lives and their health.

My daughter Kathy was diagnosed with rheumatoid arthritis when she was 27-years old. Although her type of arthritis is not preventable, she has actively worked on developing the nutrition-activity-attitude habits I explained in the last chapter. They have successfully postponed its crippling consequences. She has taken personal responsibility to fight the disease by seeking out the best foods to eat, identifying the right exercises to strengthen her joints, and routinely seeking the counsel of a physical therapist. She consciously maintains an attitude of cheerful persistence. But it was not this way in the beginning.

Her physical therapist/personal trainer asks her the same question repeatedly, "Why didn't you come to me sooner?" The answer is easy. In the thirteen years since she was diagnosed, she has not deteriorated to the extent that any of her physicians have ever considered sending her to physical therapy as a way of managing her condition.

Fortunately, she decided to take a very proactive role with her health and asked her rheumatologist to recommend a physical therapist. Now she receives physical therapy wrapped up in personal training.

She begins by warming up on a stationary bike for fifteen minutes, increasing her heart rate while lubricating her knees (which heats up the synovial fluid). Next, she and her therapist/trainer work to strengthen the muscles that surround her joints and increase core strength and flexibility. Throughout the sessions, they stretch various muscles to prevent soreness or pain, and finally they stretch or focus on specific areas that require special attention.

Is it difficult? Well, sticking to any consistent workout program is not easy. However, Kathy will tell you that it is the best relief she has had. While her regimen may not be for everyone, it could be the right method for many people that suffer from rheumatoid arthritis but have never had a doctor suggest it.

While Kathy is not cured and still has bad days, she has chosen to take control of her health using a non-traditional physical program that has worked for her. She had initially accepted her insurance company's view that she was not in "bad" enough shape to warrant a recommendation from her doctor for physical therapy or a personal trainer. Think about that. She, like many others, was put in the position of waiting until she had deteriorated enough to qualify for help instead of getting the help she needed so she did not get worse in the first place. She now only wishes that she had been more proactive from the start.

While Kathy can afford it, not everyone with rheumatoid arthritis can hire a professional physical therapist/personal trainer. However, a 21st Century System of Health and Healthcare, utilizing personal health accounts, should provide everyone the opportunity to learn about and engage in such alternative treatments. If it is important to your life and it is your money, you should be able to get the treatment to stay healthy not merely to recover from terrible problems.

In a more difficult and courageous case, actor Christopher Reeves contin- ues to push his physicians and himself to discover new treatments and pro- cedures available so that he is able to experience the maximum mobility possible and achieve the highest quality of life despite his present physical limitations.

Laura Landro, a *Wall Street Journal* reporter, describes undergoing a bone marrow transfusion to survive leukemia in her book, *Survivor*.[3] She walks the reader through her choices between four different hospitals and four different approaches to the management of bone marrow transplants. She tells you what Web sites she found helpful and how she used her comput- er as a survival tool. Laura's book is a model of the interactive, informed patient health system of the future; and she is proof that an informed patient-centered system can exist today.

Kathy, Christopher, and Laura are witnesses to the power of a personal responsibility system and to the tremendous improvement in quality of life that it brings.

Empower People to Take Control of Their Lives and Their Health with Technology

Technology has allowed consumers to become dramatically more informed about the products they buy in everything but healthcare. With the Internet you can evaluate quality and cost and compare many different products from different stores at the same time. Before making a choice, you can even read the comments of consumers who have already pur- chased the product. Ten years ago it was necessary to purchase a plane ticket through a travel agent. Today a variety of Web sites make it routine to comparison shop for the flight times at the best price and in some cases even choose your seat. Scrambling to the bank before it closed on Friday is also a thing of the past. ATM cards have completely changed our notion about accessing and spending money. With a personal computer, paying bills or managing bank or brokerage accounts on-line is relatively easy.

Many of us take conveniences like these for granted. They are user-friendly, provide a quality service, and give us access to the information we need with a high degree of accuracy. Contrast the level of control we have over our financial relationships with the healthcare system that we accept today. It is not for lack of technology; the same technologies we use in banking and traveling can be applied to healthcare. We are simply not in the habit of demanding the same level of service or control in healthcare that we expect in other areas. Moreover, the healthcare system is constructed as if we were incapable of being accountable or responsible for our health and healthcare decisions. In all other areas of our lives, we are expected to manage life's complications from home ownership to investments to maintaining vehicles to making our own travel arrangements. The expectation of knowledge, ability to learn, and responsibility is common everywhere except in healthcare. Only in healthcare are we assumed to be unqualified to choose a doctor or understand our treatment options.

It is unacceptable that we are still at the mercy of an insurance company to understand care options and provider choices and costs. The role of the patient has evolved into a dependency relationship in the healthcare delivery system rather than the driver of the system. Access to information and knowledge about healthcare will empower consumers to make the best healthcare choices in deciding which procedures, treatments, and preventive care will best meet their needs mentally, emotionally, and physically.

Technology and scientific advancements are providing opportunities to transform the healthcare model at breathtaking speed. Using the same technologies that already work in other parts of our lives, we can design a healthcare system that is accessible 24/7, offering you consistent quality and access to the information you need.

Just as you have a variety of ways to communicate with your bank securely and privately, you should expect the same standard of real-time, confidential access with your healthcare provider. Several innovative companies are leading the way and are already providing a better health future. Today you can monitor all your vital signs from home. If your blood pressure is too high for the third day in a row, or a family member has flu symptoms, you can electronically communicate these new developments with your healthcare provider and receive immediate feedback, shortening your road to recovery.

The Internet also provides easy access to many resources that can help us understand our conditions and possible treatments. Companies like WebMd.com, WorldDoc.com, and PDr.net provide us with the ability to comparison shop for medications, hospitals and doctors on-line just as many do now for other goods and services. Quality, credentials, and financial information about the providers are also available. There are discussion groups specific to medical conditions such as the treatment of AIDS, diabetes, breast cancer, or arthritis. Web sites can assist us in diagnosing ourselves or in finding a doctor. And the Web provides access to emotional support and education groups not only for the patient but also for family members who are providing care. Just having the right knowledge and information can relieve anxiety, fear, and uncertainty.

We should utilize technology to create individual electronic medical records that are password protected like your ATM card, allowing you to easily give a care provider an accurate account of your personal health history, medical conditions, the medications you are taking, and insurance information. This would be particularly useful if you are seeing a new doctor or are in a medical emergency. An electronic record would allow the physician to focus their time and energy on treating what truly ails you.

Information Is the key

In order for you and your familiy to exercise the individual choice and accountability that has the power to transform the system, you need access to information. It is impossible to have a free market without information. Yet even in this information age it is still very difficult to obtain data about a doctor's experience providing medical care in a specific area. For example, numerous studies have shown that your chances of an optimal outcome for a high-risk surgery would be much greater if you elected to go to a hospital that does a high volume of that particular surgery. Studies have found as much as a threefold difference in surgical mortality rates across hospitals.[4] Picking the wrong, under-experienced doctor and hospital can make it three times as likely that you or someone you love will die. In fact

Dr. R. Adams Dudley of the University of San Francisco studied hospitals in California and identified ten different surgical procedures for which hospital volume had a significant impact on outcomes. He estimated that 500 deaths a year could be saved in California alone if patients who needed one of these ten procedures chose a hospital that met the frequency benchmarks.[5] Dr. Dudley's study proves that the difference in accessing this kind of information and not accessing it can literally be your life or your death.

However, obtaining that kind of information can be very difficult, if not impossible, unless you live in a state that mandates that hospitals report it. Unfortunately, few states collect this kind of data. The Pennsylvania Health Cost Containment Council, www.phc4.org, may be the best working model of how a state is attempting to measure hospitals. PHC4 publishes annual reports for over 80 different procedures and treatments ranging from congestive heart failure to diabetes. With personal control of your healthcare, you can identify the care providers and care institutions in your community that have the best indicators of optimal health outcomes and spend your health dollars there. As people have both a psychological sense of control and a personal sense of financial power and incentive they will spend more time learning about maintaining and improving their own health.

Transformational Human Resources

As we mentioned earlier, making insurance more affordable and easier for individuals to purchase from a variety of risk pools (company, trade association, religious institution) is a vital step to restoring market forces in the healthcare industry. However, this transformation does not exonerate the group-purchasing agency from implementing sound business principles and quality systems in administering the insurance plan. In fact, the competition will make it imperative that these principles are applied.

There are a number of sound principles that are at the heart of Peter Drucker's life-long work on management and at the center of Edwards Deming's equally long commitment to the quality movement. Almost every seasoned manager will recognize these principles. What is amazing is how

seldom senior executives have applied these principles to meet the challenges of health and healthcare. Here are six principles that we distilled
from these quality experts.

1. Use the health-oriented, wellness model
2. Know your costs and risks
3. Focus on the outcomes
4. Make health information available to your employees
5. Use health management programs to increase health and
   decrease cost
6. Incentivize healthy behavior through rewards and prizes: when
   all else fails, mandate

Health-Oriented, Wellness Model

Keeping you healthy is better for your quality of life and less expensive to
the individual and society. The CDC's report, "Best Practices for
Comprehensive Tobacco Control Programs," illustrates that cost savings
from moderately-priced, effective education to get people to stop smoking
pays for itself within three to four years.[6] Presently neither the individual
nor financial systems are incentivized to focus on health first, nor are they
capable of shifting to a health-oriented, wellness model. Bringing about
this change requires optimizing individual health and creating methods to
allow people access to information and resources to sustain their own
health.

Knowing Your Costs and Risks

Healthcare is different than other business activities in that companies that
know intimately every other cost center often know remarkably little about
the costs of their health system. Transparency and accountability in healthcare remain rare. As explained earlier, market dynamics, such as supply
and demand, and the application of information technology have enabled
corporations and consumers to become sophisticated purchasers in every
other area. Corporations have invested in sophisticated software to track,
monitor, and analyze their costs in every cost center except health. The
foundation of an entrepreneurial approach to purchasing must start with
knowing your costs.

Any company that purchases health benefits for its employees should demand, as a condition of their contract, to be given sophisticated analytical health data for its employee group. It is surprising how accepting Fortune 500 companies are of insurance company practices that would be intolerable from any other supplier. For example, it is absurd that a company spending millions of dollars on health insurance is denied information about the claims their employees are making. Of course companies should not be permitted to obtain health information on a specific individual, but receiving aggregate data about what kind of drugs employees are purchasing, what hospitals and doctors are serving the majority of employees, and what the most common chronic diseases are among their insured population would be invaluable for effective benefits design. Insurance companies should offer you easy and understandable outcomes information as a condition of your using them.

It is imperative for companies to have access to cost information that is not filtered through a party with a vested interest. The Gannet Company, McDonalds, AOL, and MBNA America are four of the companies implementing a new software system called VitalSpring@Work. VitalSpring collects an employer's claims data from insurance and health-plan companies and provides the employer with software to analyze aggregate demographics, costs, and claims details while maintaining the workers' privacy rights. By using this kind of information, companies can closely monitor their costs through the year and compare it with benchmarked data. This information allows benefits designers to create benefits packages that cover the most needed services and eliminates costly benefits their employees do not need or are not using. VitalSpring integrates costs from all silos of benefits including medical, dental, pharmaceutical, short- and long-term disability, worker's compensation, and disease management. With the VitalSpring technology, a health-benefits manager will be able to measure the effectiveness of the benefits and programs the company is offering and make modifications based on that data. It provides leverage for negotiating future benefits packages as well. VitalSpring estimates that clients can expect annual savings of 3% to 5% of their total healthcare benefits expenditures during the first year following deployment of VitalSpring@Work. The end result is increased effectiveness for every dollar spent on healthcare and potential cost savings.

Knowing your costs is the first step in becoming an entrepreneurial health purchaser. Knowing your costs is a necessary means to achieve the ideal end, better health outcomes for employees at lower cost.

Focus on Outcomes, Not Costs

It is imperative to base coverage decisions on health outcomes and not just costs. Put simply, health outcomes are the measure of the effects of the resources you are expending. Wiser health strategies and systems should lead to better outcomes for the invested resources. However, that requires focusing on outputs rather than inputs. A health outcome is not necessarily measured by how you feel at the end of a physician appointment or a hospital visit. Measuring health outcomes is a process in which a focused effort is made to evaluate the effectiveness of the strategies, systems, therapies, and care so best outcomes can be developed with varying costs attached. The entrepreneurial purchaser asks, "Of all possible best outcomes which one is the least expensive?"

Suffering caused by an unfocused, shortsighted, bookkeeping approach to health and healthcare is not legitimized merely because traditional, annual accounting cannot figure out how to account for the long-term benefit of preventive services that keep you healthy. The quarterly report is often antithetical to an outcomes-based budget. Corporate governance and financial analysts must have more long-term thinking if companies will be able to take an outcomes-based approach to their benefits design. Only this system will result in healthy workers and a healthier bottom line in the long run.

Coverage decisions should not be based on the price of a particular procedure in a vacuum. These shortsighted views distort reality. For example, the current non-outcomes-based budgetary process every company accountant currently uses (we have been searching for a company that does dynamic, outcomes-based budgeting and cannot find one) notes the increasing cost of drugs without accounting for the savings in productivity, because of fewer days lost to illness thanks to those drugs, or the savings from surgery that those drugs are preventing. Likewise, the current non-outcomes-based budgetary process registers the costs of health management and other preventive programs without accounting for their measurable long-term savings. Healthcare does not fit into the typical cycle of quarterly, or even yearly, reporting.

We have met with some entrepreneurial companies who are investing in cost tools and targeting the needs of their employees. One specific company aggressively tracked the cost and their employees' overall health outcomes and noticed that people with diabetes in Plan A had significantly more hospital and doctor visits than people with diabetes in Plan B. As they investigated and analyzed the data further, they discovered that Plan A had a much higher co-pay for insulin (the drug that keeps people with diabetes healthy) than Plan B. The result was less compliance and more complications that resulted in increased doctor and hospital visits. After lowering the co-pay in Plan A, the employees got healthier and the company's costs decreased.

By having an intimate understanding of the needs of employees, purchasers can more aggressively manage the outcomes that matter. The decision of an entrepreneurial purchaser to track and manage outcomes will yield improved health, improved quality of life, improved employee satisfaction, decreased production losses, and less use of healthcare resources.

Make Clinical Health Information Available to Your Employees

Health is one of the most searched topics on the Internet, and there is a massive amount of information from which to choose. A Yahoo search on diabetes provided over five million matches. People want to know everything about a disease they or a loved one have. They do not just "surf the net," they become self-identified experts by digging through scholarly journals of technical scientific studies. In fact, patients make up one-third of the people who search for articles on MEDLINE, the most comprehensive source of life science and bibliographic information. People want first-hand knowledge about healthcare. Employers have to understand that the issue is not "Are my employees searching for information on the Internet?" Rather, "What kind of information are my employees reading on the Internet and is it accurate?"

Because of the legitimate concern about the accuracy of information on the Internet, the entrepreneurial purchaser would want to provide accurate reference guides for use. Many employers are doing just that. Healthwise (www.hcp.org) is a nonprofit company that offers companies, hospitals, and health insurance providers the ability to subscribe to their medical knowledge base. The knowledge base is available in written or electronic forms and provides information based on medical literature and outcomes research that has been filtered through their eight physician medical board. One large publicly owned financial-service corporation recently initiated an employee health program with the purpose of increasing employee access to information, decreasing unnecessary utilization, increasing employee self-care, and improving early interventions. One survey completed by the employer found:

- 77% of their employees surveyed agreed that what they had learned would help improve the quality of care they received
- 88% of employees surveyed agreed that the Healthwise program gave them the confidence to handle health problems at home
- 86% agreed that the program helped avoid unnecessary trips to the doctor
- 73% agreed that they would save money on care for health problems
- 90% agreed that they would be more prepared when seeing a doctor

Empowering employees with accurate, reliable, and easily accessible health information dramatically increases the quality of care and decreases overall costs.

Use Health-Management Programs to Increase Health and Decrease Costs

Entrepreneurial 21st century health purchasers who understand the relationship between prevention, high quality, and cost management implement health-management programs (a psychologically better name for disease management). Health-management programs work. They help us stay healthy, and they have a proven return on investment.

Health management is one of the fastest growing segments of the health industry. It provides people suffering from chronic diseases with information, counseling, and access to healthcare professionals to help them manage their health. Insurers and companies are realizing dramatic, positive outcomes from the implementation of serious disease-management programs for policyholders and employees who live with chronic diseases such as diabetes, heart disease, asthma, or depression.

These programs should be focused on keeping people healthy before they even get a disease. Programs like these should be pervasive in our health system so that people without chronic diseases can take the necessary steps to prevent their onset. Most people want to be healthy and want to know what to do to maintain their health. If we can provide them with the information and the assistance they need to stay healthy, people will suffer less, costs will go down, and quality of life will go up.

The Steelcase Company was an early adopter of systematic prevention initiatives through health-management programs, which resulted in better health and lower cost. Back in the mid-1980s, the company implemented a series of initiatives including health awareness education, early disease screening, health risks appraisals, on-site mammography, extensive prevention and rehabilitation programs, self-care educational materials, on-site counseling, special programs for high-risk employees, fitness and recreation programs, and a wellness center. A ten-year University of Michigan study conducted with Steelcase found that employees with high-risk lifestyles spend 75% more on medical care than their low-risk counterparts. Focusing on educating the employees about the health risks and costs of those lifestyles led to changed behavior, healthier lives, and lower costs.

In addition to educational materials and periodic calls or visits with a nurse, some companies and organizations are using sophisticated yet user-friendly technologies to better assist clients in managing their health. The Veterans Administration in Florida contracted with the Health Hero Network (HHN) (www.healthhero.com) to implement a technology platform for their case-management nurses assigned to work long term with patients with chronic disease to help them manage their health. A group of veterans were given the "Health Buddy," a small device with a large screen and large buttons that sits on a countertop in their homes. HHN also has an Internet interface, but the Health Buddy was effective with the seniors who do not use computers. Every day the patients interacted with the Health Buddy for about five minutes, answering some questions about how they were feeling, what their clinical values were (i.e., blood-glucose level, blood pressure, etc.) and were quizzed about their disease. Every night the Health Buddy securely downloaded information over the Internet to a computer program so the case managers could review all their patients and react to the data. The nurse also had categorized, risk-stratified information at his or her desktop to better prioritize which patients had the highest need for intervention. The outcomes of a study the Veterans Administration completed are amazing.

- 40% reduction in emergency-room visits
- 63% reduction in hospital visits
- 60% reduction in nursing-home admissions
- 88% reduction in nursing-home bed days of care
- significant improvement in quality of life[6]

Incentivize Healthy Behavior Through Rewards and Prizes: When All Else Fails, Mandate

I am a huge fan of positive incentives. I think that carrots work much better than sticks in a free society. Systems that punish, too often fail. Systems that reward, lead to positive change in a positive manner.

One of the strongest motivators of change in human and institutional behavior is money. The 21st century entrepreneurial purchaser would work to design benefits packages that incentivize preventive, healthy behavior among the people they insure and also incentivize high-quality care for providers and institutions.

Currahee Health Benefits Solutions (see Transforming Examples, Appendix A) is one of the most effective health management programs we have seen. Their focus has been to contract with employers to provide specific health management services to their employees. They aggressively incentivize and recruit eligible employees into their programs. In addition to the educational materials, clinical advising, and access to nurse case managers, they provide economic incentives for compliance with the course of action designed for each individual. As a result the employees have improved health, and the organizations and companies who have enlisted Currahee have seen a measurable return of $3 to $5 for every $1 invested.

Purchasers, both private and governmental, should design their benefits to encourage positive behavior as well as look for ways outside of the typical insurance-based system to keep their employees healthy. Beyond the moral correctness of that position, a healthy employee is a productive employee. Innovation and risk-taking are important elements to design the right kind of incentives. There are plans that eliminate the out-of-pocket costs on drugs taken consistently. There are employers raffling off trips to Disney World only for those individuals who got their flu vaccination. There are numerous other creative ways to employ incentives to encourage the right health behavior in people.

The amount of hours we worked and the time my staff and I spent in the Speaker's office made it very easy to make poor dietary choices and not exercise. Leftover cookies and appetizers from meetings and receptions, fast food, and tuna melts from the grill led to almost everyone in the office gaining weight over the first year. Someone in the office started a weight contest, who could lose 8% of their body weight in eight weeks. Everyone who wanted to participate put in $20 and weighed in with the weight keeper. It became a team approach to healthy behavior. After eight weeks, two of the staff had achieved their goal, winning about $150 each, and quite a few others were close behind. This is not a revolutionary idea but the kind of healthy, team-building activity that could be replicated in any workplace. It just takes leadership.

A system that is incentive rich would add value to medical care while taking out needless cost. For example, there should be increased reimbursement for risk-adjusted (difficult cases), high-quality care. There should be financial incentives for electronic filing of claims. There should be lower co-pays for patients who are compliant with their health-management requirements. In short, there should be incentives for good health management for both patient and provider.

Because insurance should be available for everyone, individuals who are working in low-paying jobs and are otherwise too poor to buy insurance should receive a tax credit for that purpose. The very poor, those on Medicaid for example, should receive vouchers for this purpose. Initiatives such as these would take much of the burden off state budgets and would return care for the poor to a true marketplace. If all the different complex and bureaucratic systems designed to deliver care for the poor were part of one budget, and that money was then distributed as vouchers, the current total federal, state, and local expenditure on healthcare for the poor would be more than enough to provide for a voucher system that returned choice to the poor and incentives to the providers.

There are other opportunities to use better financial incentives and individual choice to lower the cost of the healthcare system. What if we could get the same pharmaceutical coverage for over-the-counter drugs as we do for prescription medications? Many of the drugs you can purchase over the counter at the pharmacy or grocery store once required a prescription. Often these medications can provide the same healing capability as drugs purchased with a prescription but at one-tenth the cost.

Yet both the insurance and the tax system have a bias in favor of purchasing the more expensive product. Today you are reimbursed if you buy the newest and most expensive product even if an equally good but older and much less expensive alternative is available. That is the opposite of a sound, market-oriented design for financing health and healthcare.

Conclusion

This system of self-definition and self-management is, of course, exactly what we do in every other aspect of spending our own resources. You decide the kind of housing you can afford and want. You decide the kind of car or clothing or vacation you can afford and want. We think you are smart enough to buy, insure, and maintain a house (which can be quite complicated). We think virtually everyone can learn to buy and maintain a car or truck. In each case we believe you can learn to be a smarter and wiser consumer of goods and services. No one has suggested we need a third-party purchaser of house and car maintenance because we are incapable of learning. Indeed, anyone who proposed it would be ridiculed.

This does not mean we believe in a wide-open, unregulated free market. We expect the government to set minimum standards for safe housing. We expect the government to license electricians because we know what they do is dangerous. We expect the government to set minimum safety standards for cars and trucks. The difference is that once these standards have been set, we expect individuals to interact in a market economy with providers of goods and services to make choices within the limits set by government. Because these providers of goods and services must meet your needs to continue receiving your business, they innovate and improve what they are doing far more rapidly and dynamically than is possible in a bureaucratic system.

Owning your own health insurance policy or health reimbursement account empowers you, the individual. Because you are deciding how to spend the money, you have a vested interest in the cost of goods and services and how your healthcare dollars should be spent. You not only reap the health benefits of taking care of yourself but also the financial benefits. You would know how much healthcare treatments and services cost and could then decide how your healthcare dollars are spent, a transparency that is completely missing today.

---

[1] President, Economic Report of the President (Washngton, DC: Government Printing Office, 2002).
[2] Department of the Treasury, Office of Public Affairs, "Treasury and IRS Issue Guidance on Health Reimbursement Arrangemgents," press release, issued 26 June 2002. <www.treas.gov/press/releases/po3204.htm>
[3] Laura Landro, *Survivor: taking control of your fight against cancer,* (New York: Simon and Schuster, 1998).
[4] G.T. O'Connor, et al., "A regional prospective study of in-hospital mortality associated with coronary artery bypass grafting. The Northern New England Cardiovascular Disease Study Group," *JAMA* 266 (1991): 803-809; S.V. Williams, D.B. Nash, N. Goldfarb, "Differences in mortality from coronary artery bypass surgery at five teaching hospitals," *JAMA* 266 (1991): 810-815.
[5] Williams Dudley RA, Johnson, KL, Brand R, Rennie DJ, Milstein A. "Selective Referral to High-Volume Hospitals: Estimating Potentially Avoidable Deaths." *JAMA* 283 (2000):1159-1166.
[6] As reported on <www.cdc.gov/tobacco/research/_data/stat_nat_data/bestprac-dwnld.htm> as of 24 April 2003.

CHAPTER SIX

Medical Culture

Over the last twenty years, knowledge and insight about health and health-care has been rapidly increased. Scientific breakthroughs continue at a breathtaking pace. Recent discoveries in the pharmaceutical industry and the Human Genome Project will help determine an individual's potential to be genetically predisposed to a disease, making it possible to anticipate potential health risks and to develop a plan to lessen the likelihood of illness.

The surge of technology and science has made it difficult for any health-care professional to stay current about the most recent advancements that save lives and ease administrative burdens. Fortunately, technology continues to generate new tools to synthesize information and provide it to healthcare professionals in a useable format. Already today, technological resources enable doctors to write prescriptions electronically, access and incorporate the latest advancements, and collaborate with experts world-wide. Unfortunately the healthcare system has historically been slow to accept, embrace, and implement these tools despite their obvious and dramatic benefits.

This will necessitate a cultural shift from a reactive patient-treatment methodology to proactively keeping individuals healthy. In a 21st Century System of Health and Healthcare, providers will use technology tools that enable patients to manage their health, own their medical record, and control their healthcare dollars.

In order to ensure the best individual care using the most advanced science, a 21st Century System of Health and Healthcare should allow providers and patients to easily access real-time information on health strategies and treatment options with a user-friendly resource system connected to the Internet. However, changing the quality of healthcare in America requires more than just changing systems. It is essential that we change the focus, attitude, and environment of the people that operate in the system. As the practice of medicine continually evolves, doctors, nurses, pharmacist, midwives, and all other healthcare workers need to be part of the evolutionary process to find better treatments and cures. Their focus should always be to get the best knowledge and implement the best practice to achieve the best outcome for the patient. That requires transformation to a system that values outcomes and allows healthcare professionals to invest time on education and on the health of their patients instead of on bureaucracy, regulation, and litigation.

However, the culture of medicine is a chief obstacle to transforming the current healthcare system into one that is innovative, high quality, technology rich, transparent, and cost effective. In this chapter we will look at the cultural barriers of healthcare providers, insurance companies, and employers.

Medical Education

It all starts here. Through years of rigorous schooling, doctors are taught to be autonomous centers of expertise surrounded by people who follow orders. They have been educated and tested in a system that stresses huge volumes of memorization. The styles of medical care have emphasized post-disease and post-trauma care, undervalued preventive care, emphasized the provider-centric system, and devalued or ignored the potential of empowering individuals in their own health. Doctors have been exploited in residencies that encouraged habits of self-reliance and endurance over teamwork. The exhausting nature of medical education has led to an over-valuation of past knowledge and an undervaluation of emerging or new knowledge. Finally, the doctor-centric model has failed to appreciate other team members and, in particular, led to a doctor-nurse style of dominance-subservience that has made it much harder to retain nurses and utilize them most effectively.

The present system fails to encourage learning about best practices. To correct this, the education of medical professionals should continue beyond the medical school experience in order to have a continual build-ing of knowledge followed by a dissemination of that knowledge through-out the system. In leading this transformation, medical schools should cre-ate an environment where science and medicine merge by taking a proac-tive role in working and focusing on the individual and collaboratively developing the pathways of care to achieve the best outcomes. In order to do that, healthcare education facilities should create an expectation that students will seek the most up-to-date resources and knowledge and access the most advanced tools for diagnosing and treating diseases. This stan-dard of lifetime learning must then be transferred into practice after grad-uation. Establishing a learning link between medical teaching institutions and those healthcare providers no longer connected to a teaching environ-ment could help reach that standard by making development and learning best practices an ongoing endeavor for each healthcare provider.

Medical schools and other health schools should also establish a strong requirement for learning about health management and helping individu-als develop their ability to use the nutrition-activity-attitude system to stay healthy. Medical training needs to broaden into healthcare planning beyond being applicable to our healthcare. You and your healthcare providers should establish a realistic strategy for you to reach and maintain your optimum health status. When assessing your health portfolio, you need to remember to realistically account for your lifestyle, exercise and eating habits, your environment, exposure to stress, and your predisposi-tion to medical disorders. Similar to evaluating and modifying your finan-cial plan according to your circumstances, this type of evaluation and flex-ibility is applicable to your health and will put you in control.

Patients have a right to expect that their healthcare provider is constantly learning about the latest information and technology. One source for ongoing education is a program known as SKOLAR, www.skolar.com (see Transforming Examples, Appendix A). Stanford SKOLAR MD is a search engine providing information to doctors regarding a variety of healthcare issues, including medication, treatment, and diagnosis. Using this system, doctors can go on-line and review all the research available from the latest journals and other medical resources. In addition, they will receive continuing medical education (CME) credit. With more accurate, real-time information, there should be as much emphasis on prevention as there is on detection and a focus on maintaining health as much as treating illness.

Incentives should be built into the system that encourage physicians to seek out additional learning. Such incentives can, like the SKOLAR model, provide continuing medical education credits. Doctors with higher levels of additional training could be compensated at a higher rate. Incentives like these would rapidly change behaviors. As a result, physicians would access the latest reports citing the latest treatments and drugs. Your physician, working with you, would then evaluate the cost, outcomes, and available treatment options.

Team Effort

Individuals should educate themselves in order to take charge of their own healthcare. No matter how much we empower individuals, the role of healthcare professionals will still be enormous and, in many ways, decisive. Doctors and nurses are especially central to transforming health and healthcare into a 21st century system. Still, the best doctor-patient relationship is a team relationship. Unfortunately, the relationship most of us presently have with our healthcare provider is episodic and erratic. We go to the doctor to be treated for an illness but rarely just to stay healthy. However, in a 21st century model, individuals would spend more time managing their own health in consultation with their doctor. The relationship would be an interactive one in which patients are able to contribute knowledge and participate in their health strategy. After all, they are the ultimate implementers of the plan.

The Internet can enable both parties to access information on almost every aspect of healthcare to keep the plan on track while actually decreasing the number of times patients visit a doctor's office.

Understandably, doctors have mixed feelings about patients walking into their office with piles of information downloaded from the Internet. Though encouraged by your desire to be responsible for your own health, they also know that they might not be able to answer all of your questions in the eighteen minutes they spend with the average patient. Some doctors resisting new technologies will argue that medicine is an art form and that technology tools actually do more harm than good because they give the patient a false sense of knowledge. While it is true that there is a lot of art to medicine, there is also a lot of science. Today, however, there are Internet tools available that you and your doctors can use to help you zero in on a diagnosis. Decision support tools like PKC Corporation's "couplers" (see Transforming Examples, Appendix A) can help you help the doctor more rapidly discern your condition, and it can help you "check" the doctor without requiring you to be an expert.

Global Medicine

It is unrealistic to think that one individual has all the answers to your health. Sometimes your doctor needs another opinion. Allowing physicians to practice medicine across state lines in order to increase the pool of experts available to the patient and their doctor would improve the quality of care. In an age of almost universal access to electronic information, it is possible to electronically consult with the best specialists in the country. It makes no sense to restrict a licensed physician in one state from practicing medicine in another state. Too often, state licensure is a technique to restrict the supply of professionals and minimize competition.

As a starting point, board certified physicians should not have to apply for a license in all 50 states. If they achieve nationally recognized competence, doctors should be able to practice throughout the nation. Markets dynamics would enable individuals to seek the best physicians and encourage physicians to be the best. Moving information electronically between doctors and patients across state boundaries would enable more convenient, timely, and effective care at a lower cost.

Another quality enhancement opportunity would allow doctors in programs like Medicare, the Veterans Administration, the military, and the Federal Employee Health Benefits programs to be reimbursed for on-line consultations. Distance medicine would bring better care at lower cost to much of rural America. Sharing medical information electronically is not only cost effective but also improves the quality of healthcare.

It is interesting to note that physicians originally acquired and incorporated computers within their medical practices to manage the billing and financial responsibilities the insurance industry was placing on them. It is only more recently that computers have been used to facilitate the delivery of healthcare. Today bone density tests and other in-office lab tests are just a few examples of computer methods currently utilized by some physicians. The next step might be to create a routine home diagnostic center to conveniently and easily monitor your health status, enabling you to engage in your own health-management system. The outcomes and findings provided could then be sent to healthcare providers electronically so that you and your doctor—as a team—stay abreast of your condition.

This type of interconnectivity is also essential between the different healthcare entities. Mayo Hospital in Jacksonville, Florida has worked to integrate treatment of the individual by uniting their technology systems. Here doctor, lab, and pharmacist all have access to your most up-to-date medical information. They are also able to communicate with one another when something looks out of the ordinary. Mayo is hoping to eventually have medical records available to the patient 24 hours a day, accessible through an intranet site with the same security as customers who use ATM machines. Having access to medical information leads to more informed decisions and better outcomes.

Healthcare Consumer

In a world where we have the ability to do our own trading on the stock market, it should be unacceptable that we are still at the mercy of an insurance company to understand care options, provider choices, and costs. The role of the patient has evolved into a dependency relationship in the healthcare delivery system rather than the driver of the system. Access to information and knowledge about healthcare will empower individuals, as consumers, to make the best healthcare choices in deciding which procedures, treatments, and preventive care will best meet their mental, emotional, and physical needs. We want to know that the physician performing our hip and knee replacement has done the procedure enough times to be proficient at it. We want to know that if we have type 2 diabetes, our doctor has a high percentage of success in treating patients with that condition.

By using the same technologies already working in other parts of our lives, we can design a healthcare system that is accessible 24/7, offering you consistent quality and access to the information you need. A good first step would be to create individual electronic medical records that are password protected like your ATM card. They would allow you to easily give a care provider an accurate account of your personal health history, medical conditions, medications you are taking, and insurance information. This would be particularly useful if you are seeing a new doctor or facing a medical emergency. An electronic record would allow the physician to focus his or her time and energy on treating what truly ails you. You would be able to monitor vital signs from home and electronically communicate symptoms to your healthcare provider. Confidential access and ease of communication between patients and providers would prevent illnesses and shorten recovery time.

Moreover, the ability to electronically share medical information does not end with individual medical records but also allows the delivery of healthcare to be global. X-rays can be viewed on computers on the other side of the country or even overseas. A world-class heart surgeon from California could consult with your physician in Virginia about treatment options. Suddenly, the best specialists in the world can be at your bedside in a virtual connection.

Listed below are two initiatives for sharing information and implementing best practices in order to get the highest quality healthcare.

- In 1998 the Pittsburgh Regional Healthcare Initiative (PRHI), www.prhi.org, was started as a result of a regional economic strategy developed by community leaders in Pittsburgh. The initiative, under the leadership of former U. S. Treasury Secretary and Alcoa Chairman Paul O'Neill and Jewish Healthcare Foundation President Karen Wolk Feinstein, was formed to focus on quality of healthcare in the community. They fundamentally believe that the cost of healthcare would lower if quality were improved. As a result, PRHI has focused on three goals. The first has been to guarantee patient safety. They established a benchmark of zero medication errors. PRHI has partnered with the Centers for Disease Control and Prevention in Atlanta in the belief that their model may lead to breakthroughs with national implications. The second goal has been to focus on achieving the best outcomes in six clinical areas: cardiac surgery, hip- and knee-replacement surgery, maternal and child outcomes, obstetrics, depression, and diabetes. Their third goal has been to perfect the patient-care system. They did this by designing a model based on the Toyota Production system that allows every healthcare provider to learn from errors and problems and improves the healthcare-delivery processes while lowering cost.

- The Institute for Health Improvement (IHI), www.ihi.org, is a nonprofit organization led by Don Berwick. It believes that advancing the quality and value of healthcare will improve delivery. IHI's primary focus includes: safety, effectiveness, patient-centeredness, timeliness, efficiency, and equity. IHI seeks out cutting-edge ideas that impact quality and then exports that learning to healthcare professionals and organizations so the ideas to improve healthcare can be shared and implemented systemwide. The more rapidly good ideas are exchanged, the quicker the best outcome can be achieved.

Just as AARP is known nationally as a source for providing information and services for people age 50 and older, a 21st Century System of Health and Healthcare should have information technology enterprises that provide specialized medical services nationwide. Institutions that meet the certification standards would be listed on the Internet so that people anywhere in America could pick an institution with which to work. The government would set the standards, but people would choose the center that best fits their circumstances.

This would be of great value to the many people (with hemophilia or other conditions) who live far from a specialist. A nationally certified institution could assist a person with hemophilia in a local emergency room by connecting the local emergency room doctors to a top hemophilia specialist who could coach them through the appropriate care. This would allow a person with hemophilia or any other specific condition to get the best possible care. There should also be a national registry of doctors, specialized surgeons, and hospitals empowered to provide the best medical care for other specific chronic conditions.

The National Hemophilia Foundation, www.hemophilia.org, and the Factor Foundation, www.factorfoundation.org, are two organizations already helping parents across the country learn how to help their children get the right treatment and learn the behaviors that lead to the fullest possible life with the least risk of real damage.

Every family could be electronically connected to a community of support the very day they discover their new baby has a chronic condition. The result would be a speed of understanding, an avoidance of confusion, a minimization of risk, and an easing of worries that would be invaluable for many families and give children the best opportunity to lead the fullest lives with the fewest possible complications.

Today we have the potential for every American with hemophilia to have a pager, a cell phone, and a laptop to reach a specialist on a 24/7 basis and to access Web pages that contain the newest information about best practices and outcomes. When dealing with a condition that costs between $25,000 and $200,000 per year, per person, a sophisticated and ethical response would be to make the investment to save not only money but also suffering.[1]

This model of best care with guaranteed access would actually save the government money over the lifetime of people with conditions such as hemophilia. Today we will pay for a very expensive joint surgery for a person with hemophilia, sometimes $1 to $2 million dollars for an operation that could have been avoided with better care and earlier intervention.[2] This model of electronically connected, national care is a classic example of saving lives and saving money.

Diabetes is another major health challenge and is very costly in lives, quality of life, and financial expense. Because diabetes is a chronic condition positively impacted by the right treatment and the right behavior, there is an enormous difference between best and worst outcomes. The 1992 Lewin VHI study showed one in four Medicare dollars were being spent on people with diabetes at that time.[3] These dollars were spent not caring for the disease diabetes only, but other diabetically driven illnesses such as heart disease, blindness, amputation, and kidney failure as well as non-diabetic incidents like broken bones, colds, and pneumonia. We should strive to create universal screening so people know if they are pre-diabetic and have simple Web-based systems for people to manage their own health.

Associations such as the American Diabetes Association, www.diabetes.org; the American Cancer Society, www.cancer.org; and the American Healthcare Association, www.ahca.org, which focus on long-term-care issues, are additional resources to help individuals make the most informed choices on healthcare providers, treatments, costs, and outcomes.

Utilize Impartial Advisor and Advocate Services

Although hospitals do not collect or offer nearly enough data to assist healthcare consumers in making informed choices, today there are tools to help employers monitor the quality of healthcare services of their employees. In healthcare, access to these advisor and "watchdog" technologies can mean the difference between life and death. These powerful human and technological resources are enabling companies to ensure that their employees are getting the best possible care.

One company, ActiveHealth Management, combines technology and medical professionals to provide "guardian angel" services to insurees (see Transforming Examples, Appendix A). ActiveHealth uses a sophisticated technology to scan available digital information, such as claims and laboratory data, then filters it through clinical data rules to identify potential "gaps in care." For example, the technology can review claims and test results chronologically and recognize when the doctor should be running a specific test or prescribing a specific medication. Once the technology identifies a potential oversight or mistake, the ActiveHealth team of medical professionals, including nurses and physicians, reviews the information, and if the "gap in care" appears legitimate, it will have an expert physician call the patient's doctor to discuss the situation.

Incentives for Prevention

A cultural shift is needed by government and employers to establish a model of prevention. To facilitate the most rapid policy changes, government and employers should be using incentives to encourage quality improvements. For example, a hospital that decreases their rate of staph infections (the most common hospital-induced illness) or is rated among the lowest in occurrences should receive a financial reward. Having payers (both governments and corporations) split the savings from lower infection rates with hospitals would be both logical and profitable. If hospitals simply received half of what they saved from the cost of average infection rates, there would be a massive incentive to focus on lowering the rate of infections, the number of unnecessary illnesses, and therefore, decrease unnecessary, preventable costs. The hospitals, the patients, and the payers would all be winners in this incentive-pulled system of positive change.

Employers could also use incentives to drive behavior. Perhaps primary-care doctors who treat people over the recommended body weight should get a higher reimbursement if they order blood-sugar level and cholesterol checks to scan for diabetes. Perhaps doctors whose patients have had open-heart surgery should get a bonus if their patient is prescribed and remains on beta-blockers for six months. I am not arguing for these specific measures or prizes but for setting standards for success. The simple fact is that rewarding achievement works. These data points may seem difficult to track, but there are existing technologies that can already do this and there are certainly technologies that could be built if the demand existed.

Another type of incentive could be a discount on malpractice insurance for using proven technologies that reduce errors, such as electronic prescriptions. Pharmaceutical companies and laboratories often provide this type of equipment free to medical professionals who prescribe their medication or access their services. Hospitals that integrate certain technologies such as electronic medical records (EMRs), computerized physician order entry (CPOE), telemedicine, and e-mail consultations could also be financially rewarded.

Still, large systems resist change. No matter how enticing the incentive, command and control bureaucracies often will not change. For example, the Mayo Clinic in Jacksonville, Florida has been using an electronic patient record and saving between $2 and $7 million every year since they began in 1996 (see Transforming Examples, Appendix A). Seven years later, despite proven reductions in medication errors and financial savings and the acceptance of the electronic records by their colleagues, the Mayo Clinics in Minnesota and Arizona have resisted adopting what is clearly a beneficial advancement. In cases where the sustaining behavior is unnecessarily costing lives and money, it is morally imperative that change be mandated, not just enticed.

Over one million medication errors occur each year in hospitals alone due to errors resulting from illegible handwriting, decimal point errors, and overlooked drug interactions and allergies.[4] According to Dr. David Bates, one-half of serious medication errors are in preventable adverse drug events of which 20% are life threatening.

The 1999 Institute of Medicine report, *To Err is Human*: *Building a Safer Healthcare System,* suggested that medication errors in hospitals alone account for 7,000 deaths annually. Furthermore, each preventable adverse drug event adds $4,700 in hospital costs that result in $2 billion per year (this does not include malpractice costs and losses in worker productivity).[5]

Computer physician order entry (CPOE) systems are electronically prescribing systems that intercept errors when they most commonly occur—at the time medications are ordered. With computerized physician order entry, physicians enter orders into a computer rather than on paper. Orders are integrated with patient information, including laboratory and prescription data. The order is then automatically checked for potential errors.[6]

According to The Leapfrog Group's November 2000 "Computer Physician Order Entry Factsheet," CPOE has resulted in better health and lower costs for both of the following institutions:

- Brigham & Women's Hospital: 55% fewer medication errors with a return on investment of $5 to $10 million in annual savings

- Wishard Memorial Hospital: length of stay fell by 0.9 days and hospital charges fell by 13%

Yet despite the evidence, only 13% to 15% of hospitals have computer physician order entry, and even at those hospitals the majority of doctors do not use the technology most of the time.[7]

If every doctor used computer physician order entry when treating inpatient Medicare patients, it would result in the prevention of over 400,000 adverse drug events, the average Medicare length of stay dropping from 6.0 to 5.1 days, and approximately $823 million of savings in Medicare hospital charges alone would be realized.[8] Can you imagine how many lives, how much pain and suffering, could be saved with $823 million?

Both employer and government healthcare purchasers need to be more proactive and creative in incentivizing, leading, and even mandating change in the healthcare system. Clearly, by 2005, we should mandate that every Medicaid prescription made without an electronic physician order entry system will not be reimbursed by the government. Hopefully private insurers would follow suit. We could incentivize and fund the migration to an electronic system by giving doctors extra money for every prescription they write electronically in 2003 and 2004.

Finally, any new model of healthcare must be transparent and report outcomes. Offering outcomes-based information has a twofold benefit. First, it arms us with important medical information to make decisions and choose healthcare providers. Second, it makes hospitals and doctors accountable. Reporting on specific metrics will result in providers working to provide better care so they can report better outcomes.

The Leapfrog Group is doing just that (www.leapfroggroup.org). Leapfrog was founded by the members of the Business Roundtable on the premise that the merely asking for information would focus hospitals on improving quality in the areas on which they were measured. Moreover, patients would receive better quality care because they would be empowered with information that could make a significant difference in their overall health outcomes. It is made up of private- and public-sector purchasers who represent approximately 33 million Americans and more than $56 billion in healthcare expenditures. By leveraging their combined purchasing power, they were able to apply pressure to the hospitals to report outcomes representative of the total quality of care. The employers of the Leapfrog Group make that information from the hospitals available to their employees. Although a hospital is not required to report their outcomes, unwillingness to report the metrics naturally raises suspicion with customers.

Legal Hurdle

Much of what is standing in the way of the cultural changes that we are seeking is the fear of litigation, as we will discuss in the chapter on health justice. Litigation has had a dramatically negative effect on medical innovations reaching the doctor's office.

Without litigation reform as it applies to healthcare, transforming the healthcare system and its culture will be impossible. The predatory behavior of trial lawyers does not allow for transparency in the system nor does it encourage healthcare professionals to report mistakes. We need a new model of health justice for transformation to occur.

[1] Neil Frick, conversation with the author (26 March 2003).

[2] Dave Madieros, conversation with Kathy G. Lubbers 24 April 2003.

[3] As reported on www.insulinfree.org/articles/touchsugar.htm as of 23 April 2003.

[4] Linda T. Kohn, Janet M. Corrigan, and Molla S. Donaldson, ed., Institute of Medicine Committee on Quality of Health Care in America (Washington, DC: National Academy Press).

[5] J.D. Birkmeyer, C.M. Birkmeyer, D.E. Wennberg, M.P. Young, "Leapfrog safety standards: potential benefits of universal adoption," The Leapfrog Group (Washington, DC, 2000).

[6] ibid.

[7] "Computer Physician Order Entry Factsheet," November 2000. As reported on <http://www.leapfroggroup.org/FactSheets/CPOE_FactSheet.pdf> as of 23 April 2003.

[8] ibid.

Toward a 21st Century System
of Health Justice

Increasingly we see the human cost of a litigation system run amok in which trial lawyers have grown stunningly more greedy and destructive, causing a breakdown in health justice. Greed has replaced equity, enrichment has replaced justice, and what was once a nuisance has grown into a genuine threat to the nation's health as the following examples illustrate.

In late 2002 the only trauma center in Las Vegas closed because of the preposterous cost of litigation insurance. The risk of dying from trauma went up exponentially for residents and visitors alike. Lawyer enrichment has put human life at risk.[1]

Also in Las Vegas, the price of litigation insurance and the threat of predatory lawsuits have led obstetricians to refuse to take new patients.[2]

Surgeons in West Virginia are being threatened by massive increases in litigation insurance. Patients have to wait longer or travel farther to undergo needed surgery. The lawyers are getting richer, but the health of West Virginians has been put at risk in the process.[3]

The difference between Pennsylvania and New Jersey litigation costs are now so great that doctors are moving from Philadelphia across the river to Camden, New Jersey where their patients now have to travel for care.[4] Unfortunately, New Jersey is not the haven we would hope; between 5,000 and 10,000 New Jersey doctors walked out of their offices for two weeks to call attention to their own unsustainable increases in litigation insurance premiums.[5]

The cost of litigation insurance in long-term care facilities, up to $1,000 per bed, per month in some states, is leading an increasing number to close their doors.[6] The unscrupulousness of trial lawyers is affecting the economy, crippling families, and risking lives.

The American College of Obstetrics and Gynecology has issued a red alert in nine states; four more are on the watch list. The current system of litigation is incentivizing healthcare professionals to quit practicing in states with high malpractice insurance.[7] The American Medical Association reports that twelve states—including Texas, New York, Florida, Ohio, Pennsylvania, Oregon, and New Jersey—are in serious danger of doctor shortages because of rapidly rising malpractice insurance premiums.[8] While trial lawyers are reaping enormous benefits, doctors are forced to abandon patients in desperate need of care.

The recent doctor strikes; closures of hospitals, trauma centers, and long-term care facilities; and the continuing outcry about the expense of the predatory litigation system are all indications that we need to rethink the way we resolve conflicts about patients' rights in our healthcare system. The key is to ensure that we do what is right for the individual who has a legitimate grievance, for care providers, and for society.

On the one hand, we do not want to block anyone from seeking justice if they have been injured or harmed. In fact we want to ensure timely justice both for the integrity and sustaining power of American values and as an added deterrent to gross negligence. On the other hand, we do not want a system that drives good healthcare professionals out of business, costs society an unnecessarily large amount of money, rewards lawyers for frivolous suits, or creates a culture that obscures accurate information about quality and errors.

Balancing the general public's interest in safety and best information with the individual's legal right to protect themselves is possible. In fact, we have a model in the aviation safety system.

When first elected to Congress in 1978, I represented the Atlanta airport and Delta Airlines, the largest private employer in Georgia, as part of my district. In addition, I had the opportunity to serve on the Subcommittee on Aviation. While fulfilling these responsibilities, a problem arose with the DC-10 aircraft. Upon takeoff, an engine would literally fall off the jet, causing the airplane to crash and killing passengers and crew.

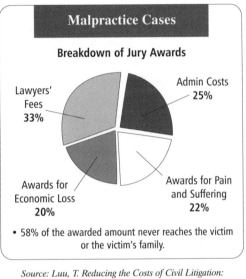

Source: Luu, T. Reducing the Costs of Civil Litigation:
What are the Costs of Litigation?
PLRI Public Law Research Institute

Because there had been two DC-10 crashes, one in Mexico City and one in Chicago, there were hearings on Capital Hill in the Subcommittee on Aviation. The National Transportation Safety Board (NTSB) surveyed the crash sites, interviewed people, and studied the airplanes' parts. By carefully reviewing mandatory records, it discovered that when overhauled in the maintenance process, the engines were reinstalled in a manner that placed too much stress on the huge bolts holding the engine to the wing. These bolts were weakened so that the pressure applied upon take-off created a stress point that fractured and caused the engines to fall off. Within 48 hours of understanding the problem and devising a solution, the Federal Aviation Administration sent out a message to every mechanic in the world who worked on DC-10s so they could understand and correct the problem. The message was simple and straightforward—do maintenance the new way, because the old way kills people.

We should apply the FAA model to healthcare. There are approximately 2,000,000 hospital-induced illnesses and 1,500,000 long-term care-induced illnesses every year. If we treated these numbers the way we treat an airplane crash, we would have a very different response. However, an appropriate response first requires an information system that gathers data, performs appropriate analysis, and then sends the results back out to change behavior. Those who insist on doing it the old way, even if the old way sickens and kills people, should simply not be allowed to practice medicine.

To implement such a systemwide change, it will be necessary for doctors to fully disclose mistakes without fear of a lawsuit. Much like how the airline industry collects maintenance records and practices to devise solutions, the healthcare industry needs to have data to evaluate and drive new procedures. Doctors who are unwilling to share information are inhibiting growth and preventing the system from generating new, improved processes to save lives. We would never accept an airline industry that kept from the public errors that caused the deaths of so many. Similarly, we cannot tolerate a healthcare system that obscures information at the expense of lives.

It is a matter of values. In the airline industry, safety is more important than litigation. Pilots and mechanics report problems without fear that they will immediately face a blackmail lawsuit from a predatory trial lawyer. Manufacturers, airlines, and the government work together on safety concerns because they know their primary interest is manufacturing better airplanes with better procedures to maximize safe travel.

In aviation we have placed the public's interest in safety and quality above the lawyer's interest in suing. In health and healthcare, we still place the lawyer's right to collect exorbitant sums above the patient's right to have the highest quality outcome based on the best possible information.

It is impossible to develop the kind of quality system of health and health-care we need as long as the predatory trial-lawyer system threatens every doctor, every hospital, and every healthcare professional.

First, it is impossible to get people to expose their mistakes and share less desirable outcomes if the consequence of honesty is litigious action. Asking people to act against their own self-interest is neither the American way nor particularly rational. It is our job to create a system of health justice that rewards truthfulness and uncovers errors and problems so they can be remedied.

Disclosure and transparency are key to protecting both healthcare providers and patients. Providers must be able to share ideas on best practices and lessons learned. As cited in the Institute of Medicine's report, *To Err is Human,* patient safety is often weakened by possible litigious implications. "Patient safety is also hindered through the liability system and the threat of malpractice, which discourages the disclosure of errors. The discoverability of data under legal proceedings encourages silence about errors committed or observed. Most errors and safety issues go undetected and unreported, both externally and within healthcare organizations."[9] In order to achieve the best practices and outcomes, it is essential to have openness among healthcare providers and with patients.

Second, the fear of lawsuits, even when nothing has been done wrong, creates a climate of defensive medicine in which medical decisions are driven by this fear rather than sound health practices. It is impossible to get health professionals to focus on a best outcomes approach when their daily practice is constrained by the desire to avoid anything that could lead them to spend years of their life fighting a lawsuit.

Philip K. Howard, chairman of the Board of Common Good (www.our-commongood.com), a group dedicated to overhauling America's lawsuit culture, wrote in the *Wall Street Journal* that "most doctors admit to regularly ordering unnecessary tests and procedures just to provide a possible defense in case there is a lawsuit. The trend will only accelerate as doctors worry about keeping up with what others do—the number of possible tests for any given patient is almost endless. The gargantuan total of malpractice premiums and legal costs, over $10 billion per year, is dwarfed by the waste attributed to legal fear. Some economists estimate that the cost of 'defensive medicine' now exceeds $100 billion."[10] One hundred billion dollars in unnecessary tests and referrals is an atrocious sum. Imagine how many lives could be saved from medical breakthroughs funded by this $100 billion.

Third, the very psychology of an adversarial, litigation-oriented model is the antithesis of a good doctor-patient relationship. The doctor and the patient should be an honest, intimate team jointly fighting the disease or condition that threatens the patient. When the doctor has to enter every conversation knowing it could be quoted back in a jury trial, there is an inhibition and distancing that impedes the process of achieving better health.

Fourth, the misallocation of resources away from health and healthcare toward predatory trial lawyers is breathtaking in scale and a major burden on the system. In Florida, long-term care facilities are paying as much as $12,000 per bed, per year in litigation insurance.[11] That is $1,000 a month that could go toward better care for your mother or your aunt. Instead of providing better care and more amenities, that money is paying for insurance against predatory trial lawyers. At a time of crises in state Medicaid programs and difficulties with the financing of health and healthcare, it is amazing so much money is being diverted to cope with our growing class of blackmailing, predatory trial lawyers.

Fifth, the profitability of the current predatory trial lawyer behavior sends the wrong signals to young Americans. At a time when it is clear the baby boomers will need more doctors and nurses as they age and retire, young people are watching trial lawyers bankrupt health professionals. The signal is clear: become a lawyer, be on the winning team, go where the money is going. It is not surprising that there has been a steady decline in applications for medicine as many of our best and brightest young people sign up for law school.[12]

It is important for every American to understand that trial lawyers are gaining more resources to develop a systematic method of making victims of patients and their families. According to Jon Opelt of Citizens Against Lawsuit Abuse, many lawsuits result in no payment to the plaintiff, yet the trend continues as trial lawyers seek to exploit the system for what one state called "jackpot justice."[13] The average U.S. medical malpractice award has more than doubled in recent years to $1,000,000 in 2000 from $503,000 in 1997, according to a recent study by Jury Verdict Research.[14] Because the stakes are so high, the resulting frivolous lawsuits contribute to the rapid rise of liability premiums for doctors.

For all these reasons, we must replace the current system of predatory lawsuits with a 21st century system of health justice. President Bush is right to call for caps on awards as an interim step. However, it is imperative to understand that this is only an interim step.

It will be far easier to develop and implement a 21st century system of health justice than it will be to directly reform the current system, although trial lawyers will fight equally hard against either strategy. Trial lawyers know that their economic future is dependent on the rules remaining rigged in their favor. For every trial lawyer who got rich off the tobacco settlement and now owns a Gulf Stream V aircraft and a baseball team, there are hundreds of other trial lawyers who want to make their fortune from productive Americans. This is the largest private-sector, wealth-transferring group in American history, and it is no surprise that they do not intend to let the law be changed to their disadvantage.

Since trial lawyers have their way of life at stake, they have a ferocity and an intensity for lobbying that is far greater than that of their victims. Everyone else wants to move away from the current predatory system so they can focus more on other things like being a doctor or nurse or running a hospital or long-term care facility. Only the trial lawyers have their entire fortune and future tied up in this struggle. With an intimate knowledge of the legal system and coffers of wealth at their disposal, trial lawyers spend money through their political action committees, run initiatives in the states, help recruit and elect judges who favor their lawsuits, and do everything possible to rig the game in their favor.

In a fight against a small but intense opposition, it is very important for Americans to understand that their health is at stake. A motivated people, especially when they are Americans, will know that change is integral to survival. Past efforts at tort reform have failed, in part, because they invoked language and ideas that did not directly affect people's lives. Most people never think about "tort reform" or "liability caps" let alone connect those concepts with the healthcare they receive.

However, quality healthcare is intimately linked to a quality health justice system. There is a deep American cultural commitment to justice, to protection under the law, and to having the ability to protect yourself against those who have the power to hurt or infringe on your rights.

Many people who seek to rebalance the system against the predatory trial lawyers underestimate or ignore this core trait of the American psyche. There is a pattern of equality before the law, which can be traced to the Magna Carta of 1215 and the rise of English common law, that is at the heart of the system transplanted from Britain to the American colonies.

Most conservatives are vividly aware of the importance of no taxation without representation. They proudly trace the right to have some control over the executive branch spending and taxes back to the Magna Carta and King John's forced agreement with the Barons that he would only raise taxes with their consent. They understand thoroughly the power to tax as a key component in the rise of Parliament and the central role of taxation in the Boston Tea Party and the American Revolution.

However, conservatives, especially those who worry about trial lawyers and the growing litigiousness of American society, fail to give appropriate weight to the central role of trial by jury and the right of appeal. Yet, the Seventh Amendment to the Constitution—the right to trial by jury in civil cases involving more than $20.00—was adopted during the First Congress under the leadership of James Madison as part of the Bill of Rights. The right to trial by jury was the second most frequently demanded right during the revolutionary period, surpassed only by the right to representation before taxation.

The founding fathers understood that the law could be used to destroy freedom just as surely as could the power to tax. They believed that judges were creatures of the King and could not, therefore, be relied upon to protect the innocent. They saw recourse to juries of their peers as the only device that could protect them from a predatory state.

During the last two hundred years, this sense of reliance on the law for protection has grown stronger and become even more ingrained in the American psyche. If trial lawyers wrap themselves in the defense of protecting the weak against the powerful, they ally themselves with some of the deepest populist strains of American culture. This is why direct assaults on trial lawyers are often turned into debates over the rights of the poor to protect themselves by relying on lawyers to sue the powerful. The movies *Erin Brokovich* and *A Civil Action* are recent examples of this persistent element of Americanism. This vision of the trial lawyer as a defender of the underdog is a staple of the Hollywood culture in both movies and television. Taking it on is an uphill cultural fight.

Rational analysts may decry this characterization of trial lawyers as defenders of the poor by asserting that litigators are often wealthy and usually seeking economic gain rather than justice. They may also note that in one out of four jury trials, doctors are forced to pay even when experts agree they did nothing wrong. As Philip Howard points out in his aforementioned *Wall Street Journal* column, "Justice today, studies show, is worse than random. Most errors go uncompensated; but 80% of lawsuits do not involve any negligence at all. Juries often let off the hook a doctor who made a mistake; but one in four cases results in payments where experts believe the doctor did nothing wrong."[15] However, these rational analysts are taking on one of the deepest beliefs in American culture.

The more powerful approach, and the most likely to succeed, will be to accept the key aspects of American cultural beliefs about justice and then offer a better, 21st century model of how individuals can truly achieve that justice in a better way with better results.

The 21st century system of health justice will start and end with patient safety. With this premise, it will provide fair and effective compensation, demand accountability, encourage disclosure, and incentivize the best standards and protocols of healthcare delivery. The system will provide resolution at less overall cost and deliver a larger share of the total damages to the injured—not to the attorney. It will also deliver that larger share a lot faster than the current adversarial system does.

A 21st century system of health justice will create health courts that can be accessed without an attorney and without the current delays. The health court will hear the case, review the material—available instantly since the electronic medical record will have captured everything as it was occurring—and render a timely judgment.

If the complaint were ruled legitimate, the patient would receive an immediate remedy without an exorbitant attorney's fee. If the individual felt justice had not been delivered, either because the health court found for the doctor or the award was too small, the patient could then hire an attorney and file in a district court. The patient's record and the judgment of the health court would accompany the filing at the district court. This provision would minimize the number of weak cases filed for blackmail purposes, because the trial lawyer would know, upon reading the record, that he or she had a weak case. No one would feel compelled to settle out of court just to avoid the risk of a runaway jury. This provision allows for the right to legal counsel and appeal if the health court did, in fact, make a mistake.

This system would preserve the right to be heard and guarantee every American a rapid and inexpensive way to present their case. It would allow the plaintiff to appeal the decision of the health court and honor the right to a jury trial for those who felt the health court had failed to treat them fairly. It would ensure that a much larger share of the compensation would actually reach the patient who had been hurt, rather than the paltry amount under the current trial-lawyer system.

When damages are awarded, there should be a cap on non-economic damages. FDA Commissioner Mark McClellan, in an article with Daniel Kessler, cited, "Our analysis indicates reforms that directly limit liability-caps on damage awards, abolition of punitive damages, abolition of mandatory prejudgment interest, and collateral-source rule reforms—reduce hospital expenditures by 5 to 9 percent within three to five years of adoption with the full effects of reforms requiring several years to appear."[16]

In a speech on January 16, 2003, President Bush called for reform of the medical liability system by advocating such a cap on awards. "It is a national problem that needs a national solution," he said. "And here it is—first, let me just say this as clearly as I can—we want our judicial system to work. People who have got a claim, a legitimate claim, must have a hearing in our courts. Somebody who has suffered at the hand of a lousy doc must be protected. And they deserve a court that is uncluttered by frivolous and junk lawsuits. If they prove damages, they should be able to recover the cost of their care and recovery and lost wages and economic losses for the rest of their life. That's fair. That is reasonable. And that is necessary for us to have confidence in the medical system and in the judicial system."[17]

This 21st century system of health justice would have one further advantage. It would require the patient with a problem to get early diagnosis and the earliest possible rehabilitation. Every expert knows that early diagnosis and rehabilitation are vital to helping people live full lives. The longer we wait for rehabilitation the greater the danger that we will be permanently injured or damaged.

Yet today's predatory trial-lawyer system actually discourages early rehabilitation. Since the lawyer's goal is to maximize the financial return, much of which will go to the lawyer, he or she often actively discourages the patient from seeking rehabilitation. After all, a rehabilitated patient is a much less sympathetic figure and, therefore, less likely to win a big judgment from a jury. In effect, the trial attorney immorally advises the plaintiff to accept a poorer quality of life in hopes of getting a much bigger payment, less than half of which ends up with the victim anyway. This may be a good bargain for the lawyer who collects extra money, but it is a tragedy for the individual who ends up debilitated, and possibly crippled, for the rest of his or her life because of delayed rehabilitation.

Sound health policy would gather thorough records, complete film and photographic evidence, and then move forward to aggressively rehabilitate the patient so he or she could return to living a full life. Quality of life should be a higher value than quantity of jury award money.

This model is neither new nor radical. New Zealand has been successfully using a system very much like this for nearly three decades.[18] After studying the lawsuit model of health justice, experts in New Zealand concluded that it was very expensive, bred adversarial attitude, shifted too much of the money away from the patient, took too long, discouraged appropriate and timely rehabilitation, and was very ineffective at punishing bad doctors.

New Zealand adopted a health justice model much more like the description above than like the current American lottery-by-lawyer system. The result has been a significantly more effective method of rehabilitating the injured, rewarding those who need the money, encouraging doctors to focus on medical issues, and minimizing the destructiveness of trial lawyers. It's saving lives and saving money.

Reforming the way medical cases are handled within the legal system is vital to transforming our healthcare system into a consumer-centric model. The current system of litigation is too expensive and fails to provide justice for patients and their families. The situation has reached a crisis in which predatory trial lawyers with more and more resources are gaming the system to enrich themselves at the expense of American society.

I believe it is possible to devise a more egalitarian, less expensive system with timely conflict resolution to protect the rights of health consumers, the health of Americans, and be less expensive for American society.

The Role of the States

The states can be leaders in bringing about the transformed system. Before 1975 patients' access to care in California was threatened by aggressive insurance premium hikes. After lawmakers realized the culprit was largely frivolous lawsuits, California passed the Medical Injury Compensation Reform Act (MICRA). Since MICRA was enacted, California has witnessed decreased numbers of frivolous lawsuits while seeing an increase in the monetary awards actually received by injured patients. Additionally, the law eliminated much of the motivation to go to trial. More cases are settled because of the law's cap limitation.[19] Numerous groups such as the Healthcare Liability Alliance, the American Healthcare Association, the National Council on Assisted Living, and the Chamber of Commerce are advocating for Congress to take swift legislative action to support federal legislation based on California's MICRA reforms.

President Bush cited the impact of California's proactive efforts to bring about change in his speech calling for malpractice reform. "Let me tell you a startling statistic. Reports from Philadelphia say that juries there have awarded more in malpractice damages than the entire state of California did over the last three years. That says two things. California's law is what people in your statehouse ought to look at, and you've got a problem in Pennsylvania. There was a good news story in Mississippi. I went down there and—it wasn't because of me, it was because the doctors and the citizens understand the cost of a trial system gone awry and they got themselves a law. And they got a medical liability law. They put caps, real caps. Guess what happened? In some counties, the malpractice claims rose dramatically before the law came into effect. Now what does that tell you about the system? It tells me that the system is less about justice and more about something that looks like the lottery. And with the plaintiffs' bar getting as much as 40% of any verdict, sometimes there's only one winner in the lottery."[20]

We should commit to replacing the currently destructive, unacceptable, and predatory trial lawyer system with a well-designed health justice system that will better serve us all.

[1] Rob Stein, "Increase in Physicians' Insurance Hurts Care," *Washington Post,* (5 January 2003): A10.
[2] As reported on <www.aamc.org/newsroom/reporter/july02/medicalmalpractice.htm> as of 23 April 2003.
[3] Frank J. Murray, "Lawsuit Fears Fuel Strikes by Surgeons," *Washington Times,* vol. 141.
[4] Neil Graves, "Hosps in a Jam As N.J. Docs Rally," *New York Post Online Edition,* (4 February 2003).
[5] Mary Jo Layton, Jeff Pillets, *The Record,*Bergen County (New York: 3 February 2003) A01.
[6] As reported on <www.ahca.org/news/nr030123.htm> as of 23 April 2003.
[7] As reported on <www.acog.org/from_home/publications/press_releaseslnr01-29-103.cfm> as of 23 April 2003.
[8] American Medical Association, *AMA Analysis: A Dozen States in Medical Liability Crisis,* (17 June 2002).
[9] Institute of Medice: *To Err Is Human: Building a Safer Health System* (Washington, DC: National Academy Press): 43.
[10] Philip K. Howard, "Legal Malpractice," *The Wall Street Journal,* (27 January 2003).
[11] *Palm Beach Post* (8 March 2003).
[12] As reported on <www.usatoday.com/news/nation/2002-07-23-grad-school_x.htm> as of 23 April 2003.
[13] Jon Opelt, "Some Class Action Lawsuits Benefit Everyone but 'The Little Guy,'" *American City Business Journal and Houston Business Journal* (22 October 1999).
[14] Jury Verdict Research: "Medical Malpractice Award Trends: Believe Government Sources, Not Doctors," (14 January 2003).
[15] See note 10.
[16] Daniel P. Kessler, Mark McClellan, "Is Hospital Competition Socially Wasteful?" *The Quarterly Journal of Economics* 115 (2000): 577-615.
[17] President, speech given at the University of Scranton (Washington, DC: Office of the Press Secretary, 16 January 2003). As reported on <www.whitehouse.gov.news/releases/2003/01/20030116-1.html> as of 23 April 2003.
[18] As reported on <www.whitehouse.gov/news/releases/2003/01/20030116-1.html> as of 23 April 2003.
[19] As reported on <http://pacificwestlaw.com/physicians/micra.htm> as of 23 April 2003.
[20] As reported on <www.whitehouse.gov/news/releases/2003/01/20030116-1.html> as of 23 April 2003.

CHAPTER EIGHT

Diabetes As an Example of the Health First, Healthcare Second Model in *Saving Lives & Saving Money*

Diabetes presents perhaps the clearest example of how transforming the health and healthcare system will save lives and save money.

The current system's treatment of people with diabetes is irrational and borders on unethical. The complications of diabetes include kidney failure, blindness, amputation, heart failure, and stroke. Medicare and many private insurance plans pay for kidney dialysis. They will pay for surgery to amputate a foot or perform bypass heart surgery. They will also pay for nursing-home care after a stroke. The government provides cash assistance to individuals who are blind or undergo amputation. However, what the system does not pay for, in many cases, is medication and patient training that can delay and even prevent these devastating and expensive complications of diabetes.

We know today from well-designed, long-term studies how to delay and prevent the complications of diabetes. We know it will save immeasurable human suffering and will save the healthcare system billions of dollars. But instead of trying to save lives and save money by preventing expensive complications from diabetes, the system tries to save money by restricting access to preventive services. That is the equivalent of trying to save money on car maintenance by not changing the oil. Our health system is on the verge of seizing up just as our car would be if we neglected preventive maintenance. It is time to manage costs by improving care and stop trying to manage costs by denying care.

What Is Diabetes?

The body of a person without diabetes breaks down food into glucose and feeds the glucose into your bloodstream. However, insulin is required to make this connection. Your pancreas produces the exact amount of insulin needed to move the glucose from the bloodstream to your cells so they can use the glucose for energy. You do not have to think about this process. Your blood-glucose levels stay within a very narrow range.

In type 1 diabetes, the cells in the pancreas that produce insulin have been destroyed by the body's own immune system. People with type 1 diabetes must take injections of insulin to live.

In type 2 diabetes, the body is either resistant to insulin or does not produce enough insulin and then needs higher than normal amounts to move glucose into cells. Some oral medications help the body make more insulin; others help the body use insulin. People diagnosed with type 2 diabetes often start treatment taking one kind of diabetes pill. As the years go by, they need to take a second and possibly a third type. Eventually, the majority of people with type 2 diabetes need injections of insulin as well.

In a person with untreated diabetes, the glucose level in the blood exceeds 126 mg/dl [milligrams per deciliter]. In effect, the body is being bathed in excess glucose that damages the kidneys, eyes, and nerves, resulting in vision loss, amputation, and potentially life-threatening consequences—all very costly and detrimental to quality of life.

The Data Dilemma

Before we outline the human and financial costs of diabetes, it is important to point out that some of the data is incomplete and/or misleading.

For example, a recent study by the Centers for Disease Control and Prevention gives these estimates:

- In 2001, 16.7 million, or 7.9% of the U.S. population, had diagnosed diabetes
- There was an 8% increase in diagnosed diabetes cases from 2000-2001
- In 2001, 7.2% of whites, 11.2% of blacks, and 9.0% of Hispanics had diagnosed diabetes [1]

Yet the authors write that these figures are "substantial underestimates" because only diagnosed diabetes was counted. The figures of people living with undiagnosed diabetes could be as high as 35% of the total population. The Centers for Disease Control and Prevention reports that there are over 5 million people with undiagnosed and untreated diabetes.

Another example of misleading statistics is the "cause of death" statement on death certificates. Although diabetes was the sixth leading cause of death listed on U.S. death certificates in 1999, the real number was likely to be significantly higher. This number is misleading because many states do not allow diabetes to be listed as the cause of death on death certificates. Instead, one of the complications of the disease is listed as the cause of death—heart attack, stroke, kidney failure, etc.

In fact, only about 35% to 40% of people who were diagnosed with diabetes at their time of death have it listed anywhere on the death certificate, and only about 10% to 15% have it listed as the underlying cause of death. In 1999, only 68,399 death certificates listed diabetes as the underlying cause of death. Diabetes was listed as a contributing cause of death on an additional 141,265 death certificates.

The former Chairman of Chrysler, Lee Iacocca, promised his first wife, Mary, that he would fight to have diabetes listed as the cause of death on her death certificate. Because her first death certificate failed to list diabetes, Iacocca petitioned the Michigan Supreme Court and got a death certificate re-issued showing that Mary died from diabetes.

Statistics such as the total number of people with diabetes and "cause of death" has far reaching public policy implications. Policymakers weigh this data when allotting research dollars and choosing public health campaigns. If we had accurate diabetes statistics, the nation could understand the true cost of diabetes, and research and prevention monies for this disease would increase substantially.

Although the statistics are not as accurate as we would like, almost every researcher will agree that the bias of these statistics is to underestimate the impact of diabetes, not overestimate. With that in mind, we would like to share the human and financial costs of diabetes as best as it can be determined.

The Human Costs

On average, people with diabetes live fifteen years less than people who do not have diabetes. In 1999, approximately 450,000 deaths occurred among people with diabetes aged 25 years and older. This figure represents about 19% of all deaths in the United States in people aged 25 years and older. Diabetes was the sixth leading cause of death listed on U.S. death certificates in 1999.

Heart disease is the leading cause of diabetes-related deaths. Adults with diabetes have heart disease death rates about two to four times higher than adults without diabetes. Doctors tell heart attack survivors that they are at higher risk for having another heart attack than people who have never had a heart attack. For people with diabetes, their risk is equivalent to the risk of a person who has already had a heart attack. Doctors often tell people with diabetes: "For all practical purposes, you've already had your first heart attack." In addition to a heart attack, the risk for stroke is two to four times higher among people with diabetes.

Diabetes is the leading cause of end-stage renal disease, accounting for 43% of new cases. In 1999, a total of 114,478 people with diabetes underwent dialysis or kidney transplantation. At least 50% of the new cases of diabetes-related kidney failure each year could be prevented.

Diabetes is the leading cause of new cases of blindness among adults 20-74 years old. Diabetic retinopathy (eye disease) causes from 12,000 to 24,000 new cases of blindness each year. Early detection and treatment can prevent up to 90% of this blindness.

About 60% to 70% of people with diabetes have mild to severe forms of nervous system damage (neuropathy). The results of such damage include impaired sensation or pain in the feet or hands, slowed digestion of food in the stomach, carpal tunnel syndrome, and other nerve problems. Severe forms of diabetic nerve disease are a major contributing cause of lower-extremity amputations.

More than 60% of all nontraumatic lower-limb amputations (of a toe, part or all of a foot, or part of a leg) in the United States occur among people with diabetes. The hospitalization costs alone associated with the more than 80,000 lower-limb amputations exceed $860 million annually. Over half of these amputations could be prevented,[2] especially with appropriate diabetes education which would have instructed individuals to examine their feet daily and report any blisters, open sores, discoloration, etc.

In addition to heart disease, stroke, blindness, end-stage renal disease, and amputations, people with diabetes are more susceptible to many other illnesses and, once they acquire these illnesses, often have a worse prognosis than people without diabetes. For example, they are more likely to die with pneumonia or influenza than people who do not have diabetes.

Most deaths from diabetes are from the long-term complications that develop over the years. But sometimes diabetes kills quickly. Uncontrolled diabetes often leads to biochemical imbalances and, if not managed, could result in hospitalization and even death.

The human impact of diabetes on people living with the disease and their loved ones is dramatic. Doris Gilbert's daughter Laurie died at age 28 after 22 years of diabetes. In 1999, Gilbert spoke to the House Appropriations Subcommittee on Labor, Health and Human Services, and Education. She talked about Laurie's creativity, her interest and work in photography and scriptwriting, and about her battle with diabetes.

"Increasingly," Gilbert told the subcommittee, "she suffered from retinopathy, neuropathy, kidney and liver disease, severe hypertension, depression, and worst of all, gastroparesis—for her, extremely painful and utterly debilitating. Flare-ups and hospitalizations happened over and over until she was just too ill to continue her master's program in screenwriting at UCLA.

"Rather than giving more depressing details, I'll let the hospital record tell the story: 1995, 116 days in the hospital; 1996, 156 days; 1997, she began the year in the hospital and never left alive. Twenty-eight years old! What a waste!"

The Financial Cost of Diabetes—Billions

The financial burden of diabetes is enormous. The nation spends $13,243 on each person with diabetes every year, compared to $2,560 per person for people who do not have diabetes. The figures take into account spending by individuals, employers, insurers, and government programs such as Medicaid and Medicare. The portion spent on diabetes is higher in Medicare because it is a progressive disease that affects older people more over time.

In 2002, the United States spent $132 billion on diabetes. Direct medical expenditures (medical bills, etc.) for people with diabetes totaled $91.8 billion. Indirect costs from lost workdays, restricted activity days, premature mortality, and permanent disabilities due to diabetes totaled $39.8 billion. No cost estimates were projected for the over five million people believed to have diabetes but who have not yet been diagnosed.[3]

Diabetes is a deceptively expensive disease because it is the complications of the unmanaged disease that make it costly. For example, Medicare costs for treatments for kidney disease average $51,000 per person; total Medicare expenditures for treating diabetic kidney failure exceed $5.1 billion each year. The estimated total first-year cost of treating preventable cases of diabetes-related kidney failure is about $842 million.[4] According to the Centers for Disease Control and Prevention, if all people with diabetes received recommended screening and follow-up care for eye disease, the annual savings to the federal budget could exceed $470 million. Over 80,000 people undergo diabetes-related lower-limb amputations each year. These amputations cost more than $860 million annually in hospitalization costs alone.

The bottom line is diabetes is a chronic condition, and until a cure is found more people will die and suffer unecessarily and more money will be spent than necessary.

The Hidden Disease: Undiagnosed and Untreated Diabetes

Why are over five million people in the United States living with undiagnosed diabetes?

If you develop type 1 diabetes, your blood glucose climbs to very high levels, and you soon have symptoms of diabetes: urinating more, thirsty, tired all the time, and weight loss. If you do not get treatment, you will soon feel very ill, and you may end up in the emergency room. You do not have type 1 diabetes very long before you are diagnosed.

When you develop type 2 diabetes, it is a different story. You have some insulin in your system. Your blood-glucose levels are higher than normal but not so high that symptoms come on suddenly. Your symptoms are more subtle and grow with time. You are a little more tired, you are getting up at night to go to the bathroom, but you may pass those off as age or stress. That is why about a third of people with type 2 diabetes are currently undiagnosed.

On average, people have type 2 diabetes for eight to twelve years before they are diagnosed. That is eight to twelve years of untreated diabetes, and it lays the foundation for complications. Indeed many people have diabetes complications when they are first diagnosed with type 2 diabetes. Oftentimes it is the complication—a foot ulcer, a heart attack—that brings the person to the doctor.

We need to do more to find the over five million people who are unaware they have diabetes and get them treated.

Two Large Risk Factors for Diabetes

Age and obesity are two factors that increase an individual's risk of type 2 diabetes. Given the trends in these areas, and the current treatment of diabetes, the number of people with diabetes is growing and will continue to grow significantly.

Because diabetes is a progressive disease which affects people more significantly as they grow older, Medicare spends more on diabetes than other insurers. As the baby boomers age and technology increases, the Medicare spending on diabetes will accelerate dramatically.

Obesity is a significant risk factor for diabetes. One can barely go a day without seeing another report about how Americans are getting heavier. "Dramatic new evidence signals the unfolding of a diabetes epidemic in the United States," said former director of the Centers for Disease Control and Prevention, Jeffrey P. Koplan, MD, MPH. "With obesity on the rise, we can expect the sharp increase in diabetes rates to continue. Unless these dangerous trends are halted, the impact on our nation's health and medical care costs will be overwhelming."

The ever-present evidence of increasing obesity is not surprising given the rapid rise of fast food chains, which notoriously have food high in fat and calories. Fast-food restaurants charge us mere pennies to super-size our meal, thus doubling or tripling our carbohydrate, caloric, and fat intake. Portion size in the United States is usually at least double of the daily recommendations, especially when eating out. A daily super-sized, 32-ounce drink sold by the average convenience store filled with regular soda contains around 26 teaspoons of sugar and could translate into a weight gain of 52 pounds. In this society, we want to get what we pay for and when we do, we generally eat it all.

Twenty years ago type 2 diabetes was known as adult-onset diabetes; developing it before age 40 was the exception. American children and teens are heavier and less active than they were ten years ago, and more and more children and adolescents are being diagnosed with type 2 diabetes and high blood pressure. If America's younger generation does not get help for obesity and early detection of diabetes and if they do not properly manage their disease, we will witness an increase of people in their mid-thirties on kidney dialysis, going blind, with amputated feet. This is the inevitable result unless we do something to reverse this trend.

The Fundamentals of Managing Diabetes

Managing blood sugar is a rigorous process. It requires the right education, the right supplies, and steadfast d e d i c a t i o n. Although diet and exercise are integral to any regimen, a person with type 1 diabetes will always be dependent on insulin to control their blood sugar and stay healthy. For example, a woman with type 1 might need to take three or

Diabetes Management Results in Better Health

- "Improving glycemic control in people with diabetes is clearly cost effective."
  - *Diabetes Care 23, 390-404, 2002*

- "Improved glycemic control of type 2 diabetes is associated with substantial short-term symptomatic, quality-of-life, and health economic benefits . . . . Favorable health economic outcomes [for improved diabetes control] included higher retained employment, greater productive capacity, less absenteeism, few bed-days, and fewer restricted-activity days."
  - *JAMA 280: 1490-1496, 1998.*

- "These data from a staff-model HMO provide evidence that sustained improvements in glycemic control among older, predominantly type 2 diabetic patients are followed fairly closely in time by reductions in healthcare utilization and costs. These observations lend support to the growing evidence that older as well as younger diabetic patients benefit from better glycemic control. The cost differences of approximately $685-$950 per year, per patient would more than pay for system enhancements required to achieve better glycemic control."
  - *JAMA 285: 182-189, 2001*

- Researchers at an HMO compared two years of healthcare costs for two groups of members with diabetes: those who enrolled in a disease management program and those who did not. Program participants made more visits to their primary care provider and had more of the recommended screening tests but made fewer visits to emergency rooms. The results: "Per member per month paid claims averaged $394.62 for program patients compared with $502.48 for nonprogram patients . . . . For the 3,118 continuously enrolled patients included in this analysis, this amounts to a total of $4,035,689.70 per year in fewer claims paid compared with nonprogram patients."
  - *Diabetes Care 25(4):684-689, 2002*

more shots of insulin a day or use some kind of insulin delivery system like an insulin pump. To determine how much insulin to take each time, she would need to prick her finger to get a drop of blood, apply the blood to a testing unit, and run a test using a blood-glucose meter.

She then must balance what insulin doses she gives herself against what and how much she eats and how much exercise she gets. In addition, she must readjust her treatment regimen depending on other factors that affect blood glucose such as other medications she may be taking, stress, and hormone fluctuations. Careful management of her blood-sugar level means the woman with type 1 diabetes is constantly watching out that she does not allow her blood sugar to get too low. This is called hypoglycemia. Hypoglycemia has immediate consequences which can be mild, such as a rapid heartbeat and numbness in the lips to severe consequences like seizures or hypothermia.

A person with type 2 diabetes, however, may not require insulin to maintain a healthy blood-sugar level. Once diagnosed she might begin with an individualized meal and exercise plan designed to help her lose weight, which will help maintain acceptable blood glucose, blood pressure, and cholesterol. She will also be doing self-blood glucose monitoring several times a week to once a day. If she is not able to normalize her blood sugar, her doctor might prescribe oral diabetic drugs. If she is still not able to normalize her blood sugar, insulin will be prescribed. The regimen of the type 2 woman at this point would be similar to the type 1 woman described above. The key to preventing the full cycle in type 2 diabetes is largely the individual's personal motivation to make diet and exercise work.

The Current System Is Broken

In the best light, the current, disjointed system hinders the efforts and good intentions of many researchers, physicians, nurses, government, and the patients themselves. In the worst of cases, it is filled with disincentives and loopholes that foster ignorance, complacency, and even tolerates negligence. The result is diabetes care remains largely disorganized and segmented, resulting in human suffering, wasted resources, and even death.

A story of a man in Littleton, Colorado highlights this tragedy. Deborah

Thomas-Dobersen, a dietitian and certified diabetes educator, and Michael Dobersen, a forensic pathologist in the Littleton, Colorado coroner's office, reported on the case of a 46-year-old man who had died of diabetic ketoacidosis: "The [primary care physician] provided medical records that failed to document assessment of or provision of diabetes self-management education. The deceased was a member of a large national health maintenance organization . . . Clearly, a lack of education, a component of medical management, led to this patient's death. In this case, the health management organization offers capitated care, which means that physicians can either provide the education themselves in their office or pay for the education to be provided elsewhere. It is possible that this manner of payment provided a disincentive to offering education. The omission of the necessary education probably constitutes medical negligence . . ."[5]

Unfortunately this example is representative of the worst our system has to offer—medical negligence resulting in the non-care of people with diabetes. Although we have the knowledge and the means to prevent or delay the acute and long-term complications of diabetes, to save lives, our system fails to give people access to those means.

Coverage Decisions Significantly Affect Quality of Care

The lack of full financial reimbursement for provider services and insurance coverage decisions are the chief barriers to optimal care for diabetes. Whether it is doctors or diabetes educators not getting reimbursed for services they perform or individuals ignoring a physician's prescription because their drug is not covered under their insurance, money has a lot to do with quality of care.

The best example of this assertion is Medicare. Medicare is one of the most archaic programs operated by the government. When Medicare was created in 1965, policymakers did not foresee the significant role prescription medications would have on treating and preventing disease. Its failure to fully reimburse for services, and not cover many preventive measures, handicaps doctors and hospitals from providing comprehensive care. The current system dictates a focus on reactive acute care and does not incentivize prevention.

Coverage for prescription medications is a paramount example. Medicare does cover testing strips but fails to help the beneficiary purchase the insulin that will modify the individual's level back to a safe zone. Medicare will cover the visit to the doctor to discuss the numbness in the foot, but it will not pay for the insulin to relieve, and stop, the problem. Medicare will pay for visits to the emergency room when a beneficiary has a heart attack, but it fails to pay for the cholesterol medication that may have prevented the incident all together. Medicare's end-stage renal-disease program (offers kidney dialysis when the kidneys no longer function) is one of the highest cost programs in Medicare, yet they will not pay for the insulin that could prevent many of those individuals from needing it in the first place.

Medication is an important element in the care of people with type 2 diabetes. Yet Medicare does not cover any diabetes drugs, not even the inexpensive, 30-year-old drugs that are still effective for many patients. Seniors on a fixed income choosing food over diabetes medications are an everyday occurrence across the United States.

Consider an American senior with type 2 diabetes. In addition to high blood-glucose levels, he may have high blood pressure and unhealthy cholesterol levels, which further increase his risk of developing diabetes complications such as a stroke, heart attack, or kidney failure. He will likely need oral medication to get his sugars under control as well as medication for managing his blood pressure and cholesterol. Yet because Medicare does not pay for prescription drugs, he goes without the needed medications.

The man ages, and his body makes less and less insulin. His blood-glucose levels start to creep up despite taking maximum doses of oral medications. His feet and toes are feeling numb. Fortunately, the man's doctor is keeping close track of his blood-glucose levels, knows the standards of care for patients with diabetes, and prescribes insulin injections. Unfortunately, however, Medicare does not cover insulin so he goes without.

The doctor informs him that his foot must be amputated and he needs to go on dialysis. But after not covering the drugs that might have prevented this outcome, Medicare will pay for this expensive and sadly, avoidable treatment and care.

We need to bring Medicare into the 21st century.

Diabetes Management Results in Better Health

The tragedy in diabetes is that although it is not curable yet, tight management of diabetes can reduce an individual's risk and prevent many complications.

Two landmark studies proved that people with diabetes who keep their blood-glucose levels down near the nondiabetic range greatly lower their risk of the long-term complications of diabetes. The Diabetes Control and Complications Trial (DCCT) showed that people with type 1 who got their blood-glucose levels closer to the nondiabetic range had a 60% reduction in risk of kidney, eye, and nerve disease.[6] The UK Prospective Diabetes Study showed that people with type 2 who got better control of blood glucose using oral agents or insulin and reduced their blood pressure had a much lower risk of diabetes complications.[7]

Individuals who seek excellence in diabetes information, excellence in diabetes care, and embrace personal responsibility for their health are achieving wonderful things.

Swimmer Gary Hall Jr. won the Olympic gold medal at the Atlanta Olympics in 1996 prior to his diagnosis of diabetes. Upon diagnosis, his first physician told him he would not be able to compete for Olympic gold again. At first Gary was devastated. Yet he refused to accept being a victim and proved to be a great example of being proactive in your care and constantly denying the status quo. He set out to find a physician and routines that worked for him—and indeed he did, as witnessed by the world when he won one gold, two silver, and one bronze medal in the Sydney Olympics in 2002. Mary Tyler Moore is another world-renowned individual who has had to manage her type 1 diabetes and taken action to limit the impact of its complications while maintaining a successful career. She has long championed the cause of diabetes research in her work with the Juvenile Diabetes Research Foundation in their campaign to find a cure. It may not be curable—yet—but people can learn to prosper despite it.

Transformational Diabetes Care in America:
Excellent Care, Excellent Outcomes

With a 21st century transformational approach to diabetes care in America, we can advance the probability of successful blood-sugar levels for every person with diabetes in America.

A transformation in diabetes care in America has its foundation in comprehensive health management for individuals. This includes early education about diabetes, its physiology, its treatment, and its consequences so that people learn to manage their blood sugar levels to achieve the optimum outcomes. This comprehensive diabetes self-management training can be provided by diabetes care teams, which may include endocrinologists, diabetes educators, pharmacists, dietitians, and social workers. Yes, it costs, but study after study shows it saves money.

Medicare is beginning to embrace this message. Although the important issue of drug coverage still needs to be resolved, coverage for diabetes has improved significantly in recent years. I know because I have been involved since I was Speaker of the House.

In 1997, as part of the Balanced Budget Act, I worked with the American Diabetes Association, the Juvenile Diabetes Research Foundation, and other diabetes organizations to ensure that coverage of blood-glucose meters and the strips they require were offered to everyone with diabetes in the Medicare program. Until then, only those people using insulin qualified for this coverage.

The legislation we passed also helped more Americans in the Medicare system receive the critical diabetes education component of care. This is important because diabetes is such a patient-managed disease. The patient has to be the lab tech, doctor, nurse, dietitian, and pharmacist. If our health system simply treats them when problems arise, we will have lost this fight. Unless they know how to manage their disease day in and day out, we will only see more and more deadly complications and more and more billions of dollars being spent on serious health problems that could have been avoided.

Another major advance occurred a few years later when the Medicare program responded to new data and made a policy decision to cover the insulin pump for some of the Medicare population. The insulin pump is increasingly popular with both young and old as a way of regulating the flow of insulin into the body. Since making the coverage decision in 1999, Medicare has already reviewed it once and has expanded its coverage somewhat.

Most recently, Congress again stepped into the coverage debate and directed the Medicare program to cover medical nutrition therapy for people with diabetes. It is more than just handing the patient a sheet of "Don't Eats." Medical nutrition therapy is a critical component to the education process for the person with diabetes. Meal planning can help with weight loss, and help the person control blood glucose and blood pressure. Medicare now offers broad coverage for general diabetes education and nutrition counseling.

Medicare is not the only government agency slowly moving to a more rational model of diabetes coverage. As of early this year, 46 states required state-regulated health insurance plans to cover medications, testing supplies, equipment, and medical services necessary for patients to manage diabetes. These laws apply primarily to small businesses and individual insurance policies. You will recognize the names of some of the then Governors who signed these laws into effect: George W. Bush, Tommy Thompson, Christine Todd Whitman, and Tom Ridge. State leaders in both political parties have seen the value of providing for diabetes preventive care. We can already see the results.

As reported by the Associated Press, diabetes education has paid off for South Carolina employees who use the state health plan. A study by the State Budget and Control Board found that patients who took a diabetes education course had $2,324 less in medical claims per year than patients with similar symptoms and problems who did not go through the Diabetes Chronic Disease workshops.

In 2000 the amputation rates in Florida showed a decrease for the fifth straight year. It is not a coincidence that Florida began requiring coverage for diabetes equipment and education in 1995.

Veterans Administration hospitals and clinics have shown incredible reductions in amputations over the last three years, since they made foot care and exams a top priority for individuals with diabetes.

Because of tight budgets in the states and the large block of money being spent on healthcare, states are looking to cut back. Cuts in the programs that have achieved these results are irrational. If states begin to cut back on diabetes coverage, whether in the private sector or in Medicaid, the result will be a dramatic increase in the human and economic costs to our healthcare system. Cutting payments and coverage will result in higher—not lower—costs. We can pay now or pay more later.

It is vital that private- and public-sector health plans cover the basic tools that a person with diabetes needs to survive and stay healthy. These tools include insulin, oral medications, blood-glucose meters, blood-glucose test strips, syringes for the injection of insulin, insulin pumps and related supplies, physician visits, laboratory services, annual eye exams, and diabetes self-management training. This coverage is necessary to ensure that people with diabetes can manage the disease and prevent its complications.

Usable Information—A Key to Transforming Diabetes Care

The public should be able to know where to go to find the latest information concerning diabetes, but we need to offer it in a wide variety of formats to best serve the needs of the individual. (We have listed some Internet resources at the end of this chapter.)

Much of diabetes education includes printed materials, whether it is given to a patient by a healthcare professional (nurse, pharmacist, dietitian, podiatrist) or whether patients find up-to-date information themselves in books and magazines and on-line.

But many people in the United States do not have the needed reading skills to take advantage of the educational material. The result is that people with diminished reading skills are less likely to have good blood-glucose control and more likely to have complications.[8]

Literacy is not the only roadblock. As we have mentioned, vision impairment and blindness can be a consequence of unmanaged diabetes. About 20% of patients with type 2 diabetes have evidence of diabetic eye disease when they are diagnosed with diabetes. A person with vision problems who has been newly diagnosed with type 2 diabetes suddenly has to learn a lot and much of it is printed.

People who cannot use printed materials are currently underserved, and that leads to complications and further burdens on our healthcare resources.

We need to do more to make sure everyone has access to health information in a form they can use. For example, patients should have access to a toll-free number where they can hear a message on diabetes self-management. Video and DVD players provide another wonderful opportunity for education. Even in the poorest of communities most people have a television and one of these players. When the patient plays the CD or tape, often others in the family will listen to the education being provided. It is important that those who provide education understand how individuals learn.

Short-Changing Doctors

We expect a lot from people with diabetes: blood tests, injections, keeping up with screening tests, and keeping themselves informed. We also expect a lot from primary-care physicians who provide care for the majority of people with diabetes. The healthcare system is not giving them the support and tools they need to provide excellent diabetes care. The system short-changes them not just on reimbursement for their services but on their training as well.

In four years of medical school, a medical student may get only one afternoon of instruction on diabetes.[9] One afternoon for a disease that accounts for one in ten healthcare dollars!

But even if doctors have the training and keep current with best practices, it takes time and money to provide quality diabetes care—costs that may not be reimbursed under today's system. Steven Leichter, MD, writes: "The profit margin for rendering quality diabetes care on an ongoing basis is very narrow . . . Limitations imposed by adverse reimbursement structures may become a primary limitation to the delivery of effective care. The present model may reward those who deliver the least care and punish those who provide the best care."[10]

Transformational diabetes care would incentivize doctors and other caregivers to work with people with diabetes to obtain optimal outcomes. This must start with full reimbursement for services that are medically necessary, such as screening tests, regular examinations, and education. We need to rethink the reimbursement system so that it rewards accountability on the part of the patient, the doctor, and the healthcare system.

Patients must be motivated, they must stay well-informed, and they must demand the best care from their healthcare providers. They must also be the center of the team; they need to determine what they are willing to do and decide how they want to live. They need access to the tools and resources that will assist them in this endeavor. They also need to ask their provider: Why this medication? Why not exercise? What is the latest research? Where can I get that information? A patient who asks the provider will truly get better care because they are regarded as active and informed patients.

We must have doctors who follow standards of care for their patients. Standards of care for the person with diabetes include regular doctor visits for a diabetes checkup, annual eye exams, foot exams, and blood work. These should all be standard practice. Doctors who do not treat their patients according to these standards of care should not be reimbursed as well as those who do.

Screenings

Most women know the importance of self-breast exams and mammography. Most men know the importance of an annual physical and colonoscopy. How many of us know that diabetes screening should be considered in the healthcare setting every 3 years for people age 45 or over with a demonstrated high risk of type 2 diabetes? Do you know if you have been tested? If you have been tested, do you know what your results were and what they mean? Healthcare professionals must be as aggressive about testing our blood-glucose level as they are in testing our cholesterol level.

It is important for you to know if you have any of the risk factors that increase your chances of being diabetic and to know what the symptoms of diabetes are. (See the end of the chapter for a listing of risk factors.)

This is one area that Medicare should correct immediately. Medicare does not cover independent screening tests for diabetes. That is right—a doctor will either eat the cost of the screening or charge you for the screening, but Medicare will not cover the expense. You are a doctor. A senior citizen comes to you and says, "Doc, I'm always thirsty, and I'm tired all the time." The patient has high blood pressure. You would like to test your patient for diabetes by doing a simple blood test. If you do, Medicare will not reimburse you. If you screen for diabetes and submit the test as something else, you could be investigated for insurance fraud. The only reimbursable way to screen a person on Medicare is to order an expensive "packaged" lab test, the only result of which the physician will check is the blood-sugar-level test. This is irrational and should be changed immediately.

Your patient, who is on a fixed income, could pay for the test himself, but it will not count toward his deductible. An informed consumer could, however, look for diabetes screenings done in their community or church and take advantage of such a test. The health practitioner has a responsibility to mention such options to their patients.

Save Lives and Save Money: Prevent Diabetes Itself

You have seen that many times we can prevent or postpone the complications of diabetes. We also know how to prevent type 2 diabetes itself.

Before a person develops type 2 diabetes, he has blood-glucose levels that are higher than normal but not high enough to be called diabetes. The medical term is impaired glucose tolerance (IGT) or impaired fasting glucose (IFG). In popular terminology, this has become know as pre-diabetes.

It is estimated that sixteen million Americans have "pre-diabetes." A person with prediabetes can prevent the onset of the disease with diet and exercise. Just losing some excess weight (even just five or ten pounds) can make a difference. Eating a healthier diet and increasing physical activity significantly lowers the risk of developing diabetes. An individual who really is interested in lowering the risk should be seen by a certified diabetes educator for instruction on diet and exercise. While everyone thinks they know about diet, these experts have many tools to assist everyone in meeting their goals.

In the Diabetes Prevention Program, a study funded by NIH's Institute for Diabetes and Digestive Kidney Disease, overweight people who are pre-diabetic received intensive nutrition and exercise counseling. They lost an average of twelve pounds, and 74% maintained at least 150 minutes per week of moderately intense activity. (This could be walking or biking just 20 to 25 minutes a day.) Over an average follow-up of about three years, the study group showed a 58% lower rate of progression to diabetes compared to those who did not receive the interventions.[11]

Dr. Allen Spiegel, director of the National Institute of Diabetes and Digestive and Kidney Diseases (NIDDK), the part of the National Institutes of Health (NIH) that sponsored the study, said, "These findings bring us closer to the goal of containing and ultimately reversing the epidemic of type 2 diabetes in this country."

Secretary of Health and Human Services Tommy Thompson said, "This research conveys a powerful message of hope to individuals at risk for type 2 diabetes, a painful, life-threatening disease that has been increasing in this country along with obesity. By adopting a moderate, consistent diet and exercise program, many people with one or more of the risk factors for type 2 diabetes can stop the disease before it becomes irreversible."

In light of the Diabetes Prevention Program and other studies, the American Diabetes Association and the NIDDK, in a position statement issued jointly, stated: "Healthcare policymakers and healthcare systems should aggressively explore low-cost ways to promote physical activity and weight loss."

The National Diabetes Education Project (a joint project of the Centers for Disease Control and Prevention and the NIDDK) promotes a program known as "Small Steps Big Rewards." This program encourages everyone to walk 10,000 steps a day. It is easy to think that doesn't take much, but when individuals put on a pedometer, they are amazed at how few steps happen as part of one's daily routine.

The rise in motorized vehicle transportation has decreased the amount we walk in our daily lifestyles. Americans think "car" first. I challenge you to change that mindset. Think first, "Can I walk?"

Can you take public transportation to work just by walking a few blocks to the stop? Is your church just a few blocks away? Carry your good shoes and walk! Park further from the store than necessary. Take the stairs. It may take more time and be less convenient, but we are talking about adopting lifestyle changes that could add years to your life.

Our Children

If you take a tour of a private or public elementary school, you will probably be shown, with much excitement, the computer lab. You will be assured that even the kindergartners have computer lab once a week. Ask about physical education, and you will likely be told that it was cut years ago due to time and budget constraints. It is the 21st century and we must teach technology. No one supports access to technology more than I do. But we cannot create a situation where one of the first things our children will need to do on their computers is access the medical information they need to treat the ailments caused by their inactive lifestyles.

Demand that physical education be part of the school curriculum. With our natural migration to a sedentary lifestyle, we need to artificially create the chance for our children to be active. Safety, disinterest, and distraction are all good reasons why suburban and urban children alike are not as active as they used to be. The only place many kids can get supervised daily activity is in school. Physical education in schools is done under a federally mandated guideline. Although it states that schools are to provide physical education classes three or four times per week, the only state holding to this guideline is the state of Illinois. Demand it.

Do not drive your child to school—have them walk or bike. Older children can walk with friends. For younger children, organize a "walking school bus"—several children supervised by an adult. If your neighborhood is two feet too close to the school to get bus service, do not sign the petition to get your neighborhood on the bus route. Make it fun. Get your children pedometers and let them figure out how to achieve 10,000 steps a day.

A certified diabetes educator once told me that there is no such thing as good foods or bad foods—it is about good habits and bad habits. By helping our children make good choices and educating them, we can establish a foundation for positive lifelong habits. It is imperative that nutrition be tied to health and be started early in life. Schools need to take more responsibility for what they offer students in terms of lunch and snacks and offer a wide range of healthy options.

In your community, vote in public transportation, vote in parks and recreation facilities, vote in zoning that encourages walking. Ask your employer to subsidize employees' use of public transportation because it encourages at least a little bit of walking.

Let us start looking and working forward. Let us change our society and ourselves today. Or we will pay dearly tomorrow.

Ultimate Victory—Eradication or Cure

The irrefutably single best way to save lives and money with any disease is to wipe it out or find a cure. It is so important that we dedicated the entire next chapter to investing in science and discovery to get the really big breakthroughs in health. We are passionate about finding a cure for diabetes and we believe that the federal government has a responsibility to invest heavily in this effort. Many private organizations are funding groundbreaking research as well. When we discuss managing or improving the life of people living with any disease, whether it is diabetes, arthritis, or cancer, we should never lose sight of the ultimate goal.

What Can You Do?

With your awareness, education, and involvement, we can transform diabetes in America.

If You Have Diabetes—Take Control!

If you have diabetes, it is your responsibility to ensure you are getting a complete review when you visit your doctor. Do not cut corners. Records show that individuals with diabetes should receive regular foot exams when they see their healthcare professional. Yet studies have found that when patients were asked if their physician had physically examined their feet during their office visit they said, "No, they just asked if they were okay." As much as we would like to allow the doctor to be in total control of our disease, the reality is that it is our job to make sure we are getting the treatment we need. Keep copies of your own personal records. Ask questions. Make notes about differences you see in your body.

Allow Medicare Diabetes Screening

Contact your members of Congress, senators, and the president and encourage them to enact legislation allowing physicians to perform diabetes-screening tests for American seniors at high risk for the disease.

Pass Medicare Prescription Drug Coverage

Contact your members of Congress, senators, and the president and encourage them to provide meaningful prescription drug coverage for American seniors.

Ensure Adequate Health Insurance

Incentivize payers including Medicaid, Medicare, medical savings accounts, and all forms of private health-insurance coverage to cover the basic things that a person with diabetes requires to survive. These items include insulin, insulin syringes, blood-glucose monitors, glucose test strips, insulin pumps and related supplies, diabetes self-management training, laboratory services, and specialty medical services to prevent and manage diabetes complications. Current plans to cut back on this kind of care in Medicaid and private plans are destructive thinking that will cost both lives and money.

Improve Care and Patient Compliance

We need a system that recognizes and promotes quality and rewards optimal outcomes. Some physicians and other healthcare providers take the necessary steps to keep Americans with diabetes healthy. They deserve higher reimbursements than providers whose care is substandard and results in more expensive care and more serious complications. Patients should know what to ask for and then comply with their healthcare teams' recommendations.

Provide Patient Education

More than any other disease, diabetes requires patient self-management 24/7. It takes time and support to learn to be your own doctor, nurse, lab tech, dietitian, and pharmacist. Health plans should invest in a system that allows patients 24/7 access to nurse educators that enable them to get a quick response to questions or concerns. Studies show clearly that this investment will pay off quickly. Medicare should also remove the barrier to diabetes education by making Certified Diabetes Educators eligible Medicare providers.

Stop Type 2 Diabetes Before It Starts

Walk. Ride a bike. Support efforts to make walking a bigger part of community activity. Walking away from home for just fifteen minutes a day (and walking back home again) might be the difference between developing type 2 diabetes or not for millions of Americans. Buy an inexpensive pedometer. You'll be surprised that keeping track of how much you walk each day can be an incentive to take a few extra steps. Be conscious of your diet. Start by simply reducing your caloric intake.

Don't Let Schools Contribute to This Disease

We all have personal responsibility. No one is responsible for us but ourselves. But adults are responsible for children. And while parents must be and always will be the first line of defense, we cannot allow our schools to be willing and active partners in America's severe crisis of overweight and obese children. If we give kids bad choices, they will take them. If they get only good choices for the six hours a day they are in school, that is six hours of the day we don't have to worry about. And if they had active physical education daily, real nutrition education, and better choices in food and vending machines and in school lunchrooms, we would soon see better outcomes.

What You Need to Know about Diabetes

Diabetes is a serious disease. Diabetes can strike anyone at any time, regardless of race, religion, or socioeconomic level.

Type 1 diabetes is an autoimmune disease in which the patient's own immune system destroys the insulin-producing cells of the pancreas. It is a genetic predisposition. Its occurrence is not related to obesity or sedentary behavior. Type 1 diabetes is most often diagnosed in children (and is being diagnosed at younger and younger ages for unknown reasons), but it can occur at any age. Because the pancreas in children and adults with type 1 diabetes does not produce insulin, people with type 1 diabetes need insulin injections or a continuous pump infusion of insulin to survive. Without insulin therapy, people with type 1 diabetes will, within days or weeks, lapse into a coma and die. It is estimated that 6% to 10% of all people with diabetes have type 1, and people with type 1 diabetes account for a disproportionate share of its most serious complications:

- Frequent thirst
- Frequent urination
- Frequent hunger
- Weight loss
- Visual disturbances
- Tiredness
- Abdominal pain

Type 2 diabetes used to occur in people over the age of 40. Today, however, with an increased incidence of obesity and lack of physical activity in our youth (especially those of African-American, Hispanic, and American-Indian ethnicity), type 2 diabetes can be found in children as young as ten years of age. Signs and symptoms of type 2 are similar but not as intense as those in type 1, which is why many put up with inconvenience and do not seek medical care for a long period of time. Type 2 diabetes affects 93% of all individuals with diabetes. Signs and symptoms include:

- Frequent thirst
- Frequent urination
- Frequent hunger
- Tiredness
- Dry skin
- Impotence / Vaginal infections
- Visual disturbances
- Wounds that don't heal

If any of these symptoms seem familiar to you and your family, seek out your healthcare provider and ask to be tested.

If You Have Diabetes:

Take charge. Your physician has hundreds of patients to care for but you have yourself and your loved ones. Know what your healthcare insurance is—know the type, the providers, and know what it does and does NOT cover. Talk to the benefits department at your place of employment—let them know what you need to care for your diabetes. Write to your state and federal legislators about your needs. They do not want to work against you, so get them involved.

Use a checklist. Have a checklist when you see your healthcare provider. If you have not seen a certified diabetes educator (CDE), ask why not. Know when your last A1C (hemoglobin) test was and what the results were. Know what that number means to your everyday life. Know how it relates to the medication, diet, blood-glucose tests, and exercise you perform daily. Does your provider check your feet at every visit or just ask how they are? When was your last dilated eye exam? When was your last test done to see how your kidneys are? Know where a diabetes center is located in your community.

Get a flu shot!! A recent study tracked 100,000 people through two flu seasons and found that flu vaccinations reduced deaths or hospitalizations from influenza by up to 50% among people greater than 65 years of age. The benefits were even greater among people over 65 years with existing illnesses. Medicare Part B pays for influenza vaccinations on a yearly basis.

Believe you can do it! Many people have been faced with this challenge and succeeded! Eighty-year-old people with diabetes can tell you today about using the newly discovered pharmaceutical called insulin when they were young and how they followed their regimen that allowed them to live a long life. Believe that you can control your blood sugar—you can follow your treatment plan.

People across the world have diabetes. Your neighbor, your boss, your baby-sitter, your pastor, and yes, even: Mary Tyler Moore, Brent Michaels, Ron Santo, Halle Berry, Gary Hall Jr., Jean Smart, Wilford Brimley, Wade Wilson, Patti LaBelle, and Jerry Mathers. They, like others less known, have taken steps to live a full and active life with diabetes. Many things in life we cannot control, but with diabetes specific actions CAN be taken to reduce the risk and even prevent its devastating complications—making it possible for people with diabetes to live an active life.

Believe you can do it, because you can!

Internet Resources

The National Diabetes Education Program
http://ndep.nih.gov
>NDEP is a partnership between the leading government agencies for research and treatment of diabetes (the National Institute for Health and the Centers for Disease Control and Prevention) and more than 200 private and public organizations. This Web site provides important information and links to other organizations.

American Diabetes Association
www.diabetes.org
>The ADA is one of the United States' largest nonprofit organizations providing information, advocacy, and research to the community of people living with diabetes.

The Juvenile Diabetes Research Foundation
www.jdrf.org
>Founded by the parents of children with type 1 diabetes, the Juvenile Diabetes Research Foundation (JDRF) is the world's leading charitable funder of diabetes research. Led by International Chairman Mary Tyler Moore, JDRF has one mission: to find a cure for diabetes and its complications through the support of research.

Diabetes Action Research and Education Foundation
www.diabetesaction.org
>Diabetes Action is a nonprofit organization dedicated to enhancing the quality of life for all people affected by diabetes through emphasis on nutritional therapies for prevention and treatment.

American Dietetic Association
www.eatright.org
>The Web site of the ADA offers a wide range of information, tools, and education on eating healthy.

WebMD Health

www.webmd.com

WebMD has an entire section of their Web site dedicated to diabetes. They have teamed up with the Cleveland Clinic to provide people with diabetes information such as self-testing, treatment, and tips on diet and exercise.

Diabetes For Patients

www.diabetes4patients.com

This Web site goes beyond general information, providing the individual with newsletters, cookbooks, personal weekly meal plans, electronic magazines, and product information.

[1] Mokdad AH, Ford ES, Bowman BA, Dietz WH, Vinicor F, Bales VS, Marks JS: "Prevalence of obesity, diabetes, and obesity-related health risk factors," 2001 *JAMA* 289:76-79, 2003

[2] Centers for Disease Control and Prevention: *Diabetes, a serious public health problem*. 2000

[3] American Diabetes Association: "Economic costs of diabetes in the U.S. in 2002." *Diabetes Care* 26(3):917-932, 2003

[4] Centers for Disease Control and Prevention: *Diabetes, a serious public health problem*. 2000

[5] Thomas-Dobersen D, Dobersen MJ: Case Study: "A 46-Year-Old Man With a 15-Year History of Type 1 Diabetes Who Died of Diabetic Ketoacidosis." *Clinical Diabetes* 18: 135-137, 2000

[6] The DCCT Research Group: "The effect of intensive treatment of diabetes on the long-term complications in insulin-dependent diabetes mellitus." *New England Journal of Medicine* 329:977-86, 1993

[7] The UK Prospective Diabetes Study (UKPDS) Group: "Intensive blood glucose control with sulfony lureas or insulin compared with conventional treatment and risk of complications in patients with type 2 diabetes" (UKPDS 33). *Lancet* 352:837-53, 1998

[8] Schillinger D, Grumbach K, Piette J, Wang F, Osmond D, Daher C, Palacios J, Sullivan GD, Bindman AB: "Association of health literacy with diabetes outcomes." *JAMA* 288:475-482, 2002

[9] Hirsch IB: "Diabetes education (for doctors)." *Clinical Diabetes* 17:50-51, 1999

[10] Leichter SB: "Cost and reimbursement as determinants of the quality of diabetes care: 3, Reimbursement determinants." *Clinical Diabetes* 20: 43-44, 2002

[11] Diabetes Prevention Research Group: "Reduction in the evidence of type 2 diabetes with life-style intervention or metformin." *New England Journal of Medicine* 346:393-403, 2002

Screening Guidelines of the American Diabetes Association

- Screening should be considered every 3 years after age 45
- Testing should be considered at a younger age or be carried out more frequently in people who are overweight and have one or more of the other risk factors or symptoms of diabetes.

Risk Factors for Type 2 Diabetes

- Age 45 years
- Overweight (BMI 25 kg/m2)
- Family history of diabetes (i.e., parents or siblings with diabetes)
- Habitual physical inactivity
- Race/ethnicity (e.g., African-Americans, Hispanic-Americans, Native Americans, Asian-Americans, and Pacific Islanders)
- Previously identified impaired fasting glucose or impaired glucose tolerance
- History of gestational diabetes or delivery of a baby weighing >9 lbs
- Hypertension (140/90 mmHg in adults)
- HDL ("good") cholesterol 35 mg/dl and/or a triglyceride level 250 mg/dl
- Polycystic ovary syndrome
- History of vascular disease

Symptoms of Diabetes

- Urinating more than normal
- Often thirsty, drinking more than usual
- Hunger
- Weight loss (sometimes even though the person is eating more)
- Blurred vision

Screening for Type 2 Diabetes in Children

Overweight (85th percentile for age and sex, or height, or a weight greater than 120% of ideal body weight) children above 10 years of age should be tested every 2 years if they have any two of the following risk factors:

- Have a family history of type 2 diabetes in first- and second-degree relatives
- Belong to a certain race/ethnic group (Native Americans, African-Americans, Hispanic Americans, Asians/South Pacific Islanders)
- Have signs of insulin resistance or conditions associated with insulin resistance: (acanthosis nigricans [dark patches of skin in neck or arm folds], high blood pressure, dyslipidemia, polycystic ovary syndrome)

Printed with permission from the American Diabetes Association [American Diabetes Association, Diabetes Care 26:S21-S24, 2003]

Could You Have Diabetes and Not Know It?

Risk Test

Printed with permission from the American Diabetes Association

Take this test to see if you are at risk for having diabetes. Write in the points next to each statement that is true for you. If a statement is not true, put zero. Then add your total score.

1. I am a woman who has had a baby weighing more than nine pounds at birth. YES 1 ____

2. I have a sister or brother with diabetes. YES 1 ____

3. I have a parent with diabetes. YES 1 ____

4. My weight is equal to or above that listed in the chart. YES 5 ____

5. I am under 65 years of age and I get little or no exercise. YES 5 ____

6. I am between 45 and 64 years of age. YES 5 ____

7. I am 65 years or older. YES 9 ____

TOTAL____

Scoring 10 or more points

You are at high risk for having diabetes. Only your healthcare provider can check to see if you have diabetes. See yours soon and find out for sure.

Scoring 3-9 points

You are probably at low risk for having diabetes now. But don't just forget about it. Keep your risk low by losing weight if you are overweight, being active most days, and eating low fat meals that are high in fruits and vegetables, and whole grain foods.

At-Risk Weight Chart for Men and Women
*Body Mass Index

Height	Weight
In feet and inches without shoes	*in pounds without clothes*
4'10"	129
4'11"	133
5'0"	138
5'1"	143
5'2"	147
5'3"	152
5'4"	157
5'5"	162
5'6"	167
5'7"	172
5'8"	177
5'9"	182
5'10"	188
5'11"	193
6'0"	199
6'1"	204
6'2"	210
6'3"	216
6'4"	221

* If you weigh the same as or more than the amount listed for your height, you may be at risk for diabetes.

CHAPTER NINE

For the Big Breakthroughs in Health:
Invest in Science and Discovery

There is no better way to save lives and save money than curing or eradicating a disease. Consider the difference between improving iron lungs for treating polio patients in the 1950s and inventing the Salk vaccine for polio. The first was an improvement in the immediate quality of life of individuals already afflicted. The second was a revolution that eliminated polio as a major threat.

It is very hard to get budget analysts to understand the power of basic scientific research and the fundamental nature of change inherent in scientific discovery. The result is an overemphasis on short-term investments in marginal improvements and an underinvestment in the fundamental breakthroughs in actually eliminating disease.

When President Richard Nixon declared "war on cancer" over 30 years ago many people thought it was a publicity stunt or a politician seeking a popular slogan. Yet the basic research at the National Cancer Institute (a branch of the National Institutes of Health) and the underlying fundamental research in math, physics, chemistry and biology at the National Science Foundation have brought us to a point where the survival rates for pediatric cancer have skyrocketed. Experts believe it is possible cancer will be defeated in another fifteen years.

Sometimes the basic research that really changes a field occurs outside the main centers of research on that topic. For example, the development of new methods of mathematical thinking combined with improved computers and electronic scanning have made possible the development of MRIs capable of scanning the brain of living people. Prior to these discoveries, brain science was largely based on knowledge derived from examining dead brains. Now there is a revolution in our understanding of the human brain driven principally by instrumentation breakthroughs outside biology and medicine. These breakthroughs were largely funded by the National Science Foundation and are a good example of why that institution should be tripled in size to fund the underlying research that drives the entire scientific system.

Sometimes the breakthroughs occur so far outside the established structures that it takes a little while for the established experts to catch up. There are new breakthroughs in nanoscale science and technology (see below for a further explanation of this field) that are totally outside the traditional methods of studying biology and medicine. I serve as chairman emeritus for the NanoBusiness Alliance, the first association formed to support the development of the growing nanotechnology and small technology industries. Because the nanoscale area of research has been largely driven by physics and chemistry, it is a whole new way of thinking about solving problems. It will take a while for people schooled and credentialed in other ways of thinking to realize just how fundamental these breakthroughs are.

This process of brand new ways of thinking, challenging the old order, is not new and not limited to health and healthcare. Thomas Kuhn wrote brilliantly about the difficult process of getting scientists to accept really new ideas in *The Structure of Scientific Revolutions*.[1] Kuhn concluded that in many cases the older scientists never accepted the new breakthroughs but simply retired believing in the order of things they had learned as young scientists. Kuhn argued that, as a general rule, new models of thought (he called them paradigms) were adopted by younger scientists who compared them to older models and found them more powerful and more accurate in explaining the natural world. The result was a generational process of change.

In a sense, Kuhn was describing the same phenomenon in science that Clayton Christensen described about industry in *The Innovator's Dilemma*. Christensen drew a very clear distinction between sustaining developments (doing better what you are already doing) and disruptive developments (doing something in a new way or doing something new). He pointed out that really powerful, successful, sophisticated systems are excellent at sustaining and improving what they are already doing but find it extraordinarily difficult to adopt something truly new.[2] Everyone concerned with the research enterprise should read Kuhn and Christensen and apply their critical principles to our current scientific system. The size of the National Institutes of Health was doubled recently. Now we need to critically rethink how it operates and what reforms are required to encourage both new paradigms and disruptive research.

We need to rethink the way in which we finance health and healthcare to ensure that we are moving new breakthroughs from the laboratory to the patient as rapidly as possible. Today the time lag between fundamentally new knowledge and applied technologies and medicines is much too long. Lives are lost and people suffer in the interim. This requires rethinking both how the Food and Drug Administration operates and how the Center for Medicare and Medicaid Services approves new approaches.

At the very heart of transforming health and healthcare is one simple fact: it will require a commitment by the federal government to invest in science and discovery. The period between investment and profit for basic research is too long for most companies to ever consider making the investment. Furthermore, truly basic research often produces new knowledge that everyone can use, so there is no advantage to a particular company to make the investment. The result is that truly fundamental research is almost always a function of government and foundations because the marketplace discourages focusing resources in that direction.

America's economic future is a direct function of our ability to take new scientific research and translate it into entrepreneurial development. Without the scientific research of the last 60 years, we would all have lower incomes, lower standards of living, and fewer choices. Be it health, aviation, agriculture, manufacturing, marketing, or entertainment—you name it, the American technological and scientific advantage has been key to our success as world leaders.

The Hart/Rudman Commission looked to the year 2025 to comprehensively assess and prioritize every threat to national security. Our final report in March of 2001 became more famous following September 11 because we felt strongly that the number one risk facing the nation was a weapon of mass destruction going off in one of our cities killing hundreds of thousands of people or more. One of our recommendations was to create a cabinet level Department of Homeland Security.

The Commission's second conclusion was that the failure to invest in scientific research and the failure to reform math and science education was the second largest threat to American security. We unanimously concluded that no conventional war was as big a threat to America as this failure in math and science. Indeed, we ranked only a weapon of mass destruction released in an American city as a bigger threat.

Our goal was to communicate the centrality of the scientific endeavor to American life and the depth of crisis we believe threatens the math and science education system. The United States' ability to lead today is a function of past investments in scientific research and math and science education. There is no reason today to believe we will automatically maintain that lead especially given our current investments in scientific research and the staggering levels of our failures in math and science education.

Our ability to lead in 2025 will be a function of current decisions. Increasing our investment in science and discovery is a sound and responsible national security policy. No other federal expenditure will do more to create jobs, grow wealth, strengthen our world leadership, protect our environment, promote better education, or ensure better health for the country. We must make this increase now.

Similarly, no reform is more important than reforming fundamental math and science education so young Americans leave high school capable of understanding the basic science and math needed to be effective in the marketplace.

In health and healthcare, it is particularly important to increase our investment in research. If America invests in scientific knowledge—not only in direct medical research but also in the physics, mathematics, chemistry, and engineering that are the underpinnings of so much of our advanced biological knowledge—we will extend life, minimize suffering, and create a healthier and less medically expensive America. If we slow our rate of investment, more people will die with greater pain and at a higher cost than necessary. These are simply the stark, unassailable facts.

Age of Transformations

Our future merely adds to this imperative. We stand at an incredibly important moment in history. We are at the dawn of an explosion of knowledge that will change everything we know about science and, therefore, the human body. We will exponentially grow our knowledge of biology, physiology, and other health sciences in ways that will profoundly change the practice of medicine.

I believe that the knowledge breakthroughs of the next twenty years will equal the entire 20th century. In other words, the rate of change is accelerating; in the next two decades it will be about five times as fast as in the 20th century. The rate will continue to accelerate, and we will match the 20th century again between 2020 and 2035.

In 1903 the Wright brothers invented the airplane. Also in that year, the first motion picture with a plot was made, the Great Train Robbery that lasted three and a half minutes. In 1908, after two years of planning, Henry Ford unveiled the first truly mass-produced automobile using standardized parts that made ownership of an automobile a reality for millions of Americans. These three changes revolutionized life. Changes on this scale will occur with five times the speed in the 21st century than they did in the

20th century. No one in December of 1903 fully understood the impact of the airplane. Similarly, today we find it hard to imagine the impact of some of the breakthroughs we see in our daily newspaper.

Chapter two explained the necessity for transforming health and healthcare instead of reforming it. That is because we have entered an age of transformations. We are living through two tremendous patterns of scientific, and technological change—the computer and communications revolution and the combination of nanotechnology, biology, and information— each of which would be powerful by itself. Combined, the two patterns guarantee that we will be in a constant state of transformation as one breakthrough or innovation follows another.

The revolution that has been dubbed the information age began around 1965. Thinkers and visionaries like Peter Drucker, Kenneth Boulding, and Alvin and Heidi Toffler noted the industrial era was ending and the era of computing and telecommunication, in which we currently live, was beginning.

The evolution of any technological change can be represented by an "S" curve. First, science and technology begin to accelerate slowly. Then, as knowledge and experience accumulate, they grow much more rapidly. Finally, once the field has matured, the rate of change levels off. The resulting pattern looks like an "S" on a timeline graph. These large "S" curves are made up of thousands of smaller breakthroughs that create many small "S" curves of technological growth.

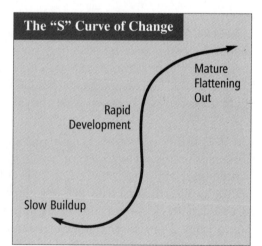

The "S" Curve of Change

Mature Flattening Out

Rapid Development

Slow Buildup

If you visualize just the growth of computers, this concept will become clear. According to Professor James Meindl, the chair of the Georgia Tech Microelectronics Department, the first computer built with a transistor was "Tradic" in 1955, and it had nearly 700 transistors.[3] The growth of computers from Tradic through the 1980s was slow and methodical. Then breakthroughs with silicon were discovered, specifically the microchip, which caused the advancements of computers and their uses to skyrocket. Today it is difficult for us to remember a world before computers. Less complicated chips are beginning to be put into almost everything we use including disposable items. Within fifteen to twenty years there will be a chip with one trillion transistors.[4]

But we are actually living through two patterns of change. The first is the enormous computer and communications revolution described above. We are at most only one-fifth of the way through it. The second, only now beginning to rise, is the combination of nanotechnology, biology, and information.

"Nano" is the space between one atom and about 400 hundred atoms. It is the space in which quantum behavior begins to replace the Newtonian physics you and I understand. The same laws of physics literally do not apply in the nanoworld. The scientists studying nanotechnology can now say with some confidence what is happening to atoms at the nanoscale level, but they still cannot explain why.

The word "nano" means one-billionth and is usually used to reference a nanosecond (one-billionth of a second) or a nanometer (one-billionth of a meter). In this world of atoms and molecules, new tools and techniques are enabling scientists to create entirely new approaches to manufacturing and to health. Nanotechnology allows us to "grow" materials by literally adding the right atoms and molecules to one another.

The "nanoworld" also includes a series of material technology breakthroughs that will continue to change how we build things, how much they weigh, and how much stress and punishment they can take. For example, it may be possible to grow carbon storage tubes so small that hydrogen could be safely stored, thus improving hydrogen fuel cell technology with dramatic implications for the economy and the environment.

According to some scientists at Georgia Tech, nanotubes are 50,000 times as thin as a human hair and 100 times stronger than steel, yet they weigh about one-sixth as much. They can conduct heat and electricity better than copper or gold. These new materials may make possible a one-hour flight from New York to Tokyo, an ultra-lightweight car, and a host of other possibilities. Originating in the NASA Ames Laboratory in California and a number of other laboratories, they are now being developed in industrial efforts across America.

This approach to growing materials rather than manufacturing them will save energy, conserve our raw materials, eliminate waste products, and produce a dramatically healthier environment. The implications for the improvement of the environment and the reduction of oil prices alone are impressive.

Whereas most of these breakthroughs are tangentially important for the health world, the direct possibilities for health and healthcare may be the most important aspect of nanotechnology. One example is that nanotechnology makes possible the ability to grow molecular "helpers." For instance, we may be able to develop anti-cancer helper molecules that penetrate human cells without damage and hunt cancer at its earliest single-cell development. Imagine drinking your orange juice with three million molecular rotor rooters to clean clogged arteries without an operation.

Biology is the second part of this three-part revolution. Not only does nanotechnology open up our understanding of biology, but biology teaches us about the nanoworld because virtually all biological activities are at a molecular level. Thus our growing capabilities in nano-tools and nano-helpers will dramatically expand our understanding of biology while our growing knowledge about molecular biology will expand our understanding of the nanoworld.

Dr. Sam Stupp is a world-class expert in using nanomaterials to develop a totally new approach to helping people recover from a variety of problems. Dr. Stupp uses molecular design to create self-assembling systems at the very basic levels of assembling atoms and molecules. In effect, he is studying how nature puts together the most basic components of our body.

Since we can now work literally at the scale of single molecules coming together to form structures by design, we are beginning to learn how nature pieces together extraordinarily complex systems. As we learn to repeat the same process, we can begin to regenerate lost parts of our body.

Imagine that a blind person could regenerate his or her retina and literally have a new organic retina made of precisely the same material as the original.

Imagine that a person in an accident who has lost the use of their arms and legs due to compression of the spinal cord could suddenly regenerate their spinal cord and have new use of their arms and legs as though the accident had never occurred.

Imagine that someone with a bad heart could grow new, healthy heart tissue instead of having a heart transplant.

Dr. Stupp believes all these breakthroughs could begin to occur by 2015.[5]

This is far from science fiction. Dr. Stupp has today, in his laboratories at Northwestern University, cell biology and animal experiments demonstrating the feasibility of these approaches thanks to this new science of regenerative medicine using molecular design and self-assembly. Dr. Stupp has created a company called NanoMateria to develop these new ideas into products that will transform how we help people live healthy lives.

This is a new and dramatically different part of biology. It is built on physics, materials science, and chemistry working back toward biological functions. It takes advantage of 40 years of progress in understanding the structure and properties of molecules and materials. It may revolutionize the way we deal with a large number of problems involving injury, illness, and aging.

Great breakthroughs are occurring in large established companies as well as small start-ups. For example, The Nestlé Research Center in

Switzerland is one of the largest and most sophisticated private laboratories of its kind in the world. The scientists at Nestlé have a very wide, and at times somewhat different, perspective on the importance and impact of nutrition on health. In addition to their interest in normal body cells, they also have a keen interest in the 70% of the cells in your body that are not "you."

Our bodies are hosts for billions of tiny beneficial bacteria which live in our small and large intestines. These organisms, referred to as probiotic organisms, help us stay healthy by, not only altering some metabolic processes in the intestine for the better but also competitively inhibiting attempts at colonization of the intestines by harmful bacteria. Consequently these probiotics act as a protective barrier for our bodies. The food you eat influences the numbers of these beneficial probiotic bacteria in our intestines in a way we are beginning to understand. As a result they have developed a yogurt which delivers these beneficial bacteria to the intestines, which is both inexpensive and practical. Once in the intestines, the probiotic bacteria can then actively play out their beneficial role. The implications for health management and disease prevention are amazing.

There are other stunning breakthroughs now occurring in biology. Breakthroughs, including the now completed Human Genome Project, will teach us more about the human body in the next twenty years than our total knowledge in history to this point. Now that we have finished documenting human DNA, Dr. Crick, the Nobel Prize-winning co-discoverer of DNA, thinks it will take us a century to understand and apply all the potential breakthroughs this new knowledge makes possible.[6] It is conceivable that in the not-so-distant future it may be possible to design an exact drug concoction specifically for you and your condition based on your genetic code.

The development of new technologies will increase our understanding of the human brain in ways previously unimaginable. Perhaps ironically, these will be largely a function of physics and mathematics because we are discovering that the brain may be one of the most complex aspects of the entire universe. From Alzheimer's to Parkinson's to schizophrenia, there will be virtually no aspect of our understanding of the human brain and human nervous system that cannot be transformed in the next two decades.

Finally, the third component is how the information revolution (computers and communications) impacts this technology in exponential ways, giving us vastly better capabilities to deal with the nanoworld and with biology.

It is the synergistic effect of these three systems together—nanotechnology multiplied by biology multiplied by information—that will lead to an explosion of new knowledge and new capabilities. This explosion itself can be represented by another "S" curve of technological development.

Consider, then, that we will simultaneously be experiencing the computer-communications revolution, which we are only one-fifth through, and the nanotechnology-biology-information revolution of which we are at the

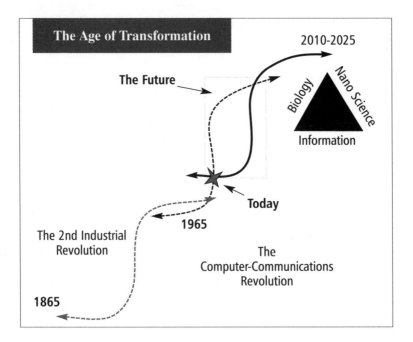

very earliest stages. The intersection of these two curves in our time creates an age of transformation that we must embrace.

Countries that study, understand, and invest in these patterns will live dramatically better lives than those who ignore them. Nations that focus their systems of learning, health, economic growth, and national security on these changes will have healthier, more knowledgeable people in more productive jobs creating better health, greater wealth, and safety.

Those countries that ignore these patterns of change will fall further behind and find themselves weaker, sicker, poorer, and more vulnerable than their more change-oriented neighbors.

That is the decision we, as a nation, are faced with today. We must choose which path we want to follow. That choice begins with whether or not we are committed to funding the basic scientific research that is the foundation of all of this innovation. We must choose whether we will commit to find a cure for cancer, AIDS, and diabetes or be resigned to just managing them. If we choose to accept the challenge, we must then be committed to the reform of math and science education that will produce young Americans able to understand and work with the new knowledge.

The Needed Investment in Science

Given the size and importance of the scientific revolutions that are beginning to occur, we need a significant increase in our investment in science throughout the federal government. I strongly supported the successful effort to double the budget of the National Institutes of Health. Looking back, however, I wish we had extended that commitment to investing in scientific research across the board and especially at the National Science Foundation.

Scientific progress in health and healthcare is a function of broad scientific progress and not of narrowly focused science. The satellite, which is looking back toward the very origins of the universe, is teaching us lessons about physics that will dramatically change our understanding of the very basic elements of our world. The weather pictures you take for granted on television are a direct product of government-sponsored programs. The research at the Defense Advanced Research Projects Agency (DARPA) has changed the pattern of our daily lives. Arpanet, as it was originally called at DARPA, became the Internet you now use. Many of the basic aspects of the computer screen you now work on were developed through contracts with DARPA.

The National Science Foundation is so vital to all scientific investment and so small relative to the National Institutes of Health that its budget should be tripled in the next few years.

We must do more than merely increase the federal budget for scientific research. We must change the way a significant part of it is thought about and allocated.

It is imperative to move away from the traditional incremental budgeting process and shift to an opportunities-based budget that takes into account a much larger perspective. The current model forces us to fund things that we know—in other words, the past and the present. It does not adequately fund or account for the larger breakthroughs of the future.

How much of an investment is too big if it launches the next 50 years of health and prosperity in our nation? If it finds the cure for cancer or AIDS? It is a difficult question to answer, but it will never be answered one budget item at a time, one year at a time. It can only be addressed in its entirety.

Not only is an investment in science and discovery an investment in the future, it is also an investment in human lives.

I serve on the board of the Juvenile Diabetes Research Foundation. The scientists who work with diabetes believe that within a decade we will have the potential to drastically reduce the impact of diabetes if not eliminate it.

How do you measure the return on an investment if it results in eliminating diabetes? What is the measure in human costs and what is the measure in revenues to the nation? Every fourth dollar of Medicare is spent treating diabetes and its side effects, which include blindness, heart disease, kidney disease, and foot amputation. If we had a capital investment model whose dividend was to recoup every seventh dollar of Medicare, we could surely justify a rather high initial investment to get that result.

Another example is Alzheimer's disease. One out of every three baby boomers may end up with Alzheimer's by their mid-eighties. The savings in human suffering makes such an investment a moral imperative. Moreover, the savings generated by a solution for this one disease would also pay many times over for the entire investment necessary to achieve it.

Recommendations

To meet the challenge of investing in science and discovery, I believe we should focus on the following areas:

1. Math and Science Education

We must fundamentally change the way we educate our citizens about science and discovery.

As I mentioned, the Hart/Rudman report became well-known after September 11 for its warnings about weapons of mass destruction. What is little known is that the second highest risk listed was our nation's inability to educate our children in math and science. We felt that the inability of our educational system to produce mathematicians and scientists posed a threat to our national security in the highest order—second only to hundreds of thousands of people being killed by a weapon of mass destruction. In fact we specifically said the danger of an inadequate education system was a greater threat to our national survival than any conceivable, conventional war in the next 25 years.

It is an objective reality that we are not producing enough properly educated 18-year olds capable of sustaining this society in the 21st century. The number of Americans who continue to invest their minds and their lives in science and math is clearly too small and getting smaller, as evidenced by our graduate schools' struggle to find enough applicants.

Barely half of the computer science graduate students working in the United States were born in the United States. Historically, we have benefited from the math and science education of other countries. The Nazis frightened a generation of scientists into migrating to America. These scholars helped us win the Second World War and have been vital to our scientific capabilities for a half-century. Another wave of scientists fled communism to live in America. For the last 50 years, our country has been a magnet to scientists and mathematicians from the third world.

Nevertheless we cannot base the most creative and vital segments of our economy and our national security on help from other nations. We can no longer assume that we can import scholars from India and China and Germany and Japan and educate them in our institutions to substitute for the collapse of educating our own young people. Especially when we, as an open society, are helping educate scientists from around the world who have a much larger incentive than before to return to their home countries in the global economy. If the present trends continue, we will be surpassed in the education of our own scientists and mathematicians by China and India in the next generation and might well be passed by Japan and Europe as well.

After fifteen years of missed opportunities in education, the depth of this problem dictates that we must be very bold in finding a solution. We must focus on results rather than intentions. This includes seriously considering notions such as waiving interest on student loans for undergraduate students that major in math and science or perhaps literally paying high school students cash for learning calculus.

We must rethink, from the ground up, how we educate our children in math and science. In my judgment it is harder than most other kinds of learning. There are many reasons in a wealthy society that people at the margin do not go into math and science. One is the fact that there is no obvious, immediate, short-term advantage to majoring in something that is harder and requires more hours and more work.

Another is the way in which we teach these subjects as facts to be memorized rather than a great adventure of discovery to be pursued. Teaching, memorizing, and testing are all familiar words. But we must return the words wonder, adventure, and discovery to our schools. We should not center on education, but on learning. We should go beyond force-feeding numbers and theories to a level of true discovery where a child wonders what the answers are and goes in search of them for the pure excitement of it.

There are opportunities for this all around us. On a worldwide scale, the opportunity for very young children to become real scientists at the discovery level is astonishing. A scientist at the Ames Research Center told me that we currently only know 3% to 5% of all species of single-cell organisms. One of the young scientists at Ames is giving students the opportunity to do real research; he currently has 10,000 students networked together through the Internet who are helping him gather data in the Pacific.

In another excellent example of involving young discoverers, the Ames Research Center hosts a program for amateur scientists who help professionals with research. NASA funds this collaborative project between Ames and the nonprofit Marine

Sciences Institute, a science education organization that runs educational cruises for teachers and students in the San Francisco Bay area. The program's director, Lynn Rothschild, has utilized the samples and physical data (temperature, UV radiation, water clarity, etc.) collected by students on the cruise to help her identify UV-absorbing pigments in plankton and to measure DNA damage experienced by plankton in the Bay at different times of the year. This information could help scientists understand far more about environmental effects on coastal communities.

Students are immersed in the research through part ownership of the scientific data. This program not only nurtures the next generation of scientists but also has allowed Ames to provide useful data that would otherwise have an economically prohibitive price tag.

We should consider almost any method that produces enough math and science students to carry out the research and development necessary for the age upon which we are embarking.

2. Increased Funding for the National Science Foundation (NSF)

Federal funding for the National Science Foundation (NSF) should be increased from $4.7 billion annually to $15 billion. Some may say that this is a very large increase. But, again, I would ask, "How large is an increase that will end diabetes? How big is too big if it cures Alzheimer's and ultimately eliminates years of pain and suffering and saves the country billions of dollars?" It is clear that the National Science Foundation could actually invest $11 billion a year within current constraints. The scale of the present shortfall was highlighted when the Director of the NSF, Rita Colwell, stated that to fund existing first-class research proposals would require more than twice as much funding as the $4.7 billion currently appropriated.[7] Yet even her testimony understates the potential shortfall in science. Dr. Colwell is describing the shortfall within the current system without looking ahead long term.

The psychology of a budget-constrained science community minimizes proposals of appropriate large-scale research projects. It is clear that instrumentation, education, and research projects could productively absorb a $15 billion annual level. It is also clear that that investment would repay itself many times over in economic growth, stronger defense, a healthier environment, and better health.

3. We Must Fund Large-Scale Marquee Projects

We must fund a new generation of large projects that could create great breakthroughs. The Defense Advanced Research Projects Agency invested millions of dollars without peer review that made possible the creation of the Internet.

In astronomy, the terabytes of data that will be produced daily ought to be captured in an open, Internet-based, archived, virtual observatory. The current plans will capture only a tiny percentage of the data. In weather and climatology, we will likely have to spend trillions of dollars to meet the Kyoto Global Warming protocol. Yet we fail to increase the current budget by less than one-tenth of 1% as much for a worldwide climatology project that would include space- and land-based ocean and atmospheric monitoring on a scale that is technically possible with modern systems. This is a clear example of an investment in science and discovery because the research done ahead of Kyoto could prove or dispel the need to join the treaty.

The National Oceanic and Atmospheric Administration is so strapped for money to keep its current systems operating that it legitimately shies away from this grandiose scale of investment in knowledge and research that should actually be the minimum investment it should be considering.

4. Room in Science Budgets Should Be Reserved for Non-traditional Research

Money needs to be available for highly innovative "out of the box" science. Peer review is ultimately a culturally conservative and risk-adverse model. Each institution's director should have a small amount of discretionary money, possibly 3% to 5% of their budget, to spend on outliers. It is important to remember that the breakthrough of plate tectonics in geology was rejected by "respectable" geologists from 1915 until 1962 although it is today the accepted interpretation of how continents move about. There has to be a modest amount available to encourage non-establishment thinking and bold, new risk takers.

5. Prizes to Advance Science

Financial incentives drive change. We would be astonished by the discoveries that could be made if we dedicated 1% of the money we currently spend on research specifically to contests with financial prizes. In 1999, I participated in a National Academy of Engineering Workshop on assessing the impact of prizes and contests on advancing science and technology. The workshop resulted in a very thoughtful report available at http://books.nap.edu/books/NI000221/html/8.html#pagetop.

The essence of the prize system is that it allows anyone, anywhere, using any methodology to try to solve a problem. The current system emphasizes scientists reviewing other scientists to invest money in culturally acceptable and reasonable risks. That has proved to be a powerful but very conservative and self-reinforcing model of advancement.

The prize system allows innovators, entrepreneurs, scientific amateurs, and anyone with a good idea to focus on the achievement rather than the process. No scientific committee would have found Charles Lindbergh and awarded him a research grant to cross the Atlantic Ocean solo from New

York to Paris. The $25,000 prize attracted him, and as a virtual unknown, he captured the world's imagination.

The Smithsonian Institution had an expensive, but failed, heavier-than-air project underway just as the Wright brothers were developing their own wind tunnels and inventing the first heavier-than-air vehicle to fly. It would have been very hard for the Wright brothers to have convinced a scientific panel that as bicycle mechanics (actually a sophisticated profession in their day) they were a better investment than distinguished scientists, yet the historical records are clear.

Most scientific money should continue to be invested through scientific peer review. Some of the money should be spent on managed large projects. One percent of the research funding should be available in prize money.

I am convinced that if we had offered a prize for the first successful and economic reusable vehicle to get into orbit, today we would have a fleet of dramatically better space-launch vehicles. If we had offered a prize for the first permanent, manned lunar base, it would have been four or five times faster than the incremental, risk-avoiding efforts of bureaucratic science.

Prizes have the virtue of integrating the hobbies and interests of amateur scientists into real discovery. Significant recent findings by amateur scientists include animal tracks in New Mexico older than dinosaurs and supernovae in distant galaxies.[8] It is important to remember that Darwin "the amateur beetle collector" nurtured Darwin "the evolutionary theorist." There is plenty to be discovered and explored by amateurs, and the Internet, combined with new instrumentation, can harness and focus the work that amateurs already do. Prizes also allow people to follow their dreams. A system that rewards creativity and innovation will see more people displaying those characteristics.

Shawn Carlson recognized the untapped resource of amateur scientists and in 1994 founded the Society for Amateur Scientists.[9] He and others guide amateur scientists in their research and enlist their help in gathering data for professional scientists. The society's Web site (www.sas.org) sends out calls for assistance on projects at universities and laboratories around the country. The potential is massive but the funds are lacking.

The history of prizes in the last three centuries is so sufficiently successful that it is worth 1% of the federal scientific endeavor to offer prizes for high-value breakthroughs. Moreover, it is hard to imagine a more efficient investment. After all, unless a scientific challenge is met, the money is not paid.

6. The Centers for Disease Control and Prevention Should Be a High Priority

Polio and smallpox have been eliminated in the United States and AIDS incidence and deaths are declining because of the research and public health leadership of the Centers for Disease Control and Prevention (CDC). Now, with the increase in deadly biological weapons, the CDC is researching immunization strategies and formulating action plans to combat epidemic outbreaks from bioterrorist attacks. It is clear that the CDC's current budget is far too small to handle the challenges of biological warfare (see Appendix B on biothreats for more details). The comfort and safety we now enjoy will continue only if future scientific funding supports the CDC's ability to do preventive research.

7. Mobilizing a Movement in Favor of Scientific Research

C.P. Snow was correct in 1959 when he described two emerging cultures—the scientific and the non-scientific.[10] Too often those who know enough about science cannot explain it in popular language. Conversely, those who are effective at communicating in popular language do not know science.

Most science professionals would rather be in their laboratories performing, at conferences learning, or in classrooms teaching than appearing in public settings to appeal for public support. Unfortunately part of their mind-set seems to be a determination that their work is so obviously important that they should not have to explain it. The same problem is found among doctors, nurses, and others involved in the healthcare industry.

Scientists have the same obligation as other citizens—if not a larger one—to go to their local town hall meeting, to show up at the door of their congressional representative, to write letters to the editor and explain why this investment is necessary—to explain exactly what is at stake. No one else has their understanding or credibility.

In my experience the only way to achieve big ideas is to mobilize popular movements behind them. The voters do matter in a free society. They can ultimately convince elected officials to meet popular demands. Perhaps the best opportunity to rally a segment of our society to the cause of investing in the future lies with the entire baby-boom generation. The baby boomers in particular have a quality-of-life interest in the rapid development of new scientific knowledge.

As I have mentioned, if nothing is done, one out of every three baby boomers may end up with Alzheimer's disease by their mid-eighties. We have the chance today to make the investment in research to prevent the suffering of so many tomorrow.

8. Space

It is impossible to write a chapter about the need for federal investment in science and discovery without mentioning our space program.

Space exploration, and the institutions, programs, and systems necessary to carry it out, has a proven record of achieving major scientific breakthroughs that directly affect our lives both from the research that takes place in space and the process itself. (Velcro is one small example.) Some of the most important research being done anywhere in the world on nanotechnology is carried out by NASA at their Ames laboratory.

But beyond these breakthroughs, space exploration has also been the most successful vehicle for translating the need to invest in science and discovery to the American people. It is a visible, tangible, results-oriented program that instills national pride and helps us quickly understand why research is important. There is something magical and passionate about space exploration that microscopes and lab coats cannot convey to young people.

The entire NASA community is aware of how incredibly important it is to continually push the boundaries of our knowledge and its benefits to our society, starting of course with the astronauts themselves. This comes across to the American people with an element of humanity too often lacking in the world of science.

I wrote the first draft of this chapter long before the loss of the space shuttle *Columbia*, but it became all the more fitting once we learned of the disaster. If it is possible for anything good to come from such a tragic loss, hopefully it is a national recognition that the heroes who lost their lives died literally in the name of bettering humanity by investing their lives in science and discovery.

We owe it to their memory to renew and redouble our efforts to venture where mankind has not gone before in space and in the rest of science. This investment will repay us again and again. That has been the lesson of America's past. And it is the promise of America's future.

[1] Thomas Kuhn, *The Structures of Scientific Revolutions,* (Chicago, University of Chicago Press: 1996).
[2] Clayton M. Christensen, *The Innovator's Dilemma,* (Harvard Business School Press, June 1997).
[3] As reported on <www.cedmagic.com/history/tradic-transistorized.html> as of 23 April 2003
[4] Dr. Meindl, correspondence with the author, March 2003.
[5] As reported on <www.matsci.northwestern.edu/stupp/sisnews.html> as of 23 April 2003.
[6] As reported on <www.salk.edu/faculty/faculty/details.php?id=14> as of 23 April 2003.
[7] House Committee on Science, Subcommittee on Basic Research, transcript of testimony from Rita Colwell, "The Impact of Basic Research on Technological Innovation and National Prosperity," (Washington, DC, 28 September 1999): 45-46.
[8] Mims, Forrest M. III, Science, 284, 55 (1999).
[9] Society for Amateur Scientists, As reported on <www.sas.org> as of 23 April 2003.
[10] C.P. Snow, *The Two Cultures,* Snow, (Cambridge: Cambridge University Press, 1993).

CHAPTER TEN

Active, Healthy Aging:
Living Healthier, Happier, and Longer

Aging is part of life. As we creep up in years our bones get achier. But the values, characteristics, and expectations of most Americans, and especially the baby boomers, are unchanged. We want to continue to lead productive, intellectually stimulating lives, have significance, and be physically active. We value our freedom and our dreams. We do not want age to define us, nor do we want age to eliminate our right to choose where and how we live. It is this American drive for independence that will lead to changes in how we think about the aging process.

In 2002 Civic Ventures commissioned a survey of 600 randomly selected people ages 50 to 75. Peter Hart, the leader of this research, stated in a summary report, "It is not the idea of shuffle board, it is not the idea of sitting back in a rocker—these people want to be engaged." Hart found that 72% of all respondents said they believe retirement is a "time to begin a new chapter;" only 16% agreed that it is "a time to take it easy."[1]

We may believe that a new chapter begins at 65. But in order to take advantage of that chapter, we need to prepare our bodies to physically and emotionally embrace the opportunities.

In the book *Living to 100*, by Dr. Thomas T. Perls and Margery H. Silver, the researchers dedicate an entire chapter to what they have learned about how to age with the best quality of life and the least pain for the longest time possible. For most of us, the chapter will truly be an eye opener. Some of the recommendations are listed below. Please consult your doctor to confirm that these strategies are in your best health interest.

- Take 400-800 IUs of vitamin E every day to help fight deterioration of your brain and to protect you from heart disease and cancer.

- The mineral selenium has proved to decrease the risk of cancer and heart attack. The recommended dosage is 100 to 200 mg per day.

- Exercise at every age to keep your body healthy and reduce stress.

- Exercise your brain. Learning new things stimulates the growth and regeneration of your brain cells. Some of the centenarians studied exercised their cognitive abilities by researching and writing books or opening and managing their own business. Others worked on crossword and jigsaw puzzles or played bridge. Still others read challenging books, learned a foreign language, took college classes, learned new dance steps, or painted. One of the most effective activities is playing an instrument because it requires us to simultaneously read, listen, memorize, perform complicated manual activities, create and relax. Consciously using your non-dominant hand to complete daily activities like brushing your teeth, washing dishes, or opening a door can also keep your mind sharp.

- Talk to your doctor about taking ibuprofen or aspirin. Aspirin has proved to lower the risk of developing Alzheimer's disease by 30% to 60%. Aspirin has also been associated with fighting Alzheimer's and has been proved to help prevent heart disease. (Although consistent use of ibuprofen can have significant side effects such as stomach ulcers and impaired kidney function.)

Seasoned Citizens Want to Stay Connected

Research indicates that the more active and more connected an elderly person is, the healthier the person tends to be. In fact, some research shows a downturn in health after a person retires from his or her full-time job. There are growing opportunities for people to stay connected and a 21st Century System of Health and Healthcare would break down barriers of isolation and encourage people to stay active. In a very real sense national retirement and tax policies ARE health policies. When these policies make it harder to stay active and easier to become indolent, we are fostering illness, decline, and actually increasing our health expenses. Good health is about a lot more than health policy.

AARP conducted a national survey in mid-2002 in an attempt to define what individuals age 45 to 74 expected for the future. Of the 1,500 employed workers in that age group who were surveyed, a substantial majority (69%) reported that they plan to work in some capacity in their retirement years. Why? Because they enjoyed working (76%) and/or they need the money (76%). Moreover, an overwhelming 84% said that they would continue working if "they won the lottery and were financially set for the rest of their lives."[2]

The part of the survey I found most interesting was that more than a third of the respondents wanted to work part time for pure interest or enjoyment. Another 10% said they wanted to open their own business, and 6% said they wanted to work full-time doing something other than what they were already doing. Clearly this group wants to stay active.

In 1998, AARP conducted a similar study for the younger boomers—those ages 33 to 52. The study found that 75% of the 2,000 people sampled said that they would work into their retirement years.[3]

The baby boomer's desire to stay active is good news for the economy. There are legitimate concerns that when baby boomers retire there will not be adequate replacements for their jobs and that the lack of their income taxes will put a substantial dent in federal and state budgets. Government budgets will be strapped just as the number of individuals on Medicare and Medicaid will swell.

In response to these trends, companies and organizations are experimenting with ways to attract older workers. Forward-looking companies and organizations are working with AARP to identify and breakdown barriers so older Americans will continue to work.

Recently, AARP launched an award program to recognize those companies that focus on opportunities for people older than 60. AARP gave awards out to the top fifteen companies.[4] Some of the winner's outstanding policies include tiered retirement structures and part-time employment. Some workers have already been experimenting with "job sharing" where a team of people work collectively to fill one job. A growing number of employers are allowing their older workers to work from home or have rehired them as short-term consultants. There are still issues to be worked out, such as continuing private health coverage for people eligible for Medicare or allowing workers who work part time to supplement their income with pensions although they are not fully retired.

We must recognize that rethinking government rules for retirement and reforming Medicare to encourage economic activity are key steps toward a better future for the baby boomers. The policies that may have made sense in earlier eras when people died younger, exhausted by farm and factory labor (most Americans died by 63 when Social Security set its payment age at 65,) are simply not applicable in an era when more people are healthier longer and want to continue to stay active. Active healthy aging requires us to rethink much more than just our health policies.

One area in which these semi-retired Americans can be of tremendous benefit is in educating and mentoring young people. The current education structure does not support the flexibility older people demand. We are losing a lot of good talent because of this inflexibility. Why not make it easier for people to teach part time or "share" a classroom with another teacher? Perhaps we should allow a teacher to offer one course a semester or quarter, which would allow them the flexibility to travel or pursue various interests during other parts of the year.

Schools that are flexible enough to include senior teachers on a part-time basis would create a richer learning experience. Seniors who know business could be teaching business courses; seniors who know science could be teaching science courses; seniors who know the world through the military could be teaching about the geography or cultures of the places they have lived. Seniors could be teaching a variety of courses bringing discipline, maturity, and perspective into schools.

It would also require changing teacher credentialing, union contracts, compensation structures (part-time teachers do not fit the current model), and in some cases curricula. It would be better for the students, the senior teachers, and the community.

As companies seek to retain employees with seasoned experience, we will need to think through the systematic improvements we can make in their work environment. For example, one profession that is already experiencing a critical shortage is nursing. The average nurse in America is older than 40 years of age. As we age, eyesight becomes a larger issue, and we can use technology, such as bar coding prescription drugs so a smart system can ensure that the right patient is getting the right treatment at the right time. This has the dual advantage of allowing nurses to be more comfortable about their nursing skills and preventing medication errors for the patient.

Financially compensated work is not the only avenue for a seasoned citizen to stay connected. Many individuals choose to volunteer their time.

Some are using technology to stay connected with programs that build virtual communities for seniors. For example, one helps students communicate with World War II veterans to supplement their history lessons and another arranges e-mailing "pen pals" (e-pals) between older and younger people. Electronic chat rooms also help people find and identify with others their own age, and they have proved to be an inexpensive way for people to connect. This is especially helpful for those who are disabled and primarily homebound.

Perhaps the most surprising data I have learned about positively influencing the health of older Americans is the connection to an animal. Significant research indicates that humans who are connected to a pet have lower cholesterol levels, fewer visits to the doctor, and have an increased optimism about life. Research also indicates that elderly pet owners have a higher sense of well-being and usefulness.

I was so convinced by the research that, while in Congress, I supported legislation that allowed seniors who moved into low-income housing to maintain their pet relationship. Families and institutions should keep this in mind when they are choosing long-term-care options for their loved ones. There are also organizations that provide "pet therapy" for elderly people. The Delta Society's Pet Partners trains and screens volunteers and their pets to visit elderly people in hospitals, nursing homes, and rehabilitation centers. Every year 6,400 Pet Partners teams visit over 900,000 people. If you would like to find a pet partner team to help an elderly person you know, or if you would like to apply to become a Pet Partner, visit www.deltasociety.org.

Helping People with Disabilities Live Healthier, Happier, and Longer

The growing number of Americans who live with significant disabilities is a new phenomenon in our society. Recent medical advances are enabling more and more people to live many years longer than previously possible with such conditions as spinal cord injury, muscular dystrophy, or Downs Syndrome. In addition, increasing numbers of people are now living into their eighties and beyond, often with age-related disabling conditions. Beyond the ethical obligation of caring for our country's most vulnerable population, we must address the health and wellness of people living with disabilities if we are to make any progress in controlling the growth of healthcare costs.

A basic principle for a 21st Century System of Health and Healthcare for people with disabilities is to keep these individuals as healthy and independent as possible for as long as possible. Unfortunately, however, preventive health measures are not always easily accessible to people with disabilities. For instance, most mammography machines do not adjust low enough for women in wheelchairs. Also, it is often difficult for people with mobility limitations to get on medical exam and X-ray tables.

Many medical practitioners perceive "disability" and "health" as mutually exclusive terms even though many people with disabilities are not sick, and many of the secondary conditions to which they are subject are easily preventable. For example, a person who sits all day in the same position in a wheelchair is at risk of developing skin sores. This risk can easily be reduced or eliminated by utilizing a wheelchair with a seat that tilts to shift pressure from one point to another during the day. As the number of people living with significant disabilities grows, preventive medical care and assistive technologies need to be made more available.

We should be exploring tax credits and other financial incentives to encourage companies to develop the right technologies for people with disabilities.

Innovative technologies are being developed every day that can improve the quality of life for citizens with disabilities and save both acute care and long-term-care dollars. Independence Technology, a division of Johnson and Johnson, has created an amazing wheelchair to help people with disabilities live more active and independent lives. The "Ibot" (www.inde-tech.com/ibot) is a wheelchair that can go up stairs, rise vertically to eye level, balance on two wheels, cross rough terrain, and still function as a standard mobility device. Unfortunately people who can benefit from technologies like these are often prevented from acquiring them because they are expensive and insurance companies are reluctant to pay for them even though they have the potential to save much more in traditional medical expenses than they cost.

When I was Speaker, we created a Disabilities Task Force in my district. I learned a great deal from the people who served on my task force about how government policies and insurance coverage decisions affect the real lives of people with disabilities and their families, both for the better and for the worse. Carol Hughes-Novak was the chairperson of the task force. Carol and her son Jonathan, who has cerebral palsy, are a true testament of a family dedicated to helping one another live as full and healthy a life as possible.

Like Carol, most families want to do as much as humanly and financially possible to enable their family member with a disability to live in their own home and participate in the community. And, from the perspective of public policy, it will be extremely difficult, if not impossible, for our country to continue providing costly institutional care for people with disabilities as the number of people needing these services grows.

When I asked Carol what could be done to help her continue to be Jonathan's primary caregiver for as long as possible, and then to ensure that he lives his entire life in the community, she offered several insights that I would like to share with you in her own words:

> 1. Recognize the value of the millions of hours of unpaid care that people with disabilities of all ages receive from family caregivers. By supplementing family caregivers' efforts with respite and other services, we can reduce caregiver burnout that in turn leads to costly institutional care for the person with the disability and health problems for the caregiver that could have been prevented. (I had 2 MRI's last year to diagnose my back problems resulting from years of lifting Jonathan and have had two epidural cortisone blocks this year that required anesthesia and an operating room—all expensive. If we had gotten Jonathan's lift and transfer system several years sooner than we did, it's likely that I would not have damaged my back.)

> 2. Promote implementation of President Bush's Olmstead Executive Order that requires state Medicaid programs to provide long-term-care services in the community whenever appropriate for the individual. In order to really achieve this, the institutional bias in Medicaid long-term-care funding must be removed. "Institutional bias" refers to the fact that anyone meeting the Medicaid means test and disability criteria is entitled to an institutional placement, but that same person must

get on a waiting list for the Medicaid Home and Community based long-term-care services that are more humane and almost always less costly. Typically the wait for these services lasts for years.

(Go to this page for a copy of Bush's Olmstead order— http://www.whitehouse.gov/news/releases/2001/06/20010619-1.html)

3. Encourage non-disabled people who are younger than 65 to buy private long-term-care insurance by making the premiums tax deductible—preferably a tax credit rather than a medical deduction. My husband and I just bought the most comprehensive long-term-care policies available at an annual cost of around $3,800 for both of us. By taking responsibility for ourselves, we will have greater freedom of choice in the event that we someday need long-term-care services—AND our care won't cost the taxpayers a cent, thereby reserving the finite Medicaid long-term-care dollars for people like Jonathan who cannot buy private long-term-care insurance.

Below are three Web sites for people with disabilities who want more information about living longer and healthier.

New Directions for Living Well
http://rtc.ruralinstitute.umt.edu/health/RuHOutreach.htm

National Center on Physical Activity and Disability
http://www.ncpad.org/

Rehabilitation Research Training Center on Health and Wellness
http://www.healthwellness.org/

How Living Healthier, Happier, and Longer Saves Money

One of the most surprising findings of the Perls and Silver study on centenarians was that centenarians do not suffer long, gradual declines in health before they die. "About 95% of their centenarians are physically healthy and cognitively independent into their nineties, with low rates of mental illness and depression. Centenarians are far more likely to have a near lifetime of excellent health, followed by a quick decline before death."[5] The more an insurance plan focuses on keeping us happy and healthy, the less likely we will need costly acute care.

An analysis of medical claims done by researchers at the University of North Carolina found that people over 65 who walk or swim could save an average of $250 per month in Medicare costs. Seniors who monitored their blood pressure and urine had estimated monthly expenditures that were on average $123 lower per month.[6] With this kind of savings, Medicare should aggressively innovate ways to encourage healthy habits. This may include giving away testing devices and providing tax credits and subsidies for community health clubs like the YMCA.

Almost $20 billion is spent each year in the United States on angioplasty and bypass surgery, much of which could be avoided if people were to make comprehensive lifestyle changes instead. Dr. Dean Ornish and his colleagues completed a study that was printed in the *American Journal of Cardiology*. It found that 80% of people who were eligible for bypass surgery or angioplasty were able to avoid it by making comprehensive lifestyle changes instead. That is a savings of $15.4 billion per year.[7]

Another study clearly shows that an investment in keeping a person healthy can save lives and save money. Unlike Medicare, Medicaid (the government's insurance program for the poor) does cover outpatient prescription drugs. When New Hampshire decided to limit the number of prescription drugs for Medicaid beneficiaries to three drugs per person, the Agency for Healthcare Research and Quality (AHRQ) investigated to see if it was an effective cost-containment strategy. After eleven months of the limitation on drugs, there was a statewide increase in hospitalizations (35%) and nursing-home admissions. In fact increased utilization of medical services was seventeen times greater than the savings in drug expenditures.[8] The result? New Hampshire removed the limitation.[9]

What Should Be Done by the Government and the Healthcare System to Encourage Active, Healthy Aging

The essence of why Medicare is in critical condition is that it focuses on sickness and not health. It pays for your open-heart surgery, but it will not pay for your beta-blocker. It pays to amputate your foot, but it will not pay for your insulin. It will pay for your drugs while you are in the hospital, but it will not pay for the same drugs that would have kept you out of the hospital. Not only should Medicare pay for drugs, but it should pay for your SilverSneakers membership and WeightWatchers, too!

Medicare must be strengthened to include a focus on outcomes-based healthcare. Immediately drugs should be reimbursed in order to de-incentivize reactive acute care. However, the current budgetary structure is clearly biased in favor of reactive care. Presently there is a different budget for inpatient and outpatient services, and there is likely to be a separate budget for drugs if the government adds drug coverage to the benefit package. Even within these larger budgets, programs are compartmentalized. A representative example of this illogical budgetary process is in durable medial equipment (DME). The DME department has to stay within its own budget; therefore purchasing decisions are made based on what the individual department can afford. No consideration is given to the fact that if DME purchases a $15,000 power wheelchair that reclines so that the user can shift his weight during the day, significantly reducing the risk of pressure sores that require hospitalization and surgery, it will save the acute-care department a minimum of $30,000.

This type of compartmentalized budgeting is not compatible with the opportunities of the 21st century. It is illogical, irrational, and unethical. It should not matter if a patient is treated in a hospital, in a doctor's office, or in their home. The flow of resources should follow the patient and not be driven by a series of bureaucratic structures. As medicine continues to develop new technology to help people avoid sickness, infection, and disease, it is illogical not to account for the money saved by the decrease in invasive and costly procedures and expensive hospitalization.

Budgetary officers should develop a single outcomes-based budget so doctors can focus on taking care of the whole person without modifying what is medically best for the patient to fit Medicare's reimbursement structure. Without a total overhaul of the budget practices of Medicare and the scoring procedures (i.e., the process of actuaries assessing how much a change in procedure being proposed in a bill will cost the government long term) of Congress and the White House, there will never be an appropriate focus on prevention.

The government should also incentivize people to purchase long-term-care insurance. Many people are surprised that Medicare does not adequately cover home care or a nursing-home stay longer than 100 days when either they or their loved ones are becoming less independent. Without long-term-care insurance, the family's only option is to spend down their assets or their parent's assets to become eligible for Medicaid. The final years of life for a Medicaid recipient involve roommates and shared televisions, telephones, and bathrooms. This fate could be avoided if we purchased long-term-care insurance for our loved ones and ourselves. Currently, long-term-care insurance, like health insurance, is not tax deductible in many states. Out-of-pocket costs and private long-term-care insurance make up roughly one quarter of all long-term-care funding. Over 75% comes from Medicare or Medicaid. A focused effort should be made to reverse that ratio. A first step would be to provide a tax credit for purchasing long-term-care insurance so people will be reminded every year that they should buy long-term-care insurance before it is too late.

What You Can Do to Improve the System

As we age, it is important to get routine screenings and physicals in order to best manage our health. Throughout this book, we have emphasized the importance of having access to quality, outcomes-based information. As we age, more medical advice will become even more important to us. The gap between our current system and the optimal system is growing. The more we need medications, the more chances we have to be a victim of a medication error. If we need nursing-home care and cannot afford to pay out of pocket, we will have to sell all our possessions to qualify for Medicaid reimbursement and then be forced to live with a stranger in a double room. When we need open-heart surgery or a hip replacement, how will we know which surgeon to choose?

We have to work to improve the system today so that it will be the system we want tomorrow. By applying the principles that we have outlined, we can create the 21st Century System of Health and Healthcare that will allow seniors to be active and healthy as long as possible.

As consumers of healthcare, we are limited by our insurance policies, presented with bills that make no sense, and have difficulty accessing a physician. As a consumer model, healthcare in America is a failure. A 21st century system of healthcare should offer a better health future with fewer illnesses, faster recovery, and greater speed and convenience at lower cost. It is what we should demand. However, for such a system to be successful, every consumer of healthcare must first accept responsibility and accountability for their own health. Managing our own health must be a fundamental part of a 21st century healthcare system that will save lives, improve health, and cost significantly less than the current system.

[1] Paul Kleyman,"Study shows how older volunteer force in U.S. could double" *Aging Today,* (Jan-Feb 03).
[2] AARP, *AARP Survey Outlines What 45+ Workers Seek from Employers,* (Washington, DC, 23 September 2002).
[3] As reported on <http://research.aarp.org/econ/boomer_seg_toc.html> as of 23 April 20003.
[4] You can find more out about AARP's award program at <http://www.aarpmagazine.org/lifestyle/Articles/a2003-01-23-top15>
[5] Dr. Thomas T. Perls, Margery H. Silver, and John F. Lauerman (contributer), *Living to 100: Lessons in Living to Your Maximum Potential at Any Age,* (New York: Basic Books, 2000), 18.
[6] S.C. Stearns, et al., "The economic implications of self-care: the effect of lifestyle, functional adaptations, and medical self-care among a national sample of Medicare beneficiaries," *American Journal of Public Health* 90 (October 2000): 1608-1612.
[7] D. Ornish, "Avoiding Revascularization with Lifestyle Changes: The Multicenter Lifestyle Demonstration Project," *The American Journal of Cardiology* 82 (1998), 72T-76T and D. Ornish, communication with Kathy Lubbers, 24 April 2003.
[8] As reported on <www.ahcpr.gov/research/cosqual.pdf> as of 23 April 2003.
[9] U.S. Department of Health and Human Services, Public Health Services, Agency for Healthcare Research and Quality, *AHRQ Research To Reduce Cost and Improve the Quality of Health Care,* special on-line report <http://www.ahrq.gov/research/costqual.pdf> as of 23 April 2003.

Transforming and Reforming

Understanding the difference between transformation and reformation is difficult. Taking a crack at transforming the health and healthcare system is daunting. The fact is transformation will not be easy. However, transforming health and healthcare is urgent, important, doable, and necessary.

Transforming health and healthcare is urgent, because it is about saving lives and saving money. Never before have we been at this historic moment in time where transforming a system as big as health and healthcare can and will mean so much to so many. The urgency comes from the real threat of bioterrorism and the need to have a system in place to even begin to comprehend how to handle such an occurrence. Additionally, the urgency comes from the ability to save thousands of lives every year if only we would transform the system to take advantage of the technology available to us right now.

Accomplishing this important goal will affect every person in the United States. It affects us as individuals by providing better quality health at lower costs. As employees and employers, we will realize lower health insurance costs due to reformed litigation and fewer medical errors, which reduces illness, which reduces costs, which reduces premiums. Transforming healthcare impacts us as citizens as we help to transform a system that accounts for a staggering 13% of our national gross domestic product. We must work together as citizen activists to create state and federal policies that lead to a 21st Century System of Health and Healthcare.

Transformation of health and healthcare is doable if we each do our share of the lifting. This is not a quick fix. This is not a short-term response. This is a call to action for each of us to consider what it is worth to live in the greatest nation on earth and enjoy the benefits of the best healthcare system in the world.

We want to encourage you to get involved in advancing the 21st Century System of Health and Healthcare. One way to do this is to join us in the discovery of transformational breakthroughs and examples, the discussion of ideas on accelerating the transformation, and learning how to apply the principles in this book to transform your organization internally by joining the Center for Health Transformation (www.healthtransformation.net). Together we can create a movement to get real transformation, but it will not happen without you. Get involved.

Join us in thinking through on a daily basis how to transform your own health and how to create a system of health and healthcare that saves lives and saves money. Think through how you could influence the thinking of our healthcare professionals and our policymakers on the state and federal levels.

As an individual, become more responsible for your own health. Think about what you can actively do to improve your health on a daily basis. Are you doing the simple things that can lead to a longer, higher quality of life? Are you encouraging your family and friends to do likewise?

As a user of healthcare, become proactive with your healthcare providers. Ask them more questions, inquire about why they are not using the latest technology, and implore them to interact with you as an informed consumer.

As a citizen, let your voice be heard. Contact the state and federal government representatives whose job it is to deal with the health issues most important to you. Become more educated and involved with the process. Insert your experiences and frustrations into their lives and into the policy debate that is being formed for you but not always with your input.

What can we do? Talk to your congressional representatives, senators, or state legislators about creating and serving on their 21st century health task force. Find out what good legislation is being proposed and lobby your legislators for its passage. Write an editorial and submit it to your paper—more people read the editorials written by private citizens than those written by the columnists. Go to town-hall meetings. They are powerful and effective ways to educate lawmakers on topics they may not be aware of. Recruit your co-workers to petition your employer to create an employee advisory group on health benefits. Identify communication sources to continue to stay abreast of what is happening in healthcare.

Transformation is hard. Transforming health and healthcare is critical. Facing a daunting task has never stopped the American people before. The time is now. It is up to you to help us create a 21st Century System of Health and Healthcare to improve the quality of life for every American while saving lives and saving money.

This appendix provides real-life examples of transformation in the healthcare industry. Some highlight high-tech solutions where information technology has facilitated everyday healthcare processes and procedures, saving lives and lowering costs, while others provide low-tech, common-sense resolutions to process-oriented problems. There are also examples of health-management practices that enable individuals to take control of their health to improve wellness through lifestyle and attitude changes.

Transforming Examples
Contents

ActiveHealth Management, Inc. — CareEngine℠ Service

Contact   Lonny Reisman, MD
CEO
ActiveHealth Management, Inc.
95 Madison Avenue
New York, NY 10016

Phone   (212) 651-8201

E-mail   lreisman@ahm-usa.com

Web site   www.activehealthmanagement.com

The Situation

According to the 2002 Institute of Medicine Report, between 44,000 and 98,000 hospital deaths occurred because of medical errors, and an estimated cost of $17 billion can be linked to medical errors. These numbers are outrageous and are primary examples of why the healthcare system must transform, and they do not even include errors on the outpatient side.

The Solution

ActiveHealth Management is a leading provider of evidence-based clinical information and healthcare quality improvement solutions. The company's clinical and technical team has developed a suite of services that empower providers, health plans, and self-insured employer groups to improve healthcare quality, reduce medical errors, and lower overall medical costs.

ActiveHealth's flagship CareEngine℠ Service couples a full spectrum of patient data (i.e., pharmacy, labs, and claims) with proprietary evidence-based clinical rules sets leading to the improved care of individual patients.

The CareEngine^{SM} System combs through high volumes of patient claims, pharmacy, laboratory, and hospital data and applies a series of clinical rules, or "matrices" designed to flag cases in which there may be a problem with the current course of treatment or a medical problem that is not being addressed. The CareEngine^{SM} System identifies problems ranging from potentially disastrous medical errors to instances in which preventive medical tests or treatment protocols are not being delivered.

The CareEngine^{SM} System contains thousands of matrices, based upon thousands of algorithmic elements, designed to identify highly specific patient problems such as misdiagnoses, flawed surgical or medical management, and a variety of pharmacy issues such as drug-to-drug, drug-to-disease, and drug-to-metabolic interactions, or lack of follow-up or preventive treatment. It also uncovers potential conditions that have not been treated including complications presented when a patient has more than one disease. The matrices have been developed over the past six years through literature searches coupled with expert clinical opinion and are reviewed and updated on an ongoing basis.

In the event that aspects of care are incompatible with established standards of clinical appropriateness, the software defines an intervention for that patient which is then validated, and in some cases expanded, by a physician specialist with expertise in the relevant discipline. ActiveHealth's technology detects medical errors by scanning physician, hospital, pharmacy, and laboratory claims for individual patients. The technology then applies the information against evidence-based clinical knowledge for the purpose of identifying patients that are not getting the best care. Once identified ActiveHealth professionals intervene with their practicing physician and necessary critical information.

In addition to staff physicians and nurses who review cases triggered by the CareEngine^{SM} System, ActiveHealth contracts with a panel of physician consultants, all of whom are Board-certified specialists with active teaching appointments at major academic institutions. These panelists are called upon to review complex cases requiring specialist opinion.

In addition, ActiveHealth provides case management, disease management and utilization-management services through its URAC-accredited clinical-services subsidiary. The company also provides population-based, data-analysis services through its Health Data + Management Solutions subsidiary.

Better Health & Lower Costs

Approximately 1.8 million patients are currently enrolled in this program. Enrollment is expected to increase to over 3 million patients in 2003 through contracts with commercial health plans, self-insured employees, and government payers.

Government subscribers include Massachusetts state employees, some FEHB plans, and some Medicare-plus choice plans. In fact ActiveHealth's tools uncovered 20,000 clinical issues in one year in a 56,000 Medicare+ Choice plan.

An academic group also conducted a prospective, randomized clinical study of 50,000 managed-care members by utilizing ActiveHealth Management tools with 25,000 members. The group discovered 2,000 instances where doctors intervened and/or provided recommendations. Using ActiveHealth's tools resulted in the following:

- 15% decrease in hospital bed days per 1000 members
- 19% decrease in hospital paid claims
- 5.5% decrease in overall paid claims

In conclusion, a Health Economic Model has shown that ActiveHealth's tools lower medical costs and provide a return over the program costs of 3 to 7 times for Medicare and Medicaid populations and 1.5 to 4 times for commercial populations. In other words, 2% to 4% savings in medical costs for Medicaid and Medicare populations could be realized (a 3% average savings for 40 million Medicare beneficiaries would save $9 billion annually).

AOM, Inc. — PRIMEXIS™

Contact Pam Martin
CEO
AOM, Inc.
4780 Ashford Dunwoody Road
A-603
Atlanta, GA 30338

Phone (678) 462-8500

E-mail pam_aom@mindspring.com

Web site www.primexis.com

The Situation

The healthcare system is plagued by problems that exist due to barriers between patients and primary-care physicians. Forty-eight percent of all national doctor visits are primary-care visits. However, primary-care physicians are increasingly unable to balance the demands of their workload with available resources—not to mention the fact that doctors are leaving medicine at an alarming rate because they simply cannot afford the cost of insurance because of trial lawyers and medical malpractice. Furthermore, over 45 million Americans are uninsured. Those that have insurance are confronted with increases in cost of coverage, which affects both employers and consumers who face large annual premium increases.

The Solution

AOM is a company born of a vision for the development of innovative solutions to the revenue-management problems currently facing primary-care physicians and other physicians. The company was founded in July of 1998 as a primary-care-practice management company.

AOM's mission is to solve the revenue management problems currently facing primary care and other physicians and to make basic medical services available to more people at lower cost. In January of 1999, AOM, Inc. implemented a pilot of the PRIMEXIS™ payment program, which is a prepaid, non-insurance program allowing a patient up to eight primary-care visits per year at a cost of $30 per patient per month. This product has no exclusionary diagnosis, a low "co-pay" ($10, $15 or $20), and requires NO CLAIMS FILING. The product forwards a monthly or weekly predictable, recurring revenue stream to the provider of care. The product has currently received approval as a non-insurance product in three states and is pending approval in five other states.

PRIMEXIS™ provides a simple solution to the complex problems faced by primary care physicians and healthcare consumers. The PRIMEXIS™ program provides expedited payments to physicians and low-cost access to basic healthcare for consumers—all without the liability, mountains of paperwork, and administrative burdens of conventional healthcare financing. Patients select a primary-care physician who agrees to provide a limited amount of primary-care services in exchange for fixed monthly payments and variable point of service administrative fees. AOM facilitates patient and physician enrollment and manages the electronic collection and transfer of patient payments, of physician compensation, and of fees and commissions paid to resellers, referrers, networks, and agents.

Better Health & Lower Costs

The outcome of the PRIMEXIS™ initiative allows access to primary care (internal medicine, family practice, and pediatrics) for the uninsured and the uninsurable for a low monthly fee. It also allows for a predictable payment of funds to capital-strapped, primary-care locations to improve paper-based systems and hire more nurses. Employers, especially small employers, will be provided with a financially manageable access to care for employees who would otherwise be seen in an emergency room of a hospital. The product, when combined with insurance coverage (such as catastrophic or PPO with high front-end deductible) reduces total "coverage" cost by 20% to 60%.

AOM's primary-care product results in an estimated overall reduction of healthcare costs between 15% and 30%. Costs will be lowered by the elimination of paperwork—cost estimated to be 15 to 30 cents of deposited dollars for physicians and insurance carriers (or self-funded employers).

Another product result is a decrease in premiums as the carriers' point of risk assumption is moved out to the eighth visit. Finally, and most importantly, the "no diagnostic exclusion feature" of the payment product gives the uninsured and/or working poor a real chance to have preventive care and the basic essentials.

Currahee Health Benefits Solutions, Inc.

Contact	Mack Bryson
	CEO
	Currahee Health Benefits Solutions, Inc.
	3575 Koger Boulevard, Suite 200
	Duluth, GA 30096
Phone	(800) 625-7556
E-mail	mack@currahee.net
Web site	www.currahee.net

The Situation

Rising healthcare costs are a reality for companies of all sizes. While many executives might feel powerless to do more than shift costs to employees or offer fewer benefits, there is an alternative. An emerging field of practice called disease management (referred to as health management in this book) helps companies significantly reduce healthcare expenses by identifying and enrolling chronically ill employees in a program that rewards them for becoming accountable for and gaining control of their personal health.

Most people are familiar with the wellness programs offered by local hospitals, community groups, and even some employers. Wellness programs generally reward individuals for adopting healthy lifestyle choices such as losing weight, giving up smoking, or reducing stress. These programs are effective in helping people who are basically healthy improve their quality of life, but there is another population of the working public that suffers from chronic illness—diseases like diabetes, asthma, heart disease, high blood pressure, or high cholesterol. In a typical company, these people comprise approximately 20% of the employees and dependents covered under the health plan.

Drilling down into a company's medical and pharmacy claims data, one can discover that the bulk of the expense of the healthcare plan—probably about 45%—goes to claims for chronic illness. In other words 20% of the insured employees and dependents are responsible for 45% of the health-care costs. Add to that expense the costs of lower productivity that result, and you can begin to see the impact chronic illness has on a business.

Disease management is a relatively new tool that offers a practical solution to this growing problem. Enrolling chronically ill employees in programs that offer them incentives for managing their condition is a proven and effective way to get individuals to take accountability for his or her own health and, in turn, lower costs for employers while increasing productivity through fewer sick days and healthier employees.

The Solution

Currahee Health Benefits Solutions is an Atlanta-based company that designs disease management and pharmacy management for employers who are savvy enough to recognize the financial and productivity benefits that come from a healthy workforce. Currahee's programs are designed to manage an individual's disease in the most cost-effective manner, while improving the quality of care and outcomes. The focus of these services is to target individuals with chronic diseases—many of which may be managed in the home and workplace—saving money and time through early intervention before an acute-care situation occurs. Once enrolled in the program, individuals receive benefits such as waived prescription co-pays, free medical equipment, and/or fitness center memberships.

Currahee is based on proven programs that include case management, educational services, utilization management, medication management, and coordination with the physician's office. Chronic conditions that are targeted include asthma, diabetes, and digestive and cardiovascular disease.

Better Health & Lower Costs

Currahee assigns case managers to help individuals obtain skills to manage their health. Case managers look at national practice standards and ensure the individual is getting the proper care. If not, they help the individual determine why they are not getting it and coach them on the proper questions to pose to their caregivers. Because case managers are in routine contact with individuals gathering medical information from them, they not only help individuals manage their chronic disease they also sometimes help determine other health-related conditions. In some instances this has been lifesaving.

Currahee seeks to provide health plan sponsors with a proven method of identifying and managing healthcare costs and to provide plan enrollees with proven disease management protocols to manage their disease states. For every dollar spent on disease-management programs, employers realize a return of $3 to $5.

One of Currahee's current projects involves the development and management of a chronic disease-management program for five hospitals in semi-rural and rural areas in mid and east Georgia. The purpose of the program is to improve members' health through early identification and management of chronic health conditions as well as through education, prevention, and lifestyle behavior modification. A secondary purpose is to develop a tool that can be used by semi-rural and rural hospitals to assist local self-insured employers in managing chronic illnesses in their populations. This, in turn, creates an additional source of revenue for the hospitals.

The impact of this program is real and justified with clinical results. Of a population of 1,525 individuals eligible to participate in this program, a total of 476 had enrolled in the first 25 months of the combined program (103 individuals enrolled for diabetes services, 99 for hypertension, 37 for high cholesterol, 32 for asthma, 25 for digestive, and 180 for co-morbid). Of the five hospitals, one program has been effective for 25 months, three for 18 months, and one for 6 months as of June 30, 2002.

The Return on Investment = 222% for the combined programs for the period aggregate (ROI=425% for 25-month program, 156% for 18-month program, and 162% for 6-month program.) Full payback of the total program comes as early as six months, and current enrollee rate is continuing to increase (net increase in 2002 was 65.5%).

Evercare™

Contact	John Mach, MD
	CEO
	Evercare™
	9900 Bren Road East
	Minnetonka, MN 55343
Phone	(866) 728-9836
Web site	www.evercareonline.com

The Situation

More than 39 million elderly and disabled Americans receive healthcare through Medicare, and 6 million of them qualify for both Medicare and Medicaid. The oldest Americans tend to be frail, have complex healthcare needs, and reside in nursing homes or assisted-living facilities.

The Solution

Evercare™ is a part of Ovations, one of five operating businesses within UnitedHealth Group. UnitedHealth Group is a diversified health and well-being company that provides a broad spectrum of resources and services to help people achieve improved health and well-being through all stages of life. Evercare™ optimizes the health and well-being of aging, vulnerable, and chronically ill individuals by using nurse practitioners or care managers and physician teams to improve healthcare delivery for individuals residing in nursing homes, assisted living facilities, or in their homes. Evercare™ enhances their quality of life while reducing hospital admissions, potentially harmful drug interactions, and side effects.

Better Health & Lower Costs

Evercare™ focuses on the timely delivery of primary and preventive care. As a result, for individuals enrolled in Evercare's nursing-home program, hospital admission rates are 50% less than comparable nursing-home patients. In fulfillment of federal guidelines, 94% of Evercare™ residents have discussed treatment options for care at the end of their lives. This compares to approximately 57% for other Medicare beneficiaries. Evercare™ has earned a 97% satisfaction rating from enrollees' family members.

As a result of Evercare's comprehensive health assessment, the average number of medications taken by Evercare™ enrollees is substantially less than the number of medications taken by other nursing-home residents. This reduction in medications reduces the chances for harmful drug interactions and side effects.

Evercare™ serves 60,000 Medicare and Medicaid beneficiaries in eleven states and is funded through both the Medicare and Medicaid programs. Approximately $20 billion in hospital costs could be saved over a five-year period if the federal government could implement this system for the costliest 5% of Medicare beneficiaries. This can be accomplished by improving preventive and primary care, and communication and involvement with the family and healthcare providers in the medical decision-making process.

HealthCare Dimensions Incorporated — SilverSneakers®

Contact   Mary Swanson
President and CEO
HealthCare Dimensions Incorporated
9280 South Kyrene Road, Suite 134
Tempe, Arizona 85284

Phone   (800) 295-4993

E-mail   mary.swanson@hcdimensions.com

Web site   www.silversneakers.com

The Situation

According to the Centers for Disease Control and Prevention, chronic diseases such as heart disease, stroke, cancer, and diabetes are among the most prevalent, costly, and preventable of all health problems. The prolonged course of illness and disability from such chronic diseases as diabetes and arthritis results in extended pain and suffering and decreased quality of life for millions of Americans.

The role of regular exercise in preventing or delaying many of these chronic diseases, reducing disability, and improving health and well-being has been well documented in medical literature. According to Medicare Health of Seniors surveys, 88% of older adults have at least one chronic condition and 68% are burdened with multiple conditions. Older adults are a fast growing segment of society, especially with the aging of the baby boomers. Yet according to Healthy People 2010, 51% of adults between 65 and 74 years of age and 65% of adults over age 75 engage in no leisure-time physical activity. Only 14% of older adults report the level of physical activity recommended by the surgeon general and the American College of Sports Medicine.

The Solution

HealthCare Dimensions Incorporated (HCD), founded in 1992, is a healthcare-services company that promotes the health of older adults nationally through unique physical-activity programs and was established on the premise that for managed Medicare to be viable in the long run, cost-effective, preventive benefits need to be incorporated into the care continuum. The company's SilverSneakers® Fitness Program was created to meet this need and has since evolved to become one of the leading senior-exercise programs in the country.

HealthCare Dimensions' vision is to integrate quality senior-fitness programming into communities through health plans and physician settings. It is documented that increasing physical-activity levels in the older adult population can reduce the risk of disability and disease. Health plans can play a significant role in prevention and wellness by providing a fitness benefit for their members. HealthCare Dimensions currently partners with fourteen major health plans across the United States to deliver the SilverSneakers™ Fitness Program to its Medicare-eligible members at no additional cost to the member. The SilverSneakers™ Fitness Program is a unique exercise and social-oriented program designed to encourage older adults to increase their levels of physical activity and motivate them to continue to exercise. SilverSneakers™ is currently available to almost 600,000 Medicare-eligible members at HCD's fourteen health plan partners.

The SilverSneakers™ Fitness Program includes unlimited access to any fitness center in a comprehensive network chosen for location, quality, and senior-friendly service at no cost to the member above his/her monthly health insurance premium. The network of fitness centers include YMCAs, Jewish Community Centers, senior centers, and family-operated fitness centers where all older adults can benefit from quality senior fitness programming.

Better Health & Lower Costs

Enrollment in the SilverSneakers™ Fitness Program has reduced members' high-risk, sedentary behaviors by 70%, and 44% of enrollees report increasing their frequency of physical activity by an average of two days per week. Members report less disability with activities of daily living and higher functional health status. Thus functional health status is maintained over time among active participants. Members also experience lower utilization of high-cost healthcare services over time resulting in the avoidance of preventable costs.

If a program such as SilverSneakers™ was offered through every Medicare+Choice health plan to its families and even 20% of them enrolled, the health plans would avoid over $300 million per year in healthcare costs. If this cost avoidance was extended to tomorrow's 15 million M+C, PPO, and PFFS Medicare recipients, it would top $1 billion per year. If the federal government provided the SilverSneakers™ Fitness Program to all 39 million Medicare beneficiaries, over $3 billion in unnecessary healthcare costs would be avoided.

Maimonides Medical Center, Brooklyn, New York

Contact	Anne C. Sullivan
	Chief Information Officer & Senior Vice President
	Maimonides Medical Center
	1045 39th Street
	Brooklyn, NY 11219
Phone	(718) 283-1877
E-mail	asullivan@maimonidesmed.org

The Situation

It may seem surprising that the site of the nation's first human heart transplant was dependent on keypunch-based processes as late as 1995. While Maimonides Medical Center—Brooklyn's leading tertiary care institution and the nation's third largest teaching hospital—was renowned for the quality of its medical care, its information environment remained in the dark ages.

As an institution with deep roots in the community, this condition had continued for decades. However, the advent of deregulation and managed competition created the need for a new business model requiring prompt access to accurate patient data and financial information. In addition, a renewed focus on patient care and improved outcomes demanded a transition to a computer-based patient record with knowledge-based decision support.

The Solution

In 1996, Maimonides executive management made a commitment—and allocated the resources—for a strong information environment that would improve the quality of care, increase patient satisfaction, reduce costs, and position the hospital for future growth and initiatives. The result is Maimonides Access Clinical System (MACS), a Computer-based Patient Record system that has transformed the delivery of healthcare at Maimonides and serves as a model for other large hospitals nationwide.

Today MACS is used by all of Maimonides attending physicians and residents, as well as more than 120 voluntary/community physicians, for entering orders and reviewing results. This puts the medical center in an elite group of healthcare organizations, as it is estimated that only 4% of hospitals in the U.S. currently have physicians entering orders and obtaining results/reports for patient care electronically.

Implementation of a Computer-based Patient Record system is a major achievement for any healthcare organization. MACS is the only known healthcare information system to incorporate four distinct electronic medical records systems from different vendors:

- Eclipsys 7000 Inpatient Computer-based Patient Record
- NextGen Ambulatory Care Computer-based Patient Record
- E&C IPRob Perinatal Computer-based Patient Record
- A4 Health Systems Emergency Department Computer-based Patient Record

Today Maimonides' integrated Computer-based Patient Record solution is used by all employed and community physicians and residents who enter orders on-line, review drug interactions, ancillary results, and digital images as well as fully document and chart clinical information. This is true for every inpatient unit, including all critical care areas and psychiatry. Utilizing concurrent decision-support and embedded capabilities, intelligent rules engines provide clinical staff with treatment recommendations, diagnostic guidelines, and suggested medical dosages. Ancillary departments access MACS to view the status of tests, while nurses use the system to document clinical information, dispense medication, and select charge information. All users can retrieve appropriate clinical data and results, including users in remote hospital locations and community physician offices.

Better Health & Lower Costs

Benefits have been remarkable. The medical center has seen a 68% decrease in medication-processing time, a 55% decrease in medication discrepancies, and a 58% reduction in problem medication orders. Duplication of ancillary orders has decreased by 20% overall, including a 48% reduction in duplicate laboratory/chemistry tests. Over a seven-year period, accessibility of clinical data has improved time of diagnosis and treatment, contributing to a 2.21 day (30.4%) reduction in average length of patient stay. These improvements have enabled 32,168 additional inpatients to be served by the medical center, representing over $50 million in increased revenue, one-quarter of which is attributable to the Computer-based Patient Record.

Many elements have contributed significantly to the success of the project and if omitted, or poorly executed, could have derailed it. Foremost among these was establishing programs and methodologies aimed at physician participation, buy-in, and ownership. Other key factors included building a clinically-focused MIS staff, selecting appropriate vendor partners, conducting training to meet the needs of all user constituencies, and winning the support of key leaders and advocates. The result is an information-system environment that has brought dramatic improvements to the delivery of patient care while positioning Maimonides to continue to fulfill its mission as a world-class medical institution in the years ahead.

Mayo Clinic, Jacksonville, Florida

Contact   John J. Mentel, MD
Chair, Department of Applied Informatics
Mayo Clinic Jacksonville
4500 San Pablo Road
Jacksonville, FL 32224

Phone   (904) 953-2000

E-mail   Mentel.john@mayo.edu

Web site   www.mayoclinic.org or www.mayoclinic.com

The Situation

Paper-based practice of medicine decreases the productivity of doctors while increasing both patient waiting time and the opportunity for medical errors. However, the shift to an electronic healthcare era is well behind the times. The business world has transformed, or is in the process of transforming, to electronic procedures and records. It is time for the healthcare industry to follow suit.

The Solution

The Automated Clinical Practice (ACP) at Mayo Clinic in Jacksonville, Florida was a project undertaken in 1993 to encompass the computer-based patient record with the addition of the mechanisms for automated charging and order creation by physicians. This vision was crystallized and communicated as the "paperless" practice of medicine that would increase patient safety and improve physician effectiveness while at the same time driving down expenses. The last paper-based record was circulated in January 1996, and the integrated outpatient practice continues to the present day, with 445,000 patient visits conducted during 2002 with the computer-based patient record.

The Mayo Clinic uses a team approach to provide medical diagnosis, treatment, and surgery. This integrated system makes it possible for patients to get evaluations, tests, and treatments in one place and in a coordinated way. Physicians and allied-health staff provide quality, compassionate care. Their goal is to meet the needs of every patient every day. Because Mayo Clinic is a tertiary care center, most physicians are specialists with in-depth knowledge of specific diseases and new treatment and research breakthroughs. Their easy access to colleagues and Mayo's emphasis on teamwork allow medical problems to be evaluated and treated thoroughly. All Mayo physicians are salaried. Their compensation is not based on the number of tests ordered or procedures done. Mayo's patient-care activities are strengthened by programs in medical education and research. Patients who need hospitalization are admitted to nearby St. Luke's Hospital, a Mayo Clinic hospital with 289 private rooms.

Better Health & Lower Costs

The Automated Clinical Practice rollout involves all clinical users and not only certain groups. Paper medical records have not been circulated since 1996 and are currently not even available on-site. The areas that are automated now include most aspects of the practice.
Some examples are:

- An electronic medical record including all clinical documents, orders, scheduling, and laboratory.
- A fully electronic filmless radiology department with speech recognition for radiologist documentation.
- An automated Intensive Care Unit with Electronic Medical Record integration and bedside medical device interfaces directly to the EMR.
- Inpatient and outpatient surgery areas consisting of surgical scheduling, material management, and nursing documentation.
- And many others . . .

From this level of automation, patient-safety initiatives have been possible. For example:

- Orders automatically generating task lists for nursing, respiratory, etc. in the hospital.
- Automated fall risk assessment and Braden skin scale assessment in the hospital.
- A medical data warehouse that allows free text searching against the entire repository of millions and millions of documents in the electronic medical record for patient care and research.
- An infectious disease application that allows bioterrorism surveillance and automated infection control monitoring.

Dictating notes shifted work from the physician and improved both legibility and medical record turnaround time. The system allowed for real-time availability of clinical information (notes, lab, X-ray, and other results), automatic checking for duplicate redundant orders, simultaneous access to the same patient chart, improved ability to answer ad hoc questions for patient calls, more timely response from physicians when they have questions, and improved flow of information to the physician enabling him or her to have a more "complete" picture of what is known about the patient's condition at the time of the appointment. The estimated expenditure to date is $21 million on the automated practice at Mayo Clinic Jacksonville. Whether using extremely conservative data or results that are more realistic but more difficult to capture precisely, the estimated savings after expenses are $2.8 to $7.1 million annually. Thus the system paid for itself by the fourth year in financial savings alone, without counting improvements in patient health, saving doctors' time, and minimizing errors.

Northwestern Memorial Hospital

Contact	Holli Salls
	Vice President, Marketing/Public Relations
	Northwestern Memorial Hospital
	251 E. Huron Street
	Feinberg, Floor 3, Suite 710
	Chicago, IL 60611
Phone	(312) 926-2121
E-mail	hsalls@nmh.org
Web site	www.nmh.org

The Situation

A nosocomial (hospital-acquired) infection is a specific illness that develops as a result of hospitalization. The incidence of these infections continues to increase as our population ages and more individuals have abnormalities in their immune systems, making them less able to fight new infections. In addition to the impact on individual patients, these infections extend length of stay in hospitals by 6 million days annually and increase cost by $7 billion each year. Nosocomial infections are spread throughout hospitals when staff members do not wash their hands between patient visits or practice other important infection-control activities.

There are many reasons why healthcare workers do not wash their hands or comply with well-accepted methods to reduce or prevent nosocomonial infections. Healthcare workers report that time constraints, inconvenience of sink locations, and a sense of discomfort when washing their hands in front of patients all contribute to their lack of compliance with infection-control initiatives.

The Solution

In 1999, Northwestern Memorial Hospital opened a new, 492-bed hospital and medical center in downtown Chicago. A team of infectious-disease specialists, microbiologists, pharmacists, infection-control professionals, and administrators developed a comprehensive, multidisciplinary approach to combat nosocomial infections as part of the new hospital. This included the installation of dedicated sinks for healthcare workers at the entrance to every patient room. Subsequently when the Centers for Disease Control and Prevention (CDC) recommended the use of alcohol-based, waterless gel, Northwestern Memorial installed dispensers in every patient room as well as throughout the medical center. In addition, the entire hospital has special filters (high efficiency particulate air or HEPA) to reduce the risk of certain fungal infections. Special rooms were designed for patients with communicable diseases such as tuberculosis and chicken pox so that these infections would not be transmitted to other patients or staff. Finally, all flooring, wall coverings, ceiling tiles, fabrics, and counter-tops were carefully selected with the intent of reducing infections and improving patient safety.

The success of this program has been nationally recognized as Northwestern Memorial was recently awarded the prestigious 10th Annual Modern Healthcare Excellence in Healthcare Risk Management Award. The title of the winning submission was "Improving Patient Safety Through Quality Promotion and Infection Prevention: Northwestern Memorial's Comprehensive Infection Control Program." Northwestern has also been designated as one of seven Prevention Epicenters by the CDC.

Better Health & Lower Costs

Not all transformation initiatives have to be high-tech. Northwestern Memorial Hospital's solutions are low-tech, common-sense solutions that have dramatically changed outcomes and quality of care. In fact Northwestern Memorial Hospital's nosocomial infection rate of 2.1% is less than half of the U.S. average (4.5%) despite the complexity of its patient population. Northwestern Memorial's comprehensive solution lowered healthcare costs and shortened patient hospital stays. If the experience at Northwestern Memorial could be replicated throughout the country, the entire healthcare system could benefit, $3.6 billion could be saved annually just by not having to treat hospital-acquired infections.

Pfizer — Florida "Healthy State" Program

Contact	John Sory
	Vice President
	235 East 42nd Street
	New York, NY 10017-5755
Phone	(212) 573-7201
E-mail	soryj@pfizer.com
Web site	www.pfizerhealthsolutions.com

The Situation

The State of Florida, operating the fourth largest Medicaid program in the U.S., faced a $650 million Medicaid budget shortfall in 2001. The state proposed reimbursement reductions for medical services and supplemental rebates from pharmaceutical manufacturers but was willing to consider proposals addressing the underlying health risks of the population to address the root cause of rising expenditures.

One of every ten Americans suffers from chronic disease, and medical costs for people with chronic diseases account for more than 70% of the $1 trillion spent on healthcare each year in the U.S. As in many parts of the country, low-income Floridians with chronic illnesses seek care designed to treat acute symptoms rather than addressing the underlying causes of chronic diseases.

In the haste to locate a provider for their symptoms, Medicaid patients often end up using the emergency department for primary-care services, an expensive, inefficient solution that drives up the overall cost of healthcare. In fact, Medicaid patients are more than twice as likely as other non-Medicaid patients with the same type of illnesses to be admitted to the hospital via the emergency room because of an acute event.

The Solution

A unique public-private partnership was created between Pfizer, Inc. and Florida's Agency for Health Care Administration involving the implementation of a large-scale, statewide disease management (or health management as depicted in this book) program that employs a patient-centered health approach for Medicaid beneficiaries suffering from heart failure, diabetes, hypertension, asthma, and any related co-morbidities and maps the intensity of the care treatment to the disease and risk severity of the individual. This network of 55 care managers at ten local hospitals taps into the experience and resources of community organizations and local physicians across the state. These specially trained and supported care managers reach more than 11,000 high risk patients on a consistent basis to help them better navigate the healthcare system, connect and interact with physicians, understand their health conditions, and take positive steps to stay healthy. In nearly all cases, individuals participating in the program have received more medical attention for their conditions than ever before. It also touches an additional 76,000 lower-risk patients through a broad array of educational interventions and 24-hour telephonic nursing support. The program has delivered more than 16,000 home-health aids such as blood-pressure cuffs for hypertensive patients, weight scales for heart-failure patients, and peak-flow meters and spacers for asthmatics while coordinating care with providers, conducting home visits, and monitoring all clinical measures.

Pfizer is currently working on the extension of disease-management services in Florida and to the creation of similar programs tailored to the Medicaid environments in other states. Concurrently, Pfizer, through its Pfizer Health Solutions group, implements and supports disease-management programs across nearly 100 sites with commercial and Medicare populations.

Better Health & Lower Costs

The Healthy State program guarantees to save the state $33 million over two years. The combined results to date include a 15% decrease in patient hospital days/1000, and a 7% decrease in Emergency Department visits/1000.

Not only have patient stays decreased but individual behavior has improved through increased awareness and better self-management. The following are a few examples of some of the outcomes:

- 70% of heart failure patients enrolled in the program are weighing, recording, and reporting their weights; an increase of 47%. Inpatient hospital days decreased by 17% in this population.
- The hypertensive population has an overall improvement in blood pressure of 45%, and their inpatient hospitalization days/1000 decreased by 6%.
- 56% of asthma patients now use peak-flow meters to assess their own conditions, up from 25%. Asthmatic inpatient hospital days/1000 decreased by 38% and Emergency Department visits/1000 decreased by 17%.
- 96% of people with diabetes are performing preventive foot exams and Emergency Department visits of people with diabetes have decreased by 17%.

Pittsburgh Regional Healthcare Initiative

Contact   Kenneth T. Segel
Director
Centre City Tower
650 Smithfield Street, Suite 2150
Pittsburgh, PA 15222

Phone   (412) 535-0292

E-mail   ksegel@prhi.org

Web site   www.prhi.org

National Funders   Centers for Medicare and Medicaid Services (CMS)
Centers for Disease Control and Prevention (CDC)
Agency for Healthcare Research and Quality (AHRQ)
Robert Wood Johnson Foundation (RWJF)

The Situation

In Southwestern Pennsylvania, healthcare is the largest sector of the economy, employing one in eight workers and conducting more than $7.2 billion in business. Yet in 1998, as civic leaders began formulating an ambitious regional renewal, the industry was under growing pressure with bankruptcies, operating losses, consolidations, and difficulty retaining qualified workers. Purchasers bemoaned the high cost of care; the region's quality indicators did not set national records.

To address these challenges, the Pittsburgh Regional Healthcare Initiative (PRHI) was formed under the leadership of then Alcoa Chairman Paul O'Neill and the Jewish Healthcare Foundation of Pittsburgh.

The Solution

PRHI's approach to redesigning healthcare requires cooperation among previously competing interests. In addition to hundreds of clinicians, PRHI's members include 40 hospitals, 4 major insurers, over 30 major and small-business healthcare purchasers, dozens of corporate and civic leaders, and Pennsylvania's attorney general. This divergent group united in endorsing one guiding principle: healthcare delivery must focus on providing perfect care to every patient.

PRHI partners have come to realize that the challenges facing healthcare are symptoms of the same root problem: not faulty people, but faulty, error-prone systems that do not focus on patients at the point of care. Every patient intervention must become an opportunity to learn, share what they learn across the entire region, and apply the discoveries.

Goals: PRHI partners signed formal commitments to collaborate on ways to accelerate progress toward these goals:

- Zero medication errors
- Zero hospital-acquired infections
- The best patient outcomes in the following areas:
    - Coronary artery bypass graft surgery
    - Hip- and knee-replacement surgery
    - Maternal and infant outcomes
    - Diabetes
    - Depression

In pursuit of these goals, PRHI supports three sequential levels of shared learning and improvement:

Working Groups/Registries

PRHI partners have constructed formal mechanisms for bringing the scientific method into the care of every patient in the region. Examples include:

- Coronary artery bypass graft surgery:
    - Regional Cardiac Registry, with all partner cardiac surgery centers collecting and sharing data on numerous processes of care, to help determine which processes help patients return to health sooner and

more completely. The registry is supported by the Centers for Medicare and Medicaid Services.

- Quarterly Cardiac Forums, where representatives from the partner cardiac surgery centers review and discuss the most recent outcomes data.

• Perfect treatment for diabetes and depression: this group of clinicians is working with insurers and quality-improvement organizations on a model that will provide all of the area's primary-care physicians with up-to-the-minute information on the status of each patient's lab values and the last time various tests were performed.

Real-time reporting and root-cause problem-solving systems

When errors are buried, the opportunity to learn from them is lost. The goal for this area of the initiative is for every medication error to be reported and investigated to root cause within 24 hours, as close as possible to where the work is done, and shared immediately with everyone in the organization.

Real-time reporting provides a searing contrast the with way error reporting and investigation are usually done in healthcare, placing enormous demands on leaders and forcing institutions to become adept at solving problems rapidly. The real-time reporting system is inspired by the one in use at Alcoa, where the lost workday rate is now 36 times better than the average American hospital.

To make real-time error reporting work, PRHI field managers visit hospitals across the region helping them install and put to fullest use the MedMARx medication error reporting system. Each hospital also has access to the Centers for Disease Control and Prevention's National Nosocomial Infection Surveillance System (NNIS) for tracking hospital-acquired infections.

Reporting, learning, and improvement take place when employees feel professionally safe and when top hospital management creates a blame-free, non-punitive environment along with the expectation that every error will be reported. Introducing MedMARx into a professionally safe environment as a tool for reporting and solving every error within 24 hours offers hospitals a means of accelerating progress toward zero medication errors through rapid, decentralized problem-solving.

Perfecting the Patient Care System

For organizations that have made a full commitment to safety and decentralized problem solving, PRHI has introduced a way to design organizations to: a) allow everyone to learn from errors and problems, and b) improve healthcare delivery processes quickly, frequently, and at low cost. PRHI adapted the Perfecting Patient Care (PPC) System for use in healthcare from the principles of the Toyota Production System. PRHI currently includes:

- Learning Lines. In several hospital units in the region, PPC Learning Lines, unique problem-solving laboratories, design solutions to problems that interfere with meeting patient needs. Working with a team leader, those on the Learning Lines apply scientific discipline to solving problems one by one, immediately, in the course of work.
- Shared Learning. Participants may enroll in classes to learn more about the application of Perfecting Patient Care principles in the course of work.

  - The PPC Introductory Session provides a chance to learn the basics of the Perfecting Patient Care System (PPC). This interactive learning session, based on a Harvard hospital case study, is an opportunity to get better acquainted with the PPC process and how it works.

  - The PPC University is an intensive, four-day course where participants "learn by doing." It is based on the original design from Harvard Business School and Alcoa, Inc. The four-day session varies in format with case studies, role-playing, videos, mini-exercises, a book discussion, and presentations-augmented with observations on a hospital learning line. The PPC University has been recognized by the Accreditation Council for Continuing Medical Education (ACCME) which grants 0.27 continuing education units (CEUs) to those who complete it.

  - National Clinical Improvement Network (NCIN). Across the country, organizations and individuals are building knowledge about how to improve healthcare delivery systems in a complex environment. PRHI founded NCIN as a way to connect people focusing on point of care improvements in an authentic way through site visits. Eventually, NCIN hopes to develop a quality partnership with a federal working group so some federal policymakers might have a place to come and learn about problem solving at the point of care. NCIN participants include:

- Rochester Health Commission, NY
- Sutter Health System, Sacramento, CA
- Luther Midlefort, Mayo Health System, Eau Claire, WI
- Atlantic Health System, NJ
- 5 Intermountain Healthcare, Salt Lake City, UT
- Institute For Clinical Systems Improvement, Bloomington, MN
- The Reinertzen Group, Alta, WY
- Jcaho, Oakbrook Terrace, IL
- Northern New England Cardiovascular Study Group, Manchester, NH

Better Health & Lower Costs

In Pittsburgh an entire region is working together with relentless focus on solving problems at the point of patient care. Doing so will improve the quality of care for every patient, improve working conditions for healthcare workers, and reduce waste and opportunities for error endemic in today's system.

Summary of progress to date:
- Regional baselines have been established in all five clinical conditions: cardiac, orthopedics, obstetrics, diabetes, and depression.
- Regional baselines have been established in two classes of infection: methicyllin-resistant staphylococcus aureus and central-line associated bloodstream infections in intensive care units.
- Over 7,000 medication errors were reported and shared last year— 18% of the national MedMARx total.

• A state report published in 2000 shows the Pittsburgh region to have the lowest post-CABG mortality in the state—a point from which PRHI hopes to accelerate improvement.

Local Community Funders:

Aetna U.S. Healthcare Foundation
Alcoa Foundation
Allegheny Technologies, Inc.
AT&T
Claude Worthington Benedum Foundation
Dietrich Industries, Inc.
Dollar Bank Foundation

Equitable Resources
Federated Investors, Inc.
FedEx Ground Package System, Inc.
Giant Eagle, Inc.
The Hillman Foundation, Inc.
Kirkpatrick & Lockhart, LLP
McKesson HBOC Automated Healthcare

Mellon Financial Corporation
Richard King Mellon Foundation
Mine Safety Appliances Company
The Pittsburgh Foundation
PPG Foundation
PNC Financial Services Group
SMC Business Councils
USS Foundation, Inc.

Problem-Knowledge Coupler (PKC) Corporation

Contact   Howard Pierce
CEO
PKC Corporation
One Mill Street
Burlington, VT 05401-1530

Phone   (800) 752-5351

E-mail   hpierce@pkc.com

Web site   www.pkc.com

The Situation

Healthcare practitioners are required to recall, match, process, and apply large volumes of complex information at the point of care. Utilizing this medical knowledge consistently and reliably is beyond the capacity of even the best human mind, given the time and resource constraints of the healthcare environment. Any mature industry looks for tools to assist with this sort of dilemma. Consumers of healthcare services are logically being encouraged to accept more responsibility for their healthcare decisions, but without easy-to-use aids, they lack the clear and personalized information needed to take on that responsibility.

The Solution

Problem-Knowledge Coupler (PKC) Corporation is working to create a future in which people are given knowledge tools for making healthcare decisions. Patients and providers will use these tools to evaluate problems more efficiently and reliably than can the unaided mind working under the time constraints of everyday practice. These tools serve as an intellectual loom for weaving together patient-specific information and medical knowledge from every specialty into the fabric of care. They will free us from the predictable limitations and errors of the unaided human mind.

PKC bridges this gap between the vast world of medical literature and well-informed medical decisions with its medical-guidance software tools called Problem-Knowledge Couplers, or simply Couplers. Couplers are software tools that prompt both the patient and provider to input all the relevant data for a problem (utilizing the patient's time and knowledge of the problem details). For over 100 separate health topics, Couplers ask an extensive list of relevant questions that the consumer/patient can easily answer. These personalized answers, along with physical exam and lab information added by a healthcare provider, allow the Couplers system to instantly assemble very specific and up-to-date medical guidance and a full range of the patient's options. The patient and provider are then equipped to make the best and safest decisions. Couplers are the ideal communication tools for patient and provider, and the most thorough encounter documentation system ever.

Better Health & Lower Costs

A basic requirement for a mature healthcare industry is the adoption of tools like Couplers. They will extend the mind of the provider much like the x-ray extended the eyes and the stethoscope extended the ears. A second requirement will be a more sensible division of labor where the patient's time is leveraged and tools like Couplers permit non-physician providers to do far more of the work, thus optimizing the physician's time and expertise. The Department of Defense has embedded Couplers tools into their new Electronic Medical Record (CHCSII) and licenses the Couplers tools across their entire medical enterprise.

In conclusion, having the knowledge in the tools saves time and money and helps avoid dangerous and costly mistakes. For example, the Veterans Administration tested the Couplers tools and found them a far better alternative for managing chronic disease. Their study extrapolated a savings over four years of $800,000 in a population of 38 chronic diabetics. Another separate study of a group practice using Couplers found a single primary-care provider with two nurse practitioners could profitably manage a panel of over 4,000 patients with high patient satisfaction.

PRMsoft

Contact Robert Sbriglio, MD, MPH
          Chief Medical Officer
          PRMsoft, Inc.
          7365 Main Street #275
          Stratford, CT 06614-1300

Phone (203) 410-7594

E-mail DrBob@PRMsoft.com

Web site www.prmsoft.com

The Situation

Healthcare providers are finding it increasingly difficult to deliver quality care in the face of declining reimbursement and mounting regulations and costs. The long-term-care industry has been particularly hard hit in recent years with declining Medicare funding and shrinking Medicaid reimbursement.

In this environment of constrained resources, most nursing homes operate with inefficient, handwritten, paper-based clinical records that decrease the productivity of nursing caregivers, increase patient waiting time, and raise the risk of medical errors. This has contributed to caregiver frustration, patient and family dissatisfaction, and quality-care problems in this vulnerable population. Under these conditions, it is very difficult to deliver patient-centric healthcare.

Because of inadequate software, nurses are spending too much time on paperwork and not enough time with patients. This has contributed to the current severe shortage of nurses in the United States. Nursing-home patients and their families could be better served if a simple, advanced information technology existed that could enable nurses to access, document, and share clinical patient information in real time.

The Solution

PRMsoft is a provider of integrated-workflow software for the long-term-care industry. PRM stands for Patient Relationship Management—a patented business-process methodology that describes how a real-time healthcare information system with authorized access by all interested parties can utilize Customer Relationship Management (CRM) principles and deliver patient-centric care, improve patient/family satisfaction, and improve clinical and financial outcomes.

The company's Web-based software puts CRM into healthcare, focusing on patient/customer service, satisfaction, and retention. The software also views healthcare-facility employees as "internal customers" giving them software tools that facilitate workflow and enabling them to provide care in a more satisfying manner.

A suite of integrated modules are accessed locally or remotely over the Internet through a simple, Web-browser user interface. These modules help nursing-home caregivers deliver more customer-focused healthcare by allowing them to document care more rapidly and efficiently, enabling them to save time and spend more time with patients.

Since the software is Web-based, written in open standards, and platform-independent, it is "future ready," able to integrate with other open-standard Web applications and business-to-business commerce solutions.

Better Health & Lower Costs

The PRMsoft software facilitates everyday healthcare processes and procedures, thus improving quality of care and lowering costs. The system increases efficiency, improves productivity, and facilitates regulatory compliance. It provides clinical alerts in real time, improves workflow efficiencies, and reduces administrative overhead. Clinical managers are provided with real-time information on resident outcomes, staff performance, and task completion.

The system has provided significant time savings. Caregivers and other nursing-facility staff including nurses, rehabilitation therapists, social workers, and recreational therapists each report saving up to one hour/day/shift with electronic documentation over paper records. This has enabled them to spend more time with patients and other care-related activities.

Regarding reduced expenses and improved productivity, one study revealed that following the introduction of the PRMsoft system, the average monthly nursing over time was reduced by 20%, mostly due to time saved with electronic over paper documentation. A survey revealed that rehabilitation-therapist productivity increased as much as 25% following implementation of PRMsoft's electronic medical record. Each rehabilitation therapist reported saving approximately one hour/day on their shift, allowing them to spend more time on patient treatments and less time on documentation. The electronic medical record also eliminated wasted time searching or waiting for paper medical records to become available.

There are other benefits to the system. The accessibility of clinical data has improved collaboration that has contributed to more efficient and effective care. The system has provided for improved legibility and quality of documentation, has increased revenue capture, and has improved staff recruitment. There is a high satisfaction level with managed-care case managers who are able to review typed progress notes rather than often-illegible handwriting.

The PRMsoft electronic medical record software system provides a strong information environment that has brought dramatic improvements in the delivery of nursing-home care. The system serves as a model for nursing homes nationwide demonstrating the advantages of low cost, browser-based software and how it can be used to improve clinical and financial outcomes which in today's modern healthcare environment is the "point of caring.

RelayHealth

Contact	Eric Zimmerman
	Senior Vice President, Marketing
	RelayHealth Corporation
	1900 Powell Street, Suite 600
	Emeryville, CA 94608
Phone	(510) 428-7820
E-mail	eric@relayhealth.com
Web site	www.relayhealth.com

The Situation

Individuals and payers face spiraling increases in healthcare costs with few solutions in sight. In fact total health benefit costs for active employees rose by over 14% from 2001 to 2002, reaching $5,616 per employee. Individuals are shouldering a greater share of cost as employers shift costs onto employees.

Technological advances are emerging that could help lower some of these healthcare costs. According to the PricewaterhouseCoopers' Healthcare 2010 Report, 20% of doctors' office visits could be replaced by on-line visits by 2010. An April 2002 Harris Interactive poll, stated that over 90% of U.S. adults with on-line access would like to be able to communicate with their own doctor on-line. Over half say that on-line access to their doctor would influence their choice of doctor or health plan.

The Solution

RelayHealth has pioneered secure, structured HIPAA-ready, on-line, doctor-patient communication services. RelayHealth features include a full array of messaging options—supporting appointment requests, medication refill requests, referral requests, lab results, and a clinically structured interchange surrounding a non-urgent medical issue, called a WebVisitSM. A growing list of health plans have begun reimbursing physicians for WebVisits conducted with their members based on the outcomes of a large-scale, independently controlled study sponsored by Blue Shield of California and others.

Independent researchers confirmed that RelayHealth's secure e-communication service significantly reduces healthcare costs while generating high levels of doctor and patient satisfaction.

Better Health & Lower Costs

A research team led by Laurence Baker, Ph.D., Chief of Health Services Research at the Stanford University School of Medicine, analyzed claims data for treatment patients with access to RelayHealth and found statistically significant reductions in spending, compared to a matched control group without access to the service. Reduction in office-based spending was $1.92 per member, per month; with total spending reduced by over $3.00 per member, per month. These reductions compared favorably to claims paid out for webVisits, which totaled $0.31 per member, per month.

Patients reported improved access to their physicians, and most physicians surveyed preferred webVisits to office visits for patients with non-urgent medical needs. The majority of patients found the service convenient (78%), easy to use (71%), and of good to excellent quality, when compared to an office visit (66%). Over half reported improved access to their doctor.

Most physicians found the service easy to use (72%), satisfying (63%), and over half (56%) preferred webVisits to office visits for patients with non-urgent medical needs.

On the strength of these results, Blue Shield of California and ConnectiCare have each announced plans to expand their programs through which physicians are reimbursed for WebVisits with their members. Other payers are now contracting to reimburse for WebVisits with announcements forthcoming. Over a dozen major health systems and medical groups around the country have now contracted to implement RelayHealth in their medical practices.

The results of the study demonstrate the benefits of offering non-urgent on-line care, one of the few instances in healthcare where payers, medical groups, physicians, and patients alike all benefit. With healthcare costs spiraling upward, WebVisits are practical, cost efficient, and satisfying for all participants and can make a meaningful impact on a health plan's bottom line.

In addition, HIPAA privacy regulations will make standard e-mail a decidedly unattractive option for doctor/patient communication. Medical groups will demand the clinical quality and structure the RelayHealth service provides to limit liability and ensure reimbursement.

On-line doctor/patient e-communication has the potential to save tens of millions of dollars annually in healthcare costs for a typical health plan while satisfying members and improving access to care. These savings can translate into reduced costs for employers and individuals and reduction in rates of uninsured and underinsured—which rise as out of pocket costs rise.

It also provides an alternate way for physicians to treat their existing patients with non-urgent needs, which frees schedule time for sicker patients, and improves service levels for all patients.

Stanford University — SKOLAR MD

Contact	Sue Sweeney
	Vice President
	1860 Embarcadero Road
	Palo Alto, CA 94303
Phone	(650) 354-3008
E-mail	information@skolar.com
Web site	www.skolar.com

The Situation

There are approximately 650,000 practicing physicians in the United States, and ongoing continuing medical education (CME) is required for physician licensure. The purpose of continuing education is to ensure that physicians are thoroughly up-to-date on the latest medical knowledge. An average of 25 hours per year of continuing education is required in most states. Today it is believed that the "half-life" of medical knowledge is about ten years, meaning that within ten years of completing post-graduate work, a doctor's medical practice knowledge is 50% outdated. Traditional, didactic Continuing Medical Education (CME) has not been shown to affect change in practice behavior.

A recent survey at Stanford University determined that on average physicians were posed with four to eight questions per day that went unanswered due to 1) a lack of time to research the questions, 2) not having the right information at their fingertips, and 3) poor organization and indexing of the information they did have. Another study at the University of Iowa College of Medicine published in the August 7, 1999 British Medical

Journal estimated that family physicians have 3.2 questions for every ten patient visits. These questions often go unanswered because of the lack of readily available knowledge resources.

The Solution

To take advantage of the huge advances in computer-processing power and speed to allow doctors to take a self-directed approach to problem solving and learning, Stanford University developed an on-line searchable database that gives physicians rapid access to well-organized, up-to-date information from an integrated set of peer-reviewed medical sources. Stanford SKOLAR MD is a medical knowledge base that provides physicians with integrated knowledge from textbooks, drug databases, practice guidelines, MEDLINE, and journal articles. Physicians using the system can obtain continuing medical education credit for the time spent researching questions arising from real patient cases.

In February 2001, the American Medical Association approved Stanford SKOLAR MD as the first participant in a new pilot program evaluating physician-initiated and physician self-directed, Internet-based continuing medical education. Dr. Dennis Wentz, director, Continuing Professional Development, American Medical Association believes that "the Internet is an increasingly important source of information for physicians."

Better Health & Lower Costs

Stanford SKOLAR MD has received 3,050 applications for continuing medical education from 845 applicants and has awarded a total of 1,534 continuing medical education hours. On 93% of the applications, the applicant found the answer to his or her medical question. On 94% of the applications, the applicant would apply his or her answer clinically.

Since many medical errors stem from knowledge gaps and incomplete drug information, and since physicians are able to answer most of their questions with SKOLAR, widespread adoption of SKOLAR would lead to a significant reduction in medical errors.

ThedaCare, Inc. — Touchpoint Health Plan

Contact   John Toussaint, MD
President and CEO
ThedaCare, Inc.
P.O. Box 8025
Appleton, WI 54912-8025

Phone   (920) 831-6706

E-mail   john.toussaint@thedacare.org

Web site   www.thedacare.org

The Situation

Nearly half of the U.S. population, more than 125 million Americans, suffers from some sort of chronic medical condition. Care of these chronic conditions accounts for 60% of healthcare spending, which topped $1.4 trillion in 2001 and is estimated to grow to $3.1 trillion by 2012. Unfortunately, in spite of overwhelming evidence that standardization of care for these conditions reduces complications, decreases costs, and improves quality of life, there remains wide variation in the care these patients receive.

This variation is exacerbated by backlogs in patient appointments within most physician practices, poor tracking of chronic disease populations, and inefficient or fragmented systems to prompt the delivery of preventive care.

The Solution

ThedaCare™ is a community-owned health system of three acute-care hospitals, more than 100 primary-care physicians practicing at 22 sites, and multiple other healthcare related businesses and services including Touchpoint™ Health Plan, which is owned in partnership with area physicians and Bellin Health of Green Bay.

Understanding that the care of chronic disease is the greatest medical and economic challenge facing healthcare, in 1998, ThedaCare and Touchpoint embarked on a four-pronged strategy to better manage chronic disease with the goal of improving clinical quality, reducing costs, and improving patient satisfaction.

1. Development of a common information technology platform encompassing all aspects of our health system—hospitals, physician practices, and the health plan—including an electronic medical record and computers in the exam room.
2. Development of a system-wide "data warehouse" to track and prompt the treatment of patients with diabetes, coronary artery disease and other chronic diseases in real time.
3. Adoption of physician-driven, evidence-based standards for preventive care as well as management of chronic disease.
4. Conversion to an "Open Access" model of clinical office practice with the goal of seeing all patients who want to be seen the same day and delivering all needed services during that one episode of care (max care), in contrast to the "old world" system of packed schedules and significant delays for appointments for all but the most acute patients.

Each of these strategies has been a key component to successfully managing chronic disease. Without the common electronic platform among all parts of the system, it would be impossible for the data warehouse to collect information about patients with chronic disease or report these results to treating physicians. Without physician-driven standards of care, including education of all providers about those standards and training of office staffs, the data warehouse would be useless. Conversion to "Open Access" means more patients are being seen when they want to be seen and are receiving more preventive and chronic care each time they are seen.

Here is an example of how this works. Mrs. Smith has diabetes and also has coronary artery disease. One day Mrs. Smith awakens with a severe sore throat, logs on to her computer at home, and makes an appointment for that afternoon with her physician who is on an "Open Access" schedule. While on-line, Mrs. Smith uses the secure Web portal to detail all of her current symptoms. After arriving for her appointment, the nurse checks Mrs. Smith's electronic record, which queries the data warehouse and informs the nurse that Mrs. Smith is due for blood tests to check her blood sugar and her cholesterol for both her diabetes and her heart disease. She also determines Mrs. Smith is overdue for her screening mammogram. Mrs. Smith agrees to the blood tests and also allows the nurse to schedule a mammogram. Mrs. Smith is shown to an exam room where her physician, who orders a throat culture, examines her. The physician tells her she may have strep throat, and assures her that he will review all of her tests and call her if there are any problems. Otherwise, he tells her she can review the tests on-line later that evening after he reviews the results, and invites her to call or e-mail with any questions. He orders bed rest and Tylenol as needed.

By the end of 2003, this "ideal" world will be the "real world" in every ThedaCare practice. The best care is predicated on readily accessible, real-time information about a patient's most current health status. Understanding that each individual is ultimately responsible for his or her individual health, patient access to his or her personal medical information via secure connection through the Internet is critical. By the end of this year (2003), all of our primary care patients will be able to review their information, schedule their own appointments, refill their prescriptions, e-mail their physician, and research and track their own chronic conditions using a Web portal from their home computer.

Better Health & Lower Costs

Last year ThedaCare and Touchpoint's diabetes-management program prevented nearly 40 major complications among 3,400 diabetes patients for a savings of more than $4 million. Based on the latest HEDIS® data, The National Committee for Quality Assurance says ThedaCare and Touchpoint are the best in the nation for effectiveness of care, setting four national benchmarks and ranking in the top 5% of the seventeen effective-ness-of-care measures including:

Breast Cancer Screening: #1
Diabetic Retinal Exam: #1
Cholesterol Control for Diabetes: #1
Beta Blocker after Heart Attack: #1

But that's not all! ThedaCare's hospitals have consistently been rated among the "100 Top Hospitals" in the nation. Theda Clark Medical Center in Neenah, WI, has earned the distinction four times and is the only Wisconsin hospital to make the "100 Top Hospitals" in 2003-2003. Both of ThedaCare's other hospitals, Appleton Medical Center and New London Family Medical Center, each have been "100 Top Hospitals" three times.
ThedaCare is the only health system in Wisconsin to be included on the American Hospital Association's "100 Most-Wired" list for their use of information technology.

ThedaCare's commitment to quality has resulted in lower costs. ThedaCare's urban hospitals, Appleton Medical Center and Theda Clark Medical Center, are the lowest-cost hospitals in Wisconsin for both inpa-tient and outpatient care. In fact, since 1992, price increases at ThedaCare's hospitals have averaged just over 5% per year over the last twelve years.

Veterans Administration Hospital — Bar Code IV Dosing

Contact   Jeff Ramirez, Pharm.D.
           Chief Management/Clinical Information Systems Pharmacy Benefits
           Management
           Veterans Health Administration
           810 Vermont Avenue
           Washington, DC 20420

Phone   (202) 273-8428

E-mail   Ramirez.jeff@mail.va.gov

The Situation

Medication dispensing errors can be life threatening. According to a recent Institute of Medicine article, almost 98,000 deaths occur in the United States each year due to medical mistakes caused by medication errors. While the nation is experiencing severe shortages in nursing staff, errors can unfortunately be more prevalent. Applying technology to a systematic process can help alleviate inaccuracies and, more importantly, help save lives.

The Solution

In 1999 the Veterans Administration (VA) developed a program to place bar codes on dose packages, IV Admixtures, and other small syringes for injection. This program was completed at the end of 2000/beginning of 2001 and is currently in use in 172 facilities with 30,000 beds. Automating this process has improved the safety of the administration of drugs by ensuring the right drug gets to the right patient at the right time. The Veterans Administration won the Pinnacle award from The American Pharmacy Association Foundation in 2002 for developing this program.

Better Health & Lower Costs

Implementation of this bar-code documentation of medication administration at the bedside has resulted in a 50% to 75% reduction in the medication error rate at most Veterans Administration Medical Centers.

Veterans Administration Hospital — Consolidated Mail Out Patient Pharmacy (CMOPS)

Contact Jeff Ramirez, Pharm.D.
Chief Management/Clinical
  Information Systems Pharmacy
Benefits Management
Veterans Health Administration
810 Vermont Avenue
Washington, DC 20420

Tim Stroup
National CMOP Manager
5000 S. 13th Street
Leavenworth, KS 66048

(913) 727-4839

Phone (202) 273-8428

E-mail Ramirez.jeff@mail.va.gov

The Situation

Because of a nationwide shortage of pharmacists, rising drug costs, and the frequency of medical errors, automated pharmacy-dispensing-technology innovations have been developed and are being used to address these issues. These systems are capable of producing larger amounts of prescriptions with much greater accuracy rates.

The Solution

The Department of Veterans Affairs (VA) has created seven highly automated dispensing factories to fill mail-in prescriptions. The Consolidated Mail Out Patient Pharmacy System (CMOPS) differs from other mail-order pharmacies in that the prescription processing and clinical interaction with physicians, pharmacists, and the patient is left with the local medical center. The individual patient does not know if the prescription is mailed locally or is coming from a Consolidated Mail Out Patient Pharmacy.

The Consolidated Mail Out Patient Pharmacy System uses a comprehensive conveyor system that incorporates the use of bar codes for error checks throughout the system in combination with automated dispensing equipment. The Consolidated Mail Out Patient Pharmacy system tracks the prescription to the different points of filling and the automated equipment will count the medication, label the vial, cap the vial, and place the finished product into a tote circulating on a conveyer belt. Additional automation can select products in manufacturers' containers such as tubes, boxes of Insulin, etc. There is a manual filling location that notifies the pharmacy technician the location of the products to select. Only when the correct product bar code is scanned will the system print a prescription label. At the end of the conveyor line, the pharmacist reviews the final product. A video image of the products dispensed is provided to the pharmacist for final visual identification. The product is checked and sent out via mail. Scaled down versions are also being used for many ambulatory care locations for dispensing prescriptions to patients waiting after clinic visits.

Better Health & Lower Costs

Prior to implementation of this automated process, one person in an efficient environment dispensed 20,000 prescriptions a year. The goal of the program was to increase the rate to 50,000 prescriptions per person, per year. It is currently dispensing 75,000 prescriptions per person, per year. In 2002, the Veterans Administration filled 105 million prescriptions overall using 90-day fills through automated pharmacies. The process is extremely efficient and has an accuracy rate of 99.997% and an error rate of seven errors per one million.

These automated procedures have resulted in a decreased workforce growth rate and an increased productivity meaning that more people are able to be treated more efficiently and more accurately.

Veterans Administration Healthcare System — My Health*e*Vet

Contact   Chief Health Informatics Officer
Veterans Health Administration
Department of Veterans Affairs
Office of Information (19)
810 Vermont Avenue, NW, Washington, DC 20420

Phone   (202) 273-8663

Web site   www.va.gov/vha_oi/

The Situation

American healthcare has been referred to as a "trillion dollar cottage industry" because of the industrial age reliance on paper-based records. In contrast, the Department of Veterans Affairs (VA) currently has a successful Veterans Health Information Systems and Technology Architecture (VistA) that supports the continuum of care extending from intensive care units and other inpatient care, to outpatient care, long-term care, and even home care environments. Veterans Administration's Computerized Patient Record System (CPRS) provides a single, windows-style interface for healthcare providers to review and update a patient's medical record as well as the ability to place orders for various items including medications, special procedures, x-rays and imaging, nursing care, diet, and laboratory tests. In fact, 91% of all pharmacy orders are electronically placed by the provider (one of the Leapfrog Group's top three safety strategies) in contrast to rates of less than 10% outside of Veterans Administration.

Although Veterans Administration is now highly computerized, achieving even better quality, safety, and cost, requires three elements: 1) a health information infrastructure for the system that provides decision support for efficient, effective population health management, 2) an integrated patient record and care system with clinical decision support for providers, and 3) a secure "portal" for patients to receive reliable, accurate health information and interact with their health records and clinicians.

The Solution

Veterans Administration's next generation system, known as "Health*e*Vet," evolves VistA from a facility-centric to a patient-centric health information system. Health*e*Vet implements a standard core collection of functions in five areas: Health Data Repository System, Registration Systems, Provider Systems, Management and Financial Systems, and Information and Education Systems. The health data repository creates a true longitudinal healthcare record including data from Veterans Administration and non-Veterans Administration sources, supporting research and population analyses, improving data quality and security, and facilitating patient access to data and health information.

With an emphasis on "eHealth," a secure patient portal known as "My Health*e*Vet" will provide access to a personal health record, on-line health assessment tools, mechanisms for prescription refills and making appointments, and access to high-quality health information. The latter information is evidence based, consistent with the clinician practice guideline, and meant to be proactive to patients such that they advocate more effectively for their own health needs, such as pneumonia vaccinations for older patients or those with chronic illness. This information dovetails with automatic clinical reminders that Veterans Administration healthcare providers receive for those same patients.

The provider "view," Computerized Patient Record System, organizes and presents all relevant patient data in a way that directly supports clinical decision making. The comprehensive cover sheet displays timely, patient-centric information, including active problems, allergies, current medications, recent laboratory results, vital signs, hospitalization, and outpatient clinic history. This information is displayed immediately when a patient is selected and provides an accurate overview of the patient's current status before any clinical interventions are ordered.

Among several features in the Computerized Patient Record System that improve safety and quality of care are the Real-Time Order Checking System that alerts clinicians of potential problems (e.g., drug-drug interactions, duplicate labs, etc.) during the ordering session, the Notification System that immediately alerts clinicians about clinically significant events such as abnormal test results, and the Clinical Reminder System that allows caregivers to track and improve preventive healthcare and disease treatment for patients and to ensure timely clinical interventions are initiated. The clinical reminder system is now the preferred mechanism for implementation of clinical practice guidelines and facilitates linking the evidence with the real-time clinical reminder, with the action (e.g., pneumoccocal vaccination in elderly or chronically ill patient), and with the automatically generated documentation, which generates a trail of standardized performance data.

Better Health & Lower Costs

Computerization has improved Veterans Administration's outcomes in quality, safety, patient and provider satisfaction, and cost. Quality has improved in preventive care and disease treatment. Pneumococcal pneumonia vaccination of at-risk patients is an evidence-based practice that reduces excess morbidity, mortality, and cost. In 1995 Veterans Administration rates of pneumococcal vaccination were 29%. Today rates exceed 80%, a national benchmark. Among patients with COPD (emphysema), this reduces cost by an average of over $100 per year and reduces rates of hospitalization by 29% and all cause mortality by 42%.

Performance improvement has similarly occurred in the areas of disease treatment encompassed by over twenty clinical practice guidelines such as coronary artery disease, diabetes, and depression. For sixteen of eighteen clinical performance indicators, critical to the care of veterans, and directly comparable externally, Veterans Administration is now the benchmark. This includes use of beta-blockers after a heart attack (halving death and reducing avoidable, excess healthcare expenditures by over $20,000 per patient episode), breast and cervical cancer screenings, cholesterol screenings, immunizations, tobacco screening and counseling, and diabetes care. By the way, Veterans Administration is essentially identical to the best private sector healthcare performance on the remaining two indicators.

Veterans Administration cares for over 50% more patients today than it did in 1995. Cumulatively, Veterans Administration's budget has only gone up by 15% since then. Thus costs per patient are down by 26% with measurably better outcomes. These improvements don't just look good on paper, they save lives, reduce hospitalizations, improve quality, lower costs, and satisfy patients.

Vanderbilt University Medical Center

Contact	Bill Stead
	Associate Vice Chancellor for Health Affairs
	Director, Informatics Center
	Professor of Medicine and Biomedical Informatics
	Vanderbilt University Medical Center
	The Informatics Center
	Room 416
	2209 Garland Avenue
	Nashville, TN 37232-8340
Phone	(615) 936-1424
E-mail	bill.stead@Vanderbilt.Edu

The Situation

Diagnostic testing is a significant cost driver in healthcare. In the event a wrong imaging choice is made, for example, the process can be time consuming and costly both to the patient and to the medical facility.

The Solution

Vanderbilt University Medical Center has been working for over ten years to bridge the gap between patient care and information technology. In December 1999 Vanderbilt University Medical Center altered its physician order entry system so it asked physicians to decide if each open-ended, ongoing test ordered was still needed. With a simple click, a normally automatic test could be stopped. Vanderbilt has documented millions of dollars of savings each year by using decision support during the ordering process to eliminate unnecessary orders, unnecessarily high drug costs, and delays in patient recovery caused by insufficient information. And in a changing business climate where hospitals are filling to capacity, the medical center is leveraging that efficiency to take care of more patients with the same level of spending on personnel and supplies.

Better Health & Lower Costs

The Vanderbilt information system has been used since the mid-1990s, and today it results in 10,000 electronic orders a day, 70% to 80% generated directly by physicians. Through utilization of this system, CHEM7 orders decreased by 60% with actual CHEM7 testing decreasing by 40%—saving $200,000 to $300,000 a year.

Portable Chest X-Ray orders decreased by 40% with actual testing decreasing by 30%—saving $1 million a year. EKG orders also decreased by 10%. Total savings are estimated at $1.3 million a year.

If this system were implemented nationally, hospital systems would save approximately $10 to $20 billion annually.

VISICU — eICU®

Contact	Brian Rosenfeld, MD
	Executive Vice-President and Chief Medical Officer
	VISICU
	2400 Boston Street, Suite 302
	Baltimore MD 21224
Phone	(410) 246-5354
E-mail	brosenfeld@visicu.com
Web site	www.visicu.com

The Situation

Hospitals are currently at or over capacity. As demographics shift and baby boomers age, the problem is only going to get worse. The number of intensive care-unit (ICU) patients will increase as will the overall number of hospital patients. In fact, it is predicted that the number of intensive care-unit patients will double in the next fifteen years. Not only will the intensive care-unit population base increase, so will the acuity of intensive care-unit patients. In other words, not only will there be more patients, there will be sicker patients.

Intensivists are physicians with advanced certification training and experience in critical care. Typically they have completed a fellowship in critical care after serving a residency in internal medicine, pulmonary medicine, anesthesia, or surgery. Dedicated intensivists provide great value to intensive care-units. Unfortunately there are only about 5,500 actively practicing intensivists in the United States. This shortage severely limits their impact. Nationwide: less than 15% of intensive care-unit patients have dedicated intensivists, and more than 50% of intensive care-unit patients have no intensivists at all. Numerous studies have confirmed that intensivist involvement in the care of intensive care unit patients leads to double-digit improvement in patient outcomes, and the Leapfrog Group (an association of Fortune 500 companies) has called for full-time intensivist staffing as a way to save more than 50,000 lives per year.

The Solution

VISICU Inc., a Baltimore-based company, is the innovator and leading provider of remote monitoring and management technology for the intensive care unit. The VISICU eICU® solution allows hospitals and health systems to reorganize the delivery of critical care patient services, creating an integrated program that effectively standardizes clinical practices. The eICU solution networks multiple hospital intensive care units together into a central facility (eICU) to reach more patients, leverage scarce intensivists, and provide a 24/7 expert safety net. The VISICU technology identifies impending problems, prevents errors, guides decision making, and tracks performance. The result is a critical care program that brings quality to a new level and achieves unprecedented breakthroughs in clinical outcomes and economic benefit.

VISICU's eICU solution offers a low-cost way to leverage scarce intensivists with a model that could be implemented in every intensive care unit. VISICU's software supports 24/7 intensive care unit monitoring by intensivists through an electronic infrastructure of real-time monitors, electronic medical records, and telephonic and video conferencing. The system is being installed at New York Presbyterian (Columbia and Cornell hospitals), Sutter Health in Sacramento, and Advocate Healthcare in Chicago, and by May 2003, 300 intensive care unit beds will have intensivists 24/7 because of an eICU hub.

Better Health & Lower Costs

The following are the major clinical results of a study by Cap Gemini Ernst & Young on two Sentara Norfolk General Hospital intensive care units that are part of three hospitals implementing the VISICU eICU solution:

- 25% reduction in severity-adjusted hospital mortality rate for the intensive care unit population
- 17% decrease in both intensive care unit and floor length of stay (LOS)
- 20% increase in intensive care unit cases as a result of capacity created by shortening intensive care unit LOS

Cap Gemini Ernst and Young also disclosed the following financial results of the program:

- 26% reduction in hospital costs for intensive care unit patients, resulting from
  - 17% decrease in length of stay (both intensive care unit and floor)
  - 15% decrease in daily costs of intensive care unit care, attributable to: 4% decrease in nursing worked hours per patient day
  - 18% decrease in ancillary costs (pharmacy, supplies, therapies, labs, etc.)
- $2,150 per patient financial benefit attributable to lower costs after adjusting for revenue loss in "fee-for-service" and "per-diem" patients
- $460,000 increase in gross monthly revenue due to additional intensive care unit cases. This generated $274,000 margin contribution monthly
- $3,000,000 annualized net financial benefit for the two intensive care units (sixteen beds) after subtracting all program costs

If you think of this from a big-picture standpoint, if VISICU's eICU was implemented in every American intensive care unit, 150,000 lives could be saved at a cost savings of over $8 billion a year. Furthermore, if every Veterans Hospital intensive care unit were networked into an eICU at its regional hub (21 regions), the Veterans Administration would save $100,000 per intensive care unit bed (equaling $350 million a year) and many thousands of lives would be saved.

WorldDoc, Inc.

Contact	Jerry Reeves, MD
	President and CEO
	500 North Rainbow Boulevard, Suite 314
	Las Vegas, NV 89107
Phone	(702) 821-0818
E-mail	jreeves@worlddoc.com
Web site	www.worlddoc.com

The Situation

The annual health costs for a family are approximately $7,000 per year and rising more than 10% per year. Employers and government fund the majority of these costs, however individuals are experiencing rapid increases in their out-of-pocket costs for medical services and treatments and are motivated to save money. Prescription costs are a major cost driver, and they are increasing at over 15% annually.

The Solution

WorldDoc's Personal Evaluation System (PES) developed by specialist physicians provides individuals with self-directed, interactive assessments of more than 200 patient symptoms and concerns. Based on the responses, it helps them understand their most likely medical conditions and treatment options. Consumers learn which self-care options are safe and when they should seek immediate medical attention. They learn what is aging them most and steps to restore their health. It assists patients with health decisions, reduces unnecessary doctor visits, and decreases healthcare costs.

A new pharmacy module details effective generic-medication alternatives for most medical conditions comparing their prices with more expensive brand medications. Consumers are empowered with information on medically sound lower-cost treatment alternatives to discuss with their physician. And they access discounts at 30,000 pharmacies.

Better Health & Lower Costs

User survey data reveal 31% reported a decrease in medical visits, 62% reduced their need for medical services, 67% found WorldDoc helped them understand their medical condition, and WorldDoc helped 35% seek care for a previously unrecognized problem. Importantly, 92% found WorldDoc was easy to use and understand.

Users save an average of 25% on prescriptions and about $500 per year, per senior choosing recommended effective generic alternatives. Projected savings for employers is $175 per employee, per year.

Widespread usage of the WorldDoc Personal Evaluation System could significantly improve the efficiency of healthcare with projected savings for acute and chronic-care conditions from improved self-management and prescription-medication savings. A savings of 10% could be realized by providing individuals with comprehensive health-decision support tools.

Biothreat: Transform or Risk Mass Deaths
By: Newt Gingrich with Bill Sanders

Disclaimer: In the course of writing this appendix, the authors discussed at length the grave issue of bioterrorism with a number of subject-matter experts. Nearly all of these experts were reluctant to comment publicly about the severity of the threat our country is facing and cautioned us not to incite panic and fear. However, we believe strongly that Americans need to know the truth about biological warfare so they can understand the threat against which to measure domestic-preparedness plans that are being developed to address the biothreat.

> No other threat can potentially kill as many Americans as a biological threat. Our nation must mobilize and think through its responses commensurate with saving the lives of 100 million Americans. Only by understanding that we must act with that speed and with that scale—because that is literally what is at stake—will we get to a resolution.

Introduction

Biological warfare, called biothreat, is the largest threat to the human race, a substantially bigger threat than nuclear war. If the United States is hit with an engineered biological agent for which no vaccines are available, we are in for problems of colossal proportions.

Outbreaks from diseases that European explorers carried aboard their ships, including measles, tuberculosis, flu, and venereal disease, decimated the indigenous population of Hawaii from 1779 to 1854 by an estimated 85%. Some Indian villages in North America lost 95% of their populations due to similar outbreaks. The Spanish Conquest of the Aztecs can only be better understood in the context of the smallpox epidemic that devastated the Aztecs after the failure of the first Spanish attack in 1520 and killed Cuitláhuac, the Aztec emperor, who briefly succeeded Montezuma. The Bubonic Plague was fatal to about a third of the European population. Today, one-third of the population of our country would mean almost 100 million Americans dying. Consider our reaction to September 11 in which over 3,000 people died. September 11 was tragic and horrifying—but still not on the scale of devastation large enough to change the very structure of society. A real biological weapon—if we are not prepared for it—could end life as we have known it.

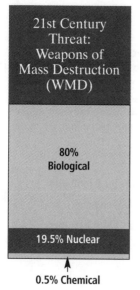

21st Century Threat: Weapons of Mass Destruction (WMD)

80% Biological

19.5% Nuclear

0.5% Chemical

In fact, biological threats, especially the threat of an engineered lethal bioweapon for which we have no vaccines, no rapid diagnostic tests, and no drug treatments are so great that we should consider the preparation of a defensive system against an engineered biological the highest priority in the American national security system and the most important job facing the new Department of Homeland Security.

In thinking about weapons of mass destruction, a good rule of thumb is to put 80% of our effort into dealing with biological threats, 19.5% into nuclear threats and a 0.5% into chemical weapons.

Nuclear war has been talked about, written about, and shown in movies far more than biological threats. Hollywood has occasionally tried to tackle this threat but usually pulls its punch. "It is one of the great scare stories of our time," wrote Robert Ebert about the movie, *Outbreak,* that challenged moviegoers in

1995 to "try to remain calm . . . the greatest medical crisis in the world is about to happen." A deadly airborne virus is tracked from Africa to the United States in a deeply disturbing and frightening film. An all-star cast and simple story line traces the ravages of a fictional "Motaba" virus to a predictable and happy conclusion.

Although *Outbreak* portrays the genuine panic and horror of a biological catastrophe, it completely fails to capture just how serious the problem could become. "Motaba" pales in comparison to a true hemorrhagic fever virus (HFV) such as Ebola or Marburg. At present, there are no licensed vaccines to treat HFVs. Given most physicians' unfamiliarity with these viruses, diagnosis would be significantly delayed. And without known treatments for HFVs, it is extremely improbable that any lab or scientist could devise a cure overnight.

In the event of an uncontrollable epidemic, America will become a different country. The experience of millions dying, the sense of helplessness and fear, the need to maintain civil order—all these factors would combine to shatter the comfortable, safe, prosperous, and remarkably free way of life we normally take for granted.

The biological threat is a very real, immediate problem. The Hart/Rudman Commission gave a devastating indictment of the "fragmented and inadequate" structures and strategies in place to respond to attacks on U.S. cities.

The commission predicted an attack on an American city by a terrorist group six months before September 11. Unfortunately many in the news media thought the conclusions of the Hart/Rudman Commission were irrelevant. In thinking about biological threats, the Hart/Rudman Commission had three key conclusions worth noting:

1. We have to assume that a weapon of mass destruction will be used in an American city.

2. We have to assume that it will happen in the next 25 years.

3. This is the number one threat to the United States.

It must be emphasized that what the Hart/Rudman Commission predicted was neither September 11 nor the anthrax event. September 11 actually understressed our systems in terms of casualties. Because so many people tragically died in the buildings, there was relatively little need for medical care. However, the anthrax event involving 22 cases and 5 deaths almost stressed the limits of involved public health agencies and hospitals.

Biothreat is a larger threat than any conceivable conventional war. There could be a crisis as early as tomorrow morning. Yet we are not prepared for a major biological event such as a large anthrax outbreak, re-engineered smallpox, or even a re-engineered influenza. The largest epidemic of the 20th century was influenza in 1918—it killed more people worldwide than were killed in the four years of World War I—so even the common flu can be re-engineered into an extraordinarily dangerous illness. Indeed, public health experts note that every generation or so a new strain of flu emerges naturally with a vastly greater lethality, killing many people.

The reality is that, whatever threat emerges, we may not have effective treatments and vaccines. Buying 300 million units of vaccine for traditional smallpox is probably the right thing to do, but it will be irrelevant if an engineered version of smallpox is released. We must build a capacity to operate in real time to identify, analyze, and respond to a new, engineered bioweapon we have never encountered before.

We must be able to detect early symptoms literally within hours of their first appearing. We must be ready to gather data nationwide so we can see where the symptoms are occurring and how rapidly it is spreading. We must also be able to communicate with doctors, nurses, pharmacists, veterinarians, laboratories, hospitals, and long-term care facilities, which will become hospitals and pharmacies in an emergency. The government will have to coordinate sample gathering, analysis, information exchange, and briefings for medical professionals and the public. Every hour will count. Only the knowledge that a well-conceptualized and already-practiced emergency health system is in operation will prevent panic. Only an all-out effort to identify the disease, develop interim treatments, and create a vaccine on a crash basis (which HIV/AIDS reminds us, may or may not be successful) will be acceptable in any real biological crisis.

We may have to maintain shadow pharmaceutical factories capable of being converted rapidly, or factories with double capacity, because we may literally have to produce a brand new vaccine for a brand new engineered disease and distribute it on a massive scale. While there may only be a 1 in 100 chance of a large-scale attack occurring, the threat is real and must be considered very seriously. If we could imagine the human costs of a nuclear weapon going off in an American city or a major biological event then it is obvious that our children and grandchildren are not going to praise us for being frugal and prudent if it ends up meaning illness and death for millions.

Biothreat Environment

Given human nature and our tendency to forget over time, preparation, driven by initial panic and fear, will subside. In a healthy world, they will get pushed to the back burner. We just need to make sure that the back burner is professional, disciplined, and ready. If there remains any doubt about the current biothreat, the data gathered (in chart below) by Seth Carus shows the explosive growth in bioagent cases over the past decades:

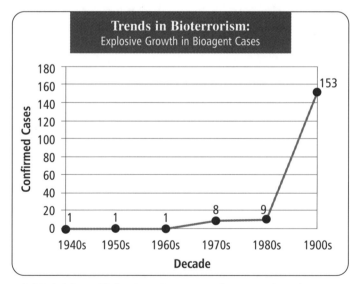

Ref: W. Seth Carus, "Working Paper: Bioterrorism and Biocrimes," Center for Counter-proliferation Research, National Defense University, Washington, DC, p.11

Carus cites concern for the fact that future bioterrorism attacks may be more deadly than past incidents based on three factors:

1. an increasing number of terrorist groups,

2. the growing technological sophistication of terrorist groups, and

3. persistent terrorists might actually gain access to the expertise generated by a state-directed, biological-warfare program.

The biothreat environment is increasingly foreshadowed as a catastrophic event born of terrorists who can become capable of using biological agents.

Richard Preston, author of *The Demon in the Freezer*, puts it succinctly: "Virus engineering is cheaper than a used car, yet it may provide a nation with a weapon as intimidating as a nuclear bomb." *The Demon in the Freezer* is a chilling, non-fictional look at the prospect of the smallpox virus being used as a bioweapon, an excellent outline of the emergency operations that took place, and the inadequate coordination between federal agencies in response to the anthrax events.

Anthrax was frightening in 2001, but anthrax is not contagious. The threat of a lethally engineered contagious disease is the greatest nightmare of all. This threat is not science fiction. This threat is clearly a potential reality today. In early 2001, Australian scientists produced an inadvertently powerful, mouse-killing virus by modifying a mousepox virus with immune system genes. Even those mice vaccinated against mousepox died when subjected to the designer virus. Judith Miller and others in the book, *Germs*, note, "Just as the super-mousepox had defeated the mousepox vaccine, so might genetically enhanced smallpox defeat the human vaccine."

A genetically modified or engineered biologic is a biothreat of a completely different magnitude. The delicate "virus-host balance" observed in nature, where viruses tend not to be extremely lethal to their hosts, is turned completely upside down when these natural environments are radically changed. Evolution may have created 100% lethal pathogens in the past, but those diseases are now extinct because they killed all of their hosts. Extinction-level events may be driven at an unprecedented rate never before seen on Earth with a genetically modified or engineered biologic.

Indeed Ken Alibek, the former director of Biopreparat and a top scientist in the Soviet warfare program who defected in 1992, describes the intimate details of the Soviet's clandestine bioweapons program that actually re-engineered microbes to make them more virulent. In his book, *Biohazard*, Alibek notes the skepticism of American scientists at descriptions of possible combined bioweapons capable of triggering two diseases. While he has not yet seen a combined agent, Alibek says: "It is clear that the technology to produce such a weapon exists" and "to argue that these weapons won't be developed simply because existing armaments will do a satisfactory job contradicts the history and logic of weapons development from the invention of machine guns to the hydrogen bomb."

In the PBS NOVA special, "Bioterror," interviews with Alibek and Bill Patrick, retired Chief of the Product Development at the Army's Fort Detrick facility, reveal shared concerns about bioterrorism. Patrick notes that his "biggest concern now is a rogue country that supports terrorism." Alibek discusses Russian co-workers who describe how easy it is to steal from biological weapon facilities and tells of a person who established a company to sell some techniques to develop genetically engineered strains. Alibek says, "Ten years ago it would require several million dollars to get one or another technique. Now you can get this information just for the cost of a translator from Russian into English or from Russian into Iranian—or any other language."

The potential of an engineered biological weapon is clearly within the reach of a dedicated opponent. Prevention will be both difficult and expensive. Even the most skeptical analyst must acknowledge that while the biothreat risk of a terrorist attack may be low, it cannot be assumed to be zero. As former Secretary of the Navy Richard Danzig notes, "The assumption that biological weapons will not be used in the future because they have not been used in the past is based on an error of fact." The disastrous consequences of an uncontrolled pandemic dictate that the U.S. government must address biothreat head on.

Important Things We Can Do

Although the United States is not entirely unprepared for bioterrorism, we are most definitely "underprepared" as noted by Senator Bill Frist in his book, *When Every Moment Counts: What You Need to Know About Bioterrorism from the Senate's Only Doctor*. False analogies such as "the average American is probably at greater risk of death or injury from driving on the highway than from exposure to anthrax" understate the potentially cataclysmic effect of a serious biological attack. Today your chance of dying in a car wreck is greater than the likelihood you will die from a biological attack. However, an engineered lethal virus, if it resembled the influenza epidemic of 1918 could easily kill more Americans than have been killed by car wrecks in the history of the automobile. Cited in a recent speech by Secretary of Defense Rumsfeld, the Dark Winter war game at Johns Hopkins University estimated a smallpox outbreak introduced in only three cities could lead to a million dead and another two million infected from a traditional, not even an engineered, virus.

The devastating costs and disruptions caused by the attacks involving 22 cases of anthrax through the U.S. Postal Service in the fall of 2001 are well known. What is lesser known is how this seemingly minor bioattack severely stressed the public health agencies in the affected states and Washington, DC. Tara O'Toole, MD, director for the Johns Hopkins Center for Civilian Biodefense, and others noted that "the United States Army Research Institute for Infectious Disease (USAMRID) performed 19,000 anthrax assays in the weeks following the mailings," "33,000 people were placed on antibiotics" and "the bill for the decontamination of the Hart building alone is estimated to exceed $23 million."

Anthrax is the BB gun of biowarfare. As New York Times reporter Judith Miller noted in NOVA's "Bioterror," the anthrax-laced letters sparked "mass disruption" rather than "mass destruction." What if the bioattack were larger and more contagious?

According to a Centers for Disease Control and Prevention (CDC) study, a bioterrorist attack could have a staggering economic impact of $26.2 billion per 100,000 persons exposed in an anthrax scenario. [Cost = (number of deaths x present value of expected future earnings) + (number of days of hospitalization x cost of hospitalization) + (number of outpatient visits x cost of outpatient visits)]. "In the absence of an intervention program for 100,000 persons exposed, the Bacillus anthracis cloud would result in 50,000 cases of inhalation anthrax, with 32,875 deaths . . . A prophylaxis program must be instituted within 72 hours of exposure to prevent the maximum number of deaths." This scenario and cost model has been described as not fully addressing the limitations of hospital facilities, lack of trained and equipped emergency personnel and drug supplies, and the low probability that an attack would be detected promptly, further leading to delays in recognition and treatment.

As recently as last fall, three out of four family physicians surveyed reported that they were not prepared to respond to a bioterrorist attack. Although 95% said they considered bioterrorism to be a real threat in the United States, only 27% thought the U.S. healthcare system could respond effectively. Findings from this study appeared in the September 2002 issue of Journal for Family Practice. Only 24% of the physicians surveyed thought they could recognize signs and symptoms of bioterrorism-related illness in their patients and only 57% said they would know whom to call to report a suspected bioterrorist attack.

Despite this ominous outlook, the national response to bioterrorism can be described in broad goals: detect the problem, control the epidemic's spread, and treat the victims. The public health system of the 21st century must strengthen infrastructure to integrate all of the health services to deal more effectively with epidemics and other emergencies. A systems approach for our preparations in dealing with bioattacks must not focus primarily on our traditional first responders, i.e., police, fire-fighters, and EMS personnel, but with health providers. Physicians, nurses, pharmacists, and public health officials must be depended upon to make the first diagnoses and take response steps. Public healthcare must take the lead in coordinating hospitals, local governments, public education programs, and national responses. New partnerships must be forged to restore national security.

Six key areas must be addressed:

1. Vision and Strategy Design

2. Information Technology Investment

3. Vaccinations and Immunization

4. Post-event Treatment

5. Civil Defense Transformation, including the transformation of the Public Health Service into a comprehensive 21st century system with a large virtual component

6. Biosecurity and Education

The defining events of 2001 have greatly sharpened the nation's focus on public health and its demand for vigilant protection and security. Only through a focused support of the six core objectives above will our country be able to effectively respond to any public health emergency in the future.

Vision and Strategy Design

Congress should set a clear benchmark for reaching the first stage of this goal within a year. A good benchmark might assume two major attacks, one nuclear and the other biological. Lay out what the United States should be capable of doing on that date. Because, if we cannot set a tough goal now, and if the unspeakable happens a year from now, we will wonder why we were not prepared. It is realistic to assume we could have a major problem in at least one city. We will be woefully unprepared if we do not cut through the red tape and insist on wartime urgency.

Because Congress appropriated a $1.1 billion bioterrorism preparedness program to the states for public health improvements in FY 2003, it is vital that goals and defined benchmarks are met by all states to insure a strong, coordinated national security plan. Project BioShield, announced in President Bush's recent State of the Union address, is a program designed to develop and make available modern, effective drugs and vaccines to protect against bioattack. It is a comprehensive effort. A clear and cogent strategic plan for bioterrorism must be produced by the newly formed Department of Homeland Security to guide funding priorities.

The federal government, along with state and local governments, has already begun to move from the tabletop exercise to field exercises. Several war games, exercises, and studies have consistently shown that even small increases in demand will overflow U.S. hospital capacity. Budget battles and healthcare inflation have gutted the surge capacity of our hospitals. Agriculture is also at risk from biological agents aimed at crops, livestock, and interstate commerce. Exercises must be designed to test all such scenarios.

Bioattack exercises focusing on senior-level policymakers such as Operation Topoff and Dark Winter revealed the effect of ill-defined legal authority in epidemic scenarios. What are the specific powers of the president, of the governor, and of the local mayor? Who sets priorities for distribution and reallocation of scarce resources? Lessons learned from these exercises must be addressed at a national level.

Maryland and Virginia counties near Washington, DC have even gone so far as to hold mock-bioterror attack drills to fine-tune their local action plans. Unfortunately these are the exceptions and many states have failed to submit plans that provide for the seventeen key preparedness objectives outlined by the HHS. Exercises and drills on all levels need to be conducted to reveal needed working relationships and coordination to successfully address a bioattack. As Theodore Roosevelt said, "The chief factor in achieving triumph is what has been done in thorough preparation and training before the beginning of the war."

Richard Danzig has proposed forming a national-level committee or task force to fully examine what needs to be done. By looking at specific scenarios built on the CDC's high priority diseases, information and lessons learned could be addressed at a national level. The CDC named six diseases that pose the highest threat to national security because they are caused by organisms that:

1. Can be easily disseminated or transmitted from person to person

2. May result in public panic and social disruption

3. Cause death in a high percentage of those infected and require special action for public health preparedness

Anthrax, botulism, plague, smallpox, tularemia, and viral hemorrhagic fevers are listed on the Centers for Disease Control Category A list as the most dangerous biological agents. Danzig suggests developing concepts of operation for each scenario and applying lessons learned to broaden biological defense measures. The key will be to not develop static plans based on scenarios but to identify core capacities and be able to adjust scales of response accordingly.

In addition, a government-wide program driven by the Departments of Health and Human Services (HHS) and Homeland Security must begin now to develop the capabilities to deal with an engineered, lethal, contagious virus. "Current efforts to sequence the genes associated with serious bioterrorist threats should be expanded and accelerated," says Rita Colwell, director of the National Science Foundation. She adds, "The importance of a system based on whole genomic sequences needs to be stressed. There are many excellent gene probes and related quick identification methods, but it takes whole genome information to detect genetically modified or engineered biologics. We risk losing the earliest response time due to lack of accuracy, poor communication, and no early warning system in place."

Information Technology Investment

A real biothreat will require an information technology investment that connects every doctor, every nurse, every pharmacist, every veterinarian, every hospital, and every nursing home in the country in real time in a virtual public health system. As a country, we need to commit to a one-time block investment to modernize the entire IT system for the health system. We should strive for information flow that is "handheld and wireless," as described by Rita Colwell, in a way that meets both our biological warfare needs and our day-to-day healthcare needs. Every person will have an electronic medical record on-line with the kind of efficiency that we now take for granted in financial services.

Only with a modernized IT system can we develop a good early-warning system. Both active and passive surveillance systems suffer from a shared handicap—by the time the data is gathered and analyzed an epidemic could have already broken out. Scott Gottlieb, MD, formerly a resident fellow at the American Enterprise Institute and now a senior official at the Food and Drug Administration, notes, "Everything America has that was designed specifically to counter bioterrorism is old, expensive, and slow."

A General Accounting Office report on infectious disease reporting systems from state and local public health offices revealed that much of the reporting data is still submitted on paper. Even when systems are electronic, people often have to reenter data by hand because systems are not interoperable. Internet-enabled public health infrastructure is urgently needed to meet the core response times required to address bioterror attacks. Bioterror attacks may go unnoticed unless key links are made, which drives the urgent need to upgrade the entire healthcare IT system.

The Department of Veteran Affairs, Deputy Under Secretary for Health Jonathan Perlin, MD, discussed the block investment needed for effective "syndromic surveillance" as critical to successfully "detect the signal that a bioweapons has been unleashed, as well as the coordinated, effective, efficient treatment of the consequences."

Additionally, a proactive communications plan is needed to coordinate actions and quell panic. Web sites, chat rooms, and e-mail are invaluable resources for getting the word out. The CDC's bioterrorism Web site is a consistently reliable source for up-to-date information and clear guidance. HHS, healthcare officials, and physicians have already pursued both public and private solutions to remedy the lack of communications associated with the anthrax event. Ronald Reynolds, MD, emergency physician in Myrtle Beach, SC notes, "Although CNN was a very good and reliable information source, we realized as physicians that it should not be our primary source of information on those agents. We should be hearing from physicians and specialists within the field." By December 2001 Dr. Reynolds had set up an Internet-based educational program on bioterrorism with Web-cast lectures. Any bioterror attack will present a unique challenge to the healthcare community. Rapid and reliable dissemination of the most up-to-date information will be of utmost importance. Physicians especially must have much more reliable information sources in the aftermath of a bioweapons attack such as the Clinician's Biodefense Network being built by the Center for Civilian Biodefense Strategies (http://www.hopkins-biodefense.org). It is designed to link practicing clinicians with biodefense experts nationwide in the event of a bioterrorist attack.

The sheer volume of patient need in the case of a contagious outbreak will require the mobilization of every medical person and every medical facility that can be made available. There should be a Public Health Service Reserve Corps, parallel to the Reserve and National Guard program we have for the military. Every doctor, nurse, pharmacist, and veterinarian in the country, including retired professionals, should be enrolled in the corps and available by e-mail at a moment's notice. Every long-term care facility in the country should be enrolled as an emergency facility the way commercial airliners are in the Civilian Reserve Air Fleet (CRAF) program. They should be paid to develop a plan for moving their healthiest and most stable residents to safe places so the facility's beds could be used in a bioattack.

The development of the nationwide information-technology network needed for a serious biological attack will actually provide the capability necessary to modernize the health field in its everyday functions. The very same equipment and connectivity that will save lives in a crisis can be used to save lives and save money in peacetime.

Designed correctly, the 21st century Biological Security Information Technology Investment is the direct parallel to the proposal by President Eisenhower to build an interstate highway system as both a national security requirement and as an enormous asset for everyday life.

In February 1955, President Eisenhower stressed the urgency of establishing the modernized interstate highway system: "In case of an atomic attack on our key cities, the road net must permit quick evacuation of target areas, mobilization of defense forces, and maintenance of every essential economic function." He went on to describe the consequences if the present system was not transformed: "The present system in critical areas would be the breeder of a deadly congestion within hours of an attack."

His urgent transportation message was echoed in his annual message to Congress in January 1956—to spearhead critical road construction "needed for personal safety, the general prosperity, [and] the national security of the American people." Eisenhower's three-pronged message provides a perfect analogy for the urgency of improving our healthcare. Critical improvements are needed, not only to improve our personal healthcare and the public health system but also to improve our ability to respond to the challenges of a bioattack.

This investment should be made by the federal government as a one-time, profound modernization that links every doctor, nurse, pharmacist, and veterinarian in every hospital, laboratory, drugstore, and long-term care facility with every agency of government that needs the information. If we are ever hit with an engineered contagious virus, we will be grateful for every second we save in discovery, analysis, reporting, and in our ability to then brief medical professionals in real time. We will be thankful for every penny we invested to make that speed and accuracy possible. This investment could save millions of lives.

Vaccination and Immunization

Vaccines are designed to prevent infections. We cannot assume that vaccines can be distributed quickly after an attack and before people develop symptoms. Gottlieb says that we cannot "assume there will be enough volunteers to administer the vaccines" and "that Americans will stand in neat lines to receive their vaccine." It is more likely, he notes, "that there will be widespread panic." In the case of smallpox, the window of opportunity for the vaccine to prevent death when administered may only be within 96 hours of exposure.

Post-Event Treatment

Vaccinations are the right choice for our front-line defenders. Nevertheless, victims of bioterrorism may not be vaccinated and strong efforts must focus on treatments and post-event treatments. For example, one source estimates that half of the population should not get the smallpox vaccine because they have a contraindication or they have intimate contact with someone who has a contraindication. So even with a vaccine, we will desperately need post-event treatments.

Gottlieb further notes that "Washington remains stuck in first gear, debating whether the development of treatments is a scientific task best handled through a command-and-control approach run by the Pentagon, or by dangling incentives before private drug companies." Congress cannot afford to continue to go back and forth on this issue. Treatments are needed on the frontlines—not on the back shelves of the laboratories.

One immediate danger is that the government has already sent a clear signal that drug manufacturers should not expect to make profits with drugs that fight bioterrorism. The knee-jerk reaction to call for stripping the Cipro™ patent away from Bayer AG to stockpile government-supply depots ran the risk of sacrificing long-term security for short-term solutions. Politicians must not attempt to gain favor by waging a public relations battle against drug companies while losing focus on the larger war against bioterrorism.

Robert M. Goldberg reinforces this point by declaring the government has "displayed a shocking misunderstanding of how profit causes the private sector to create and distribute the amazing new drugs we have come to expect." As the market's largest demander and supplier of vaccines in the country, the government's mandate for profitless prices sends a red-light signal to drug innovators and suppliers. Goldberg correctly notes, "We need to strengthen our war against bioterrorism with private capital, not impoverish such an important mission by stripping patents from the best technologies."

A key industrial-base issue is that our country is heavily dependent upon products produced overseas. For the smallpox vaccine, we are using a British-owned company with production facilities in Austria. The vaccinia immune globulin (VIG) used to help people who have certain serious reactions to the smallpox vaccine comes from a Canadian company. Key antibiotics in the pharmaceutical stockpile are also imported: Cipro™ comes from Germany and the raw material for Doxycycline™ is mostly made in China.

The defense industrial base of the 21st century must include our pharmaceutical companies. They must help form the foundation of our nation's security as ship-builders did in the 18th century, our steel companies did in the 19th century, and our aircraft manufacturers did in the 20th century. Partnering relationships are critical and must reflect a coordinated defense effort.

Expeditious development and licensing of products to diagnose, treat, or prevent epidemic outbreaks from bioterrorist pathogens must remain a high priority for the President's Project BioShield. The U.S. Food and Drug Administration (FDA) must fast-track and accelerate approval processes with priority reviews for emergency-use licensure. Careful attention to risk management and benefit analysis dictates close and early coordination between the FDA, sponsors, and end customers to improve the efficiency of product development. This resource-intensive process must be supported by increased FDA labor force and funding.

It is acknowledged that human efficacy trials are not feasible or ethical when dealing with drugs and biologicals to fight bioterror. Effective use of animal efficacy data must be accepted as scientifically appropriate. A need for honest and effective (versus legalistic) risk will challenge progress unless trusting relationships are developed. The public expects safe and effective products and will continue to look to the FDA for protection. Tort litigation must be reformed to acknowledge and understand the need for risk and benefit. We must resolve the political debate over liability or continue to risk a delayed response to a legitimate biothreat.

Under the Federal Response Plan, HHS maintains and secures the

National Pharmaceutical Stockpile, including 600 tons of emergency medical supplies distributed among twelve strategic locations ready to reach any part of the U.S. within twelve hours. Remarkably, a rushed package of 50 tons of drugs and medical supplies was delivered to New York City within seven hours of the attacks on the World Trade Centers. Unfortunately, as recently as November 2002, Florida was the only state deemed ready and prepared to receive such an emergency shipment. The continued growth of critical federal and state partnerships through planning and exercises is essential.

The nation's pharmaceutical distributors who already manage the inventory of one component of the National Pharmaceutical Stockpile are saving the government millions of dollars by rotating stock. Pharmacies are an intersection for virtually every health-system player, and pharmacists are the nation's most accessible health professional. Most states allow pharmacists to administer vaccines. A federal law could be passed so that upon presidential emergency declaration, all pharmacists could be authorized to administer and dispense needed prescriptions and vaccines.

Fostering relationships and continued involvement with pharmacies and pharmacists is urgent and vital to the need for a rapid response defense system to combat bioattacks. This would provide 55,000 "virtual public health facilities" in the drugstores people frequent. This 21st century solution is far more cost effective, far more comprehensive, and much less expensive than trying to rebuild the 1935 public health service. Both pharmacists and drugstores have expressed a strong willingness to develop a partnership for biological defense with the federal government, but the traditional public health bureaucracy has been far too turf and budget conscious to respond. Veterinarians could also play a vital role as part of our virtual public health service, especially in key rural areas. The Department of Homeland Security should immediately reach out to the drugstore chains, the pharmacy profession, and veterinarians to create partnerships that could save lives and save money.

Civil Defense Transformation

Civil defense needs to be carefully thought out—especially when it comes to volunteer and part-time personnel. First, we ought to have a public health corps of volunteers so if we have a biological event in a city like New York, we can mobilize 100,000 people to deal with it. We want those to be part-time volunteers who are trained twice a year and are actually practicing their duties, much like World War II bomb shelter wardens did in Britain.

Second, we want a civil defense system, much like we had in the 1950s, in which the Department of Homeland Security would organize people. Third, after a careful analysis, we may want or need nearly half of the National Guard efforts redirected to medical, public safety, and construction challenges. The present Guard hierarchy will probably fight any such change. Every governor who brings their emergency leadership together to play a biological or nuclear civil defense game will rapidly find they need a new set of capabilities which their World War II-focused National Guard is incapable of giving them. They will quickly appoint leaders for their state's National Guard who understand that the most important mission for the Guard in the 21st century is to be the first line of defense and recovery if something horrific happens right here at home. To have the rapid, local response capabilities needed for our country's future, we must match the requirement with the most effective and lowest cost resource.

Biosecurity and Education

The final critical issue in the age of bioterrorism is biosecurity. The skyrocketing pace of progress in the field of genomics and other areas of biological and medicine research presages a new era of biothreat. The actual technology and infrastructure that has made our lives increasingly comfortable may be exploited by those who wish to do us harm. Gigi Kwik and others from the Johns Hopkins Center for Civilian Biodefense Strategies aptly describe the challenge as "how to constrain malignant applications of powerful bioscience responsibly without damaging the generation of essential knowledge." A clear system of checks and balances must promote scientific progress while at the same time protecting powerful knowledge so that it cannot be used for evil purposes.

Kwik further notes, "Future processes and techniques available for purchase will no doubt make advanced biotechniques more accessible to a determined terrorist, which could lead to the creation of new and more dangerous bioweapons." Biosecurity cannot be achieved with specific legislative action or corporate measures. The Center for Civilian Biodefense Strategies is currently trying to detail measures for increasing biosecurity without impeding necessary research:

- increased awareness of biosecurity and bioterrorism risks among scientists and the scientific leadership

- security provisions to be organic to the culture and practices of biological research

- biosecurity to be a "bottom-up" approach imagined and embraced by all scientists

- biosecurity to include processes or measures for periodic assessment of how well the system is working

- biosecurity systems to provide the means of making applications and test systems increasingly pervasive and global

- biosecurity is a critical link in the fight against bioterror

Joshua Lederberg, 1958 Nobel Prize winner in physiology and medicine who also shared the Time Man of the Year award in 1960, has expressed a concern that "growing anthrax is as easy as baking a pie" and that "biowarfare is an evil that cannot be tolerated . . . out of a sense of moral outrage." It is of the utmost importance to follow Lederberg's lead to instill a "globally shared ethos in condemnation of any possible use of biological warfare" in adherence to the strict mandates of the 1972 Biological and Toxins Convention.

Speaking at a Rand Bioterrorism Conference in February 2000, Lederberg said, "It is very important that we enhance the international consensus that biowarfare is an evil that cannot be tolerated. It cannot be tolerated out of a sense of moral outrage, and of concern about our own welfare for sure, but it cannot be only our own survival. Civil life depends on the frustration of individuals' capacities to disrupt the entire community at a whim. If people can resort to maximum violence in settling their grievances, and this becomes habitual, we have no civil life any further. It's in that sense that these are weapons that our community cannot tolerate."

Future Scenario

Reminiscent of the influenza epidemic one century earlier, a future world could find itself battling for survival with a horrific viral disease—one that threatens the very existence of our population. A disease that started in sub-Saharan Africa has now slowly but steadily spread to the entire globe. The modern-day globalization of commerce, food, and low-cost air travel has rapidly dispersed the infectious disease throughout the world. Populations remain unvaccinated and some experts are worried that the virus, with no known natural enemies, will continue to ravage our world until it burns out of its own accord.

Historians have noted that, except for the slower spread of the disease, the new virus is similar in lethality to the Black Death that raged across Europe from 1346 to 1352 killing more than one-third of Europe's population. The virus has already killed 23 million and infected 60 million more. The United Nations now projects that by 2020 another 68 million deaths will occur in the 45 nations most heavily affected by the disease, far eclipsing the 55 million estimated dead from World War II.

Of course, you now realize that this is not a future scenario. This is the health devastation brought on by the HIV/AIDS virus. Our frustration in dealing with HIV/AIDS is apparent. Our results do not support an optimistic view of our ability to respond to an unexpected, high-powered virus.

Developing effective broad-spectrum therapeutic drugs, vaccines, diagnostic techniques, and new ways to improve human response to infectious disease is the 21st century challenge that parallels the nuclear weapons program of the 1940s or putting a man on the moon in the 1960s. Prevention and preemption must drive early detection, containment, timely analysis for the best possible treatment, and the ability to rapidly develop and deploy vaccines to prevent future outbreaks.

Conclusion

We find ourselves at a crossroads when it comes to dealing with biothreat. Our nation's healthcare organizations are struggling to balance bioterrorism preparedness with already tight budgets and inadequately staffed facilities. Soon after last fall's federal call to action, analysts at the American Hospital Association concluded that it will cost the nation's 4,900 hospitals upwards of $11 billion—more than double the federal lawmakers' pledge of $4.6 billion—to improve their ability to respond to an attack. At the current budget of $513 million for FY03 and FY04 it would take over twenty years to upgrade our hospitals.

Ultimately the biothreat will not go away by throwing billions of dollars at it. Without a vision and a strategy, it will become remarkably clear that this is not a one-time problem—it is a process that must be defined and improved. Much of what needs to be improved upon is also going to enhance the healthcare system overall. Julie Geberding, MD, director of the Centers for Disease Control and Prevention notes, "We are building terrorism capacity on the foundation of public health, but we are also using the new investments in terrorism to strengthen the public health foundation."

As the biothreat challenge emerges as an ever-greater risk, we cannot lose sight of the fact that America will almost assuredly be struck again by terrorist blows. In the September 2002 National Security Strategy, President Bush warned, "History will judge harshly those who saw this coming danger but failed to act. In the new world we have entered, the only path to peace and security is the path of action." The path of Winston Churchill would be a wise one to follow: "It is no use saying, 'We are doing our best.' You have got to succeed in doing what is necessary." In the field of biothreats we have barely begun.

Biothreat Resources

Web Sites

There are several outstanding Web sites with up-to-date information on bioterrorism. These are some of the ones we have found to be most helpful:

Biosecurity and Bioterrorism: Biodefense Strategy, Practice, and Science *(on-line journal)*
> http://www.liebertonline.com

Center for Civilian Biodefense Strategies, Johns Hopkins University
> http://www.hopkins-biodefense.org/

Centers for Disease Control and Prevention (CDC)
> http://www.bt.cdc.gov/

Center for the Study of Bioterrorism and Emerging Infections, St. Louis School of University Health
> http://www.slu.edu/colleges/sph/csbei/bioterrorism/

Medical NBC Online Information Server
> http://www.nbc-med.org/

Monterey Institute of International Studies
> http://cns.miis.edu/research/cbw/index.htm

National Association of County and City Health Officials
> http://www.naccho.org/project63.cfm

National Institutes of Health (NIH)
> http://www.niaid.nih.gov/publications/bioterrorism.htm

State Public Health Locator
> http://www.statepublichealth.org/

United States Army Medical Research Institute of Infectious Diseases (USAMRIID)
> http://www.usamriid.army.mil/

United States Department of Health and Human Services (HHS)
> http://www.hhs.gov/

United States Senator Bill Frist, MD
    http://frist.senate.gov

World Health Organization
    http://www.who.int/health_topics/bioterrorism/en/

Books

Some of the most reliable and in-depth information is contained in books you can buy or find on the shelves of your local library.

Alibek, Ken, *Biohazard: The Chilling True Story of the Largest Covert Biological Weapons Program in the World—Told from Inside by the Man Who Ran It*, (New York, Random House, 1999).

Carus, W. Seth, Working paper: "Bioterrorism and Biocrimes," "(Washington, DC: Center for Counter-proliferation Research, National Defense University, 2002).

Diamond, Jared, *Guns, Germs, and Steel*, (New York, Norton, 1999).

Eberhart-Phillips, Jason, *Outbreak Alert: Responding to the Threat of Infectious Diseases*, (Oakland, CA, New Harbinger Publications, Inc., 2000).

Frist, Bill, *When Every Moment Counts: What You Need to Know about Bioterrorism from the Senate's Only Doctor*, (Lanham, MD: Rowman & Littlefield Publishers, Inc., 2002).

Garrett, Laurie, *The Coming Plague: Newly Emerging Diseases in a World Out of Balance*, (New York, Farrar Straus & Giroux, 1994).

Henderson, D.A., Thomas Inglesby and Tara O'Toole, eds., *Bioterrorism: Guidelines for Medical and Public Health Management*, (Chicago, IL, American Medical Association, 2002).

Kohn, George C., ed., *Encyclopedia of Plague and Pestilence*, (Facts on File, Inc., 1995).

Lederberg, Joshua ed., *Biological Weapons: Limiting the Threat*, (Cambridge, MA: Harvard University, 1999).

Mangold, Tom and Jeff Goldberg, *Plague Wars: The Terrifying Reality of Biological Warfare*, (New York, St. Martin's Press, 1999).

McNeill, William H., *Plagues and Peoples*, (New York, Anchor Books, 1998).

Meade, Glenn, *Resurrection Day*, (London, Hodder & Stoughton, 2002).

Miller, Judith, Stephen Engelberg, and William J. Broad, *Germs: Biological Weapons and America's Secret War*, (New York, Simon & Schuster, 2001).

Osterholm, Michael T. and John Schwartz, *Living Terrors: What America Needs to Know to Survive the Coming Bioterrorist Catastrophe*, (New York, Dell, 2000).

Preston, Richard, *The Cobra Event*, (New York, Random House, 1997).

Preston, Richard, *The Demon in the Freezer*, (New York, Random House, 2002).

Preston, Richard, *The Hot Zone*, (New York, Random House, 1994).

Ryan, Frank, *Virus X: Tracking the New Killer Plagues*, (New York, Little, Brown, and Company, 1997).

U.S. Government, *21st Century Complete Guide to Bioterrorism, Biological and Chemical Weapons, Germs and Germ Warfare, Nuclear and Radiation Terrorism*—Military Manuals and Federal Documents with Practical Emergency Plans, Protective Measures, Medical Treatment, and Survival Information, (Progressive Management, 2001).

Web Site Reference

INTRODUCTION

www.currahee.net
www.evercareonline.com
www.gingrichgroup.com
www.healthtransformation.net
www.newt.org
www.pfizerhealthsolutions.com/healthystateframe.htm
www.pkc.com
www.prhi.org
www.va.gov/vista_monograph
www.visicu.com
www.worlddoc.com

CHAPTER 1

www.prhi.org

CHAPTER 5

www.healthhero.com
www.hpc.org
www.phc4.org

CHAPTER 6

www.ahca.org
www.cancer.org
www.diabetes.org
www.factorfoundation.org
www.hemophilia.org
www.ihi.org
www.leapfroggroup.org
www.prhi.org
www.skolar.com

CHAPTER 7

www.ourcommongood.com

CHAPTER 8

http://ndep.nih.gov
www.diabetes.org
www.diabetes4patients.com
www.diabetesaction.org
www.eatright.org
www.jdrf.org
www.webmd.com

CHAPTER 9

www.sas.org
http://books.nap.edu/books/NI000221/html/8.html#pagetop

CHAPTER 10

http://rtc.ruralinstitute.umt.edu/health/RuHOutreach.htm
http://www.healthwellness.org/
http://www.ncpad.org/
http://www.whitehouse.gov/news/releases/2001/06/20010619-1.html
www.deltasociety.org
www.indetech.com/ibot

EPILOGUE

www.healthtransformation.net

APPENDIX A

www.va.gov/vha_oi/
www.activehealthmanagement.com
www.currahee.net
www.evercareonline.com
www.mayoclinic.com
www.mayoclinic.org
www.nmh.org
www.pfizerhealthsolutions.com
www.pkc.com
www.prhi.org
www.primexis.com
www.prmsoft.com
www.relayhealth.com

www.silversneakers.com
www.skolar.com
www.thedacare.org
www.visicu.com
www.worlddoc.com

APPENDIX B

http://cns.miis.edu/research/cbw/index.htm
http://frist.senate.gov
http://www.bt.cdc.gov/
http://www.hhs.gov/
http://www.hopkins-biodefense.org
http://www.liebertonline.com
http://www.naccho.org/project63.cfm
http://www.nbc-med.org/
http://www.niaid.nih.gov/publications/bioterrorism.htm
http://www.slu.edu/colleges/sph/csbei/bioterrorism/
http://www.statepublichealth.org/
http://www.usamriid.army.mil/
http://www.who.int/health_topics/bioterrorism/en/

Acknowledgements

This book is the product of many people helping develop and nurture a process of rethinking the current system of health and healthcare.

First, we have to acknowledge the extraordinary effort of Rick Tyler in coordinating the entire book project, ensuring that the ideas and language were clear and understandable, and providing an initial concept for the design of the front cover. Without his long hours of work, this book would have taken many more months to develop.

Second, we have to thank Kathy Lubbers for working with the Alexis de Tocqueville Institution in bringing the book to publication in such a timely manner. Kathy also managed the overall book project and coordinated the writing schedules for nine people who helped in various ways to get the book ready for the de Tocqueville editor. At the Alexis de Tocqueville Institution we must thank Ken Brown for his vision in taking on this project and Jennifer Rowe for having the stamina to see it to completion. Additionally, we thank Randy Evans for introducing us to the wonderful people at the Alexis de Tocqueville Institution and for making the partnership a reality.

Steve Hanser, Newt's mentor and adviser for over 30 years, once again played a key role in thinking through the entire project, advising as it grew into fruition, and then helping rewrite the early drafts of the book.

Vince Haley, Sarah Murphy, Bill Sanders, and Mike Shields deserve special recognition for their large contributions to the chapters on health justice, transforming examples, bioterrorism, and science respectively. Jackie Cushman, Nancy Desmond, Joe Gaylord, Sonya Harrison, Amy Pearman, and AJ Young also helped significantly on this project.

Chris DeMuth, the remarkable President of the American Enterprise Institute has been invaluable throughout the entire project and remains our best advocate in growing the ideas over time.

Thanks to Chris we had a chance to work with Mark McClellan at AEI before he joined the Council of Economic Advisers and then moved on to become Commissioner of the Food and Drug Administration. Mark's extraordinary contribution in drafting the health chapter of the 2002 CEA annual report created a benchmark of free-market thinking for the future of health.

Secretary of Health and Human Services Tommy Thompson has shown great leadership, boldness, and vision in improving the health of all Americans. Tom Scully, the director of the largest single health purchasing system in the United States, the Center for Medicare and Medicaid, has been a friend and adviser throughout the growth of these ideas. Bobby Jindall, the former Assistant Secretary of HHS for Policy also played a powerful role in encouraging new thinking.

Mitch Daniels, Director of OMB, and Jim Capretta, his deputy for health, have been consistently supportive as has been Assistant Secretary of Defense for Health Affairs at DOD Bill Winkenwerder Jr., MD.

Rick Klausner was inspirational while leading the National Cancer Institute; many of his insights shaped our project on transforming health.

Bill Gimson has arranged for CDC to educate Newt on a wide range of issues over the years; the remarkable talents at CDC contribute greatly to better health in America.

Phyllis Gardner at Stanford; Molly Coye, MD, MPH, President, Health Technology Center at the Institute for the Future; Ben Lytle of Anthem; Lucian Leape at Harvard; and Don Berwick, MD, MPP, President and CEO Institute for Healthcare Improvement, have each taught us to think a little differently about the challenges of American health.

Many people have contributed to the ideas in the diabetes chapter. Several of the outstanding advisors included Martin Soeters, Steve McGill, Lynne Wentz and Susan Bales of Novo Nordisk. John Graham, Mike Mawby, Browyn Reynolds, and Marie McCarren of the American Diabetes Association. Peter Van Etten, Larry Soler, and all our friends at the Juvenile Diabetes and Research Foundation. Chris Laxton, Jerry Meese, Carolyn Leontos, and the dedicated membership of the American Association of Diabetes Educators.

Bill Novelli and Chris Hansen for their visionary leadership at AARP.

Dean Ornish, maybe the leading thinker on natural systems of staying healthy, has been an inspiration for us to think outside the normal established medical channels. He is one of the great contemporary examples of individual Americans creating change because they have the courage to believe.

Former Secretary of the Treasury Paul O'Neill taught us to think about quality and systems in healthcare with new rigor and new energy. His leadership in the Pittsburgh project is historic.

Senator Bill Frist and his staff encouraged us to continue developing new solutions and new approaches. Senator Frist's combination of being a world-class transplant surgeon and a naturally positive political leader may prove vital as America wrestles with its health future.

The Honorable Anthony J. Principi, Secretary of Veterans Affairs and Jonathan B. Perlin, MD, PhD, MSHA, FACP, Deputy Under Secretary for

Health for their desire to make the Veterans Administration system the best it can be for America's veterans. Thank you for your willingness to share many of the department's advancements.

Many people have contributed to the development of the ideas in this book. It would be impossible to name them all but several should receive special recognition: Ed Kutler, Howard Cohen, Pam Bailey, Deb Steelman, Chip Kahn, Gail Wilensky, Missy Jenkins, Dan Crippen, David Winston, Jeannine Bender, Joe Antos, Dan Freier, Joyce Larkin, Jack Riggs, John Goodman, Greg Scanlon, Bob Helms, Jack Calfee, Steve Forbes, Karen Wolk-Feinstein, Tom Emerick, Bob DuFour, Laura Linn, Mary Swanson, Carol Novak, John Iglehart, Joe Weller, Angelo Iantosca, Ron Bachman, Sam Lin, Chip Roadman, Bob Windom, MD, Fred Telling, and Marily Rhudy have helped and continue to be valuable advisors.

To the interns who have provided valued research, team work, creativity and enthusiasm to our ongoing work: Kyla Brooke, Mary Derr, Andrew Doughtery, Ted Dove, Kristopher Grajny, Laura Kurland, Andrew Long, Sarah Lowery, Jim Lunsford, Michael Mann, Lacy Martin, Zubin Master, Bob Nardo, Maureen O'Rearden, Ronni Padberg, John Raney, Jade Shipman, Peter Stone, Vince Tanciongco, April Taylor, Steven Ujvary, Melissa Winters, and Barbara Zaucha.

A special thanks to Jan Blair for sharing her proofing gifts and Robin Krauss for sharing his graphic design gifts.

Finally, we have to thank the many people who developed specific projects on which we report in this volume as transformational examples. Their leadership and their willingness to break the mold have given us the evidence that we really can save lives and save money.

To the families of the Gingrich team, especially Callista, Jeff, Tamara, Paul, Kevin, Bob, Martha, Monet, Krys, Jimmy, Willie, and Robert for their patience and support throughout the long hours of this project.

Newt, Anne Woodbury, and Dave Madeiors, Executive Director of the
Factor Foundation of America. 2003

Newt with Jane Carr of AID Atlanta, in Washington,
DC. April 21, 1991

Newt with Robert Smalley of the Arthritis Foundation
in Washington, DC. May 1, 1987

Newt visiting with medical students, surgical resident, and veteran
at the VA Medical Center in Atlanta, GA. July 1990
Courtesy of Atlanta VA Medical Center

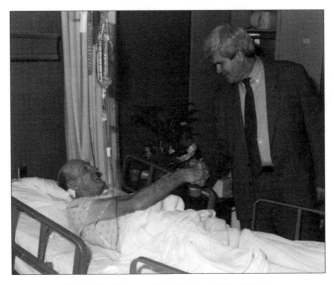

Newt at the Veterans Administration Medical Center
in Atlanta, GA. February 14, 1992
Courtesy of Atlanta Veterans Administration Medical Center

Newt visiting the zoo with a group of children from the Spina Bifida Association. April 1995
Courtesy of Spina Bifida Association.

Bill Sanders with Secretary of Defense Donald Rumsfeld at a strategic policy forum
following a bioterrorism crisis-simulation exercise, "Silent Prairie," conducted
at the National Defense University for Congressman involving top military
and government officials. February 2003

Newt with daughter Jackie Cushman and grandchildren Maggie and Robert Cushman—
continued inspiration for *Saving Lives & Saving Money*. December 2002
Courtesy of Callista Gingrich

Newt with constituent from the Sixth Congressional District of Georgia. 1991
Courtesy of Friends of Newt Gingrich

Newt with YMCA youth participants of the 1991 Washington, DC seminar from the
Sixth Congressional District of Georgia. October 1991

Discussing the future of healthcare. 1992
Courtesy of Friends of Newt Gingrich

Newt with children—the next generation of *Saving Lives & Saving Money.* 1992
Courtesy of Friends of Newt Gingrich

Newt with Arnold Schwarzenegger on the Speaker's balcony at the United States Capital Building, Washington, DC. 1997

Arnold is Co-founder and Chairman of the Board of Inner City Games, which gives inner city kids the forum and the chance to be their best in all aspects of life.

Newt with Carl Lewis in Washington, DC. March 1990

Carl is an advocate for the fight against diabetes, and he is Co-organizer of the Mayors' Sports Challenge, which motivates youth to run, nurtures their self-confidence, and builds school spirit.

Newt meets Ronald Reagan
during Reagan's presidential campaign. 1979

William Rabucha, Duanne Red, Newt, Ann Griffith, and Elleyn Yeager
from the Alzheimer's Association of Georgia. April 24, 1992 in Washington, DC.

Anne Woodbury, Newt, and Dana Pavey.
April 2003

Saving Lives & Saving Money

by Newt Gingrich with Dana Pavey and Anne Woodbury

If you would like to purchase copies of this book in quantities of 100 or more, please contact us at

THE CENTER FOR HEALTH TRANSFORMATION

1301 K Street, NW
Suite 800 West
Washington, DC 20005

(202) 414-4437

www.healthtransformation.net